FRENCH CHEFS COOKING

French Chefs Cooking

Recipes and Stories from the Great Chefs of France

Michael Buller

Foreword by Paul Bocuse

with Paul Bocuse, Jean Troisgros, Pierre, Michel, Claude and Georges Troisgros, Roger Vergé, Gerard Boyer, Paul Haeberlin, André Soltner, Daniel Boulud, Jean-Louis Palladin, Jean Banchet, Ariane Daguin, Georges Perrier, Michel Chabran, Jean-Paul Lacombe, Pierre Orsi, Roger Jaloux, Jean Fleury, Christian Bouvarel, Bernard Loiseau, Jean Ducloux, Georges Blanc, Alain Ducasse, Patrick Henriroux, Maurice Bernachon, Gilbert Le Coze, Pierre Franey, Jean Vergnes, Hervé Riou, Lea Linster, Regis Marcon, Etienne Sordello, Lionel Poilane, The Mère Brazier, Fernand Point, Henri Clos-Jouve, Margaridou

IDG BOOKS WORLDWIDE

To Jeannie

IDG Books Worldwide, Inc.
An International Data Group Company
919 E. Hillsdale Boulevard
Suite 400
Foster City, CA 94404

The IDG Books Worldwide logo is a registered trademark under exclusive license to IDG Books Worldwide, Inc., from International Data Group, Inc.

For general information on IDG Books Worldwide's books in the U.S., please call our Consumer Customer Service department at 800-762-2974. For reseller information, including discounts and premium sales, please call our Reseller Customer Service department at 800-434-3422.

Cataloging-in-Publication Data is available from the Library of Congress

Manufactured in the United States of America
10 9 8 7 6 5 4 3 2 1

Designed by Amy Trombat

FOR MICHAEL BULLER, the friend of all chefs, from fashion to gastronomy, from *haute couture* to *haute cuisine*, was only a step twenty-five years ago. When you are born in England, you keep near at hand your sense of humor, your calm in hard times, and the cherished umbrella. Crossing the Channel, after working behind the scenes of radio, theater, and fashion, he turned his talents to the service of the world's chefs.

Going to America, he was there when we needed him to give support as we chefs arrived on this soil to be discovered for our cuisine.

He quickly became a trustworthy *homme orchestre*, advising us, ready to work with us wherever we had our food and wine events. *Grand connoisseur* of wines, as journalist and author he wrote about us. His dedication and boundless admiration for the chefs across the world have made him indispensable.

This book is not about what he knows, but rather illustrates perfectly his passion for the cuisine. I take this opportunity to express warm thanks in the name of us all who have experienced that depth of heart given without counting.

All my wishes for the well-deserved success of this book.

PAUL BOCUSE, COLLONGES, 1999

CONTENTS

INTRODUCTION

As a young English schoolboy I stood on a cliff in North Devon for days on end, watching the convoys of ships on their way to the D-Day Normandy landings. Then peace, and, at the age of fourteen, I took my brother with me to cycle across the barren war-scarred north of France. Eight years later, in 1955, some friends suggested that I should come to Paris for a couple of weeks. I stayed fifteen years, working in radio, theater, fashion, and wine, enamored by this land, overflowing with cream and butter and cheeses and fine wines. Clearly, France was in my blood.

In the early seventies, I came to America, accompanying and translating for the great winemakers of France. The appreciation of dining and fine wines, especially French cuisine and French wines, was taking center stage in American living. A strong contingent of French chefs had already come to America, including André Soltner at Lutèce, Pierre Franey and Jacques Pepin at Le Pavillon, and René Verdan at the White House. There was a colony of French bistros on Manhattan's East 40s. France's ambassador-at-large of cuisine—the Paul Bocuse of his day—was the warm, outspoken chef Raymond Oliver, the first French chef to conduct a regular series of cooking lessons on television. I had interviewed him several times in the French radio studios and in his two-centuries-old Grand Vèfour Restaurant in Paris, behind the Palais-Royal, where Colette lived. I had met my first great chef of France.

In 1975, there was a revolution going on in the kitchens of France. I met this new generation of chefs coming out of their restaurants for the first time, ready to travel to America.

It was *nouvelle cuisine* time and the chefs were flying in.

Regional Cuisine

A sense of regional cuisines can be understood more clearly in France than perhaps anywhere else.

In a land only twice the size of Texas, France has some thirty regional cuisines, traditions of cooking handed down from generation to generation. In the passing from one to another, the recipes and dishes are adapted, sometimes modernized, but one thing is constant among the best cooks and chefs, in homes, and in restaurants, there is always the search for the best quality produce.

Paul Bocuse, at home and overseas, has been the flagbearer and defender of national and regional cuisine. "Whether we are from France or America, what is important is to defend our own cuisine— our *boeuf bourguignon*, our *coq au vin*, our *cassoulet* and *bouillabaisse*. In your country, you have the good crayfish of New Orleans, soft-shell crabs of the East Coast, the lobsters of Maine, the Virginia ham, the Idaho potatoes and the beef of Texas and the Southwest. Real cuisine is country cuisine. The cuisine of the regions. The cuisine of the seasons."

The chefs in this book are from eleven of these regional cuisines. Seven of them crossed the Atlantic and stayed to cook, while still conserving certain touches of regional cuisine in their repertoire. Some, like André Soltner from Alsace, and Ariane Daguin and Jean-Louis Palladin from Gascony, are a delight to the ears with strong accents of their home country.

I began with two of them, Paul Bocuse and his best friend the late Jean Troisgros, both leaders of the chefs of France at home and abroad.

Friends of my radio days in Paris, Christian Millau and Henri Gault whose food magazine *Gault-Millau* had launched *nouvelle cuisine,* sent me to Jean; Jean called up Paul and sent me across to him, Paul sent me on to other chefs.

Looking at those first dinners in America, some recipes from which are included here, there was little *nouvelle cuisine* about them. For a Bocuse dinner at Lutèce, Paul cooked a classic *quasi* of veal, a salute to his grandmother (see below) and to colleague Raymond Oliver. I learned from Paul and Jean that the legendary Fernand Point at La Pyramide and the Mère Brazier in Lyon had been cooking their green beans *nouvelle cuisine*-style decades earlier, as did the good folk, such as a Madame Margaridou in Auvergne, who cook in the villages.

By the eighties, as wine and food consultant for Pan Am, I was one of the people flying in the chefs regularly. They participated in my "in-flight tastings" and wine and food summits. Paul and his colleague Roger Vergé planned with me the First Class food service for the airline's flagship route, Nice to New York.

Paul's sole advice in the seventies, as it was twenty years later when I told him I was starting work on this book, was "Bring in the other chefs." In twenty years with the chefs, I learned that one chef leads to another. On French rail stations, a notice warns, *Attention!*

One train may hide another. As Paul puts it, "*Attention!* One chef may hide another." My life has been a series of meetings and memories, and at the writing of this book, I stopped to gather them together as a family gathers.

Going to France, and coming to America, we met. The station master waves his flag, blows his whistle, and we leave with a wagonful of chefs and recipes and memories, *bons souvenirs*.

The Recipes

THE CHEFS THEMSELVES chose their own recipes and wrote them out for me. The recipes are as clearly from the country, from the soil they grew up on, as the chefs themselves, working with fresh produce from the soil, *le terroir*. Recipes are handed down from generation to generation and adapted. "Manual laborers," is how Paul refers to himself and his colleagues.

One man, as is clear, has made it all possible, throughout this book. Paul Bocuse. He understands. Many of the chefs here have been through his kitchens. He is always there for them. He has always been there for me.

So the country, the chefs and the recipes—the land, the man and the produce—overlap marvelously. The deeper we go, the closer they grow. And all of the chefs love to come to America. For them America is "out there," a dream on the horizon.

A Family Cookbook

EARLY COOKBOOKS WERE COLLECTIONS OF RECIPES handed down from mother or father to son or daughter, sometimes grandparents to grandchildren.

The first time I visited with the great chefs of France, Jean Troisgros handed me a book, as I was leaving his kitchen, saying he believed this was one of the great cookbooks of all times.

Margaridou, the Journal of an Auvergne Cook has been at my bedside for twenty years. It begins:

These recipes of my grandmother, I was truly afraid to spoil them by writing them out. They were spoken recipes with images of a life that one had to know to understand. They were almost fairytales.

Every evening, going up to my room after work, I would write down my memories of this tradition I was born and brought up in. Every evening I would see the faces of my grandmother and her friends, a phantom circle dressed in blue aprons, coming out of the mist of time. They went to the market to shop for what they needed without looking for glory, not knowing in their marvelous simplicity that they were artists, that in this topsy-turvy world they were preserving a regional art, permitting me one day to tell a story of a region's cuisine.

A couple of days after telling Paul I was starting work on a book about the great chefs of France as I knew them, I received from him three recipes used in the Bocuse family kitchen by his mother and grandmother.

The first recipe was a Purée of Potatoes, purée *de pommes de terre*.

"My best memory is certainly the purée my mother made that had nothing sophisticated about it.

"In fact, she quickly peeled the potatoes she had just dug up in the garden, cutting them into quarters and without washing them putting them to cook slowly in some salted milk that she always watched over.

"Then at the end of the cooking, she drained off the potatoes, mashing them with a fork and adding some butter and cream (we had a cow in those days and my mother always put aside the cream from the milk which was what we called quite vulgarly 'the skin' as it formed on the top of the milk when the milk cooled off), she seasoned to taste and served this purée immediately to accompany the veal.

"I could always find in the purée some small pieces of potato that had not been mashed and that was heaven for me. I would make a well in the middle of my plate and fill it with the slightly fatty juice.

"As for the milk, once cooled off, it was saved for the cats and the dogs of the house. This way everyone was satisfied."

His second recipe was Rump of Veal, *le quasi de veau*.

"In those days, it was more the roast that accompanied the purée and my mother liked best the piece of veal called the *quasi* that was most gelatinous and deliciously soft, *moelleux*, of all.

"At the bottom of her large cast iron stock pot or cocotte, she would melt some butter, often with a piece of veal tail to give more taste to the juice.

"As soon as it was melted, she placed the roast in the pot and, turning it often, browned it on all its sides over a fire that was fairly lively, adding finally two or three white onions and a carrot cut in slices.

"Then she would salt it with coarse salt, all we had in those days as fine salt was still a luxury. Lowering the heat and covering the pot, she would leave it to simmer, returning from time to time to turn the roast and add a little hot water to dissolve the sugars."

His third recipe, dessert for this family meal, was a Compote of End of Summer Fruit, *compote de la fin d'été*.

"During my early childhood, we had a garden with fruit trees of all the fruit one finds in our region. My grandmother would always, come the last summer days, walk out under the fruit trees and gather up in her apron all the fruit that had been discarded for being badly ripened, too small or fallen and left on the ground apples, pears, plums and the first quince.

"She sorted them out, peeled them, cut them in pieces and cooked them in butter in her large black cast iron frying pan, throwing on top a large handful of crystalized sugar that caramelized the fruit, before serving it to us with some fresh cream."

This is the way recipes were passed on in those days. My cookbook is built upon those three recipes from Paul, together with the spirit of the Margaridou's cookbook Jean Troisgros gave me.

Over the years, Paul and Jean introduced me to the "big family" of the great chefs of France, some of whom are assembled here together with one or more of their recipes in this family cookbook.

Acknowledgments

THIS BOOK COMES FROM OVER TWENTY-FIVE YEARS of kindness and hospitality from the great chefs of France on both sides of the Atlantic, at the table and in the kitchen. Above all thanks to their leader, *chef extraordinaire*, Paul Bocuse and his best friend, the late Jean Troisgros. To each and every chef here, my deep thanks and *bons souvenirs*.

Paul also introduced me to his friend and neighbor, Alain Vavro, the brilliant designer of menus, tableware, and decor for the chefs of France. Since Alain knows all the chefs, I had direct lines to Collonges and we had fun. I consider Alain a close friend and one of the family of chefs.

Special thanks to André Soltner, a friend of thirty years and another direct line, always there for me with his calls, *"Ça va, Miche?"* at least once a week. André gave me the young, talented chef, Hervé Riou, native of Brittany and apprenticed in some of the fine old kitchens of France, who has been working in America since the eighties as chef, chef-owner, chef-instructor and consultant. Hervé spent long, stimulating hours with me working in his home and mine.

Others checking recipes and texts: Joel Somerstein, chef de cuisine of Waters Edge, New York; Jean Laffont of Oz, Dallas; Janie Masters of Mel's, Denver; Scott and Ann Kraft, Evan and Mike Smith, Marie MacMahon, Eloise Seigel, and my wife Jeannie Rowan, in New York.

Thanks to my editors at IDG Books. Jennifer Griffin, who put me in the hands of Sharon Bowers who marvelously understood this cookbook, writing on the last page of the first draft, "this glorious collection of recipes." And on to the final stage of editing, the careful hands of Jim Willhite, my editor. And my agent and good friend, Bobbe Seigel.

Finally, thanks to the one without whom this book could not have had such love and happiness running through it, my wife, Jeannie. Like many of you, she had never been to France. Eight years ago I took her on our honeymoon staying in the great châteaux of Bordeaux, three days with Paul at Collonges, over to the Troisgros family in Roanne, a week in Beaujolais while we assembled my Beaujolais book, and back to Paris. In her last two-and-a-half years with cancer, I wrote this book in her little house in the country, with her at my side. She would tell friends, "These are the happiest years of my life"—of my life too. So on we go. To France.

MICHAEL BULLER, NEW YORK, 1999

Paul Bocuse and Michael Buller, Collonges-au-Mont d'Or, France, 1991

IN COMPILING THIS COLLECTION OF RECIPES, I've listed ingredients in the order as used by the chef. All ingredients, unless otherwise indicated by the chef, are fresh, from fruits and vegetables to herbs, fruit, milk, butter, and cream.

- ❋ Measures are given but, as Paul Bocuse and Jean Troisgros say clearly (see Appendix—page 290), sometimes a little more or little less can depend on you. Exceptionally, there are the chefs who demand precise measures in their recipes. Nothing more or less. They are who they are because of this brilliance and precision.

- ❋ Cooking times depend on many factors: the freshness of the produce, your kitchen equipment and oven, even how you like your meat or fish. We give some tips on when a dish is cooked, but so much is common sense. Taste. Prod with a sharp knife. Look. Smell. Repeat a recipe another day. Each time we learn something. Chefs cook a dish several times daily. To add to the fun, change an ingredient or a little something in the cooking.

- ❋ Warm plates—but don't make them too hot or the sauce will separate. To warm, put them in a low oven or run them under hot water. Warm food should be served on warm plates, cold food on cold plates.

- ❋ Preheating the oven, if required by the recipe, is indicated at the start of the instructions, so you have time for your oven to reach the necessary heat. Some of the cooking in the oven is fast. The correct temperature must be assured from the start. Use an oven thermometer if your oven does not have a heat gauge. Our friends the chefs are used to working for hours on end with ovens at the right temperatures.

- ❋ Set aside and keep warm. The chefs work in kitchens where the ovens are always warm. They keep a dish warm on top of the stove or in a warm oven. Easy. For us, a double strainer, *bain marie*, with hot water, covered, is one way. Or place the dish in your oven, preheated to a low heat, leaving the oven door open while the dish is inside. Remember to turn off the heat before you leave the kitchen.

Modern ovens are being built to include an oven for warming the plates. My grandmother's Aga cooker in London, had one of its ovens designed for warming, day and night. Old country ovens, says Hervé, always had a place to put the plates or a pot to keep warm.

* Main ingredients, in particular some fish, are occasionally available only in France so we offer alternatives. In days gone by, there was freshwater fish from the rivers and the lakes. Unless we fish ourselves or know a friendly fisherman or fisherwoman, our freshwater fish today comes from farm to fish store or supermarket. Since this book is so much about French cuisine with roots in yesterday, we choose to keep alive a little longer our fantasies, like the just-caught freshwater fish from rivers and lakes. As in fishing, if you do not find what the recipe calls for, try another fish that looks fresh.

* Butter and cream are present in the recipes since, as Jean Troisgros would say, you do not go to France to diet. As André Soltner would say, You come to dine on my cuisine and I make it a little special for you.

* Not one of these chefs went to a cooking school. They had to learn at home and as apprentices in restaurant kitchens. They will tell you they are still learning, especially on their travels.

* They gave me their recipes. I have not tried to standardize them. How can you standardize 38 Frenchmen and some very individual women. General de Gaulle wondered how to govern a country with over 350 different cheeses. *Vive la différence!*

* Finally and important, the recipes are largely from the chefs' family kitchens, evolving over the years as they were passed down in a family, from one cook to another, or as the chef decides to change a detail or more. He may find another way of cooking the recipe, today he leaves out an ingredient, tomorrow he adds another, depending on what is in the market or in season or how he feels that day.

You too, as Paul Bocuse and Jean Troisgros, must feel free to evolve a recipe just as chefs do, depending on your market, your kitchen, your tastes, and those who dine with you.

Out of 120 recipes, a half a dozen are *difficult* recipes, given us by a chef proud of his skills, his kitchen and his brigade of chefs. The artist at work. These recipes give some idea of what is demanded of a Michelin three-star restaurant in France. Let us enjoy them, as I suggest in the text. Sit back, read them, dream a little. When you can, return to the source: dip into the chefs' cookbooks (see page 302) or, best of all, visit them and dine in their restaurants (see page 306).

Soups

Before lunch, at Collonges-au-Mont-d'Or. Paul Bocuse is in the kitchen. He will be out in a few minutes. His guests are sitting in his oak-paneled bar.

Vintage black and white photos of Fernand Point, the Mère Brazier, Jean Troisgros, and Paul Bocuse hang on the walls. *"Monsieur Bocuse arrive,"* the maitre d' announces. A waiter carries in a tray with the traditional glass of welcome, the kir with champagne and black currant liqueur, *crème de cassis.* In Bordeaux, the château owners would always offer a glass of champagne to guests before sitting down to the meal. "Champagne whets the appetite," says the champagne winemaker, Prince Alain de Polignac.

Black Truffles Soup Elysée V.G.E.

Soupe aux Truffes Noires V.G.E.

Paul Bocuse,
Restaurant Paul Bocuse,
Collonges-au-Mont-d'Or, Lyon

WHEN PAUL BOCUSE WAS INVITED BY THE PRESIDENT OF FRANCE *to the Elysée Palace in Paris in February 1974 to receive the Legion d'Honneur, he was the first chef to be so honored at the palace. As might be expected of him, he asked President Valery Giscard d'Estaing if he could cook the lunch and bring a colleague or two with him.*

In the palace kitchen, Jean and Pierre Troisgros created their escalope of salmon with sorrel sauce, Michel Guerard cooked a duck, Roger Vergé brought the salad from his garden, and Paul prepared a soup that he named after the President, Black Truffles Soup Elysée V.G.E.

When the President and Madame Giscard d'Estaing were seated with the chefs, the soup in front of them, the President turned to Paul and asked him how to start. Taking up his spoon, Paul replied, "Mr. President, vous cassez la croute." Literally, you break the crust, from the French slang expression for a bite of lunch, casse-croute.

Paul has had this soup on his menu at Collonges ever since. This dish is a celebration.

SERVES 4

Vegetable mixture (*matignon*)
8 tablespoons

1 tablespoon butter

4 teaspoons finely
    chopped onion

4 teaspoons finely chopped
    carrot, without core

4 teaspoons finely chopped
    celery stalk, peeled
    and washed

4 teaspoons finely chopped
    white mushroom heads,
    peeled, washed, and dried

7 ounces fresh truffles,
    cut in irregular slices

Preheat the oven to 425°F.

Heat the butter in a medium skillet and cook the chopped vegetables, covered, on medium heat for 5 minutes.

Into each individual ovenproof soup bowl (called a *gratinée lyonnaise*), put 2 tablespoons of vegetable *matignon*, adding the truffle and the foie gras, and ladle the consommé to 1/2 inch below the top of the bowl.

Prepare the flaky pastry.

Cover the soup bowls with a layer of flaky pastry, pressing down to seal the edges tight and brushing the edges with egg yolk.

Set the soup bowls in the oven, where the mixture cooks very fast. The flaky pastry should expand in the heat and turn golden, a sign it is cooked. Serve immediately.

Use the soup spoon to break the flaky pastry, which should fall into the soup.

❋ *A word from the chef. "This was my interpretation of an old, traditional dish, a vegetable soup popular with the peasants of the Auvergne and Ardèche regions, with a sprinkle of grated truffle. All I added was the light top layer of flaky pastry, making it similar to the chicken pie of England, where they knew about these kinds of pies ages ago. The layer of pastry preserves the fragrance of the dish until it's ready to be eaten."*

❋ *Fresh truffles are seasonal, readily at hand, and in the best condition in Paul Bocuse's kitchen in France, or in André Soltner's Lutèce, where the chef would buy forty pounds of truffles each December to January, cook, and bottle them for the year. Fresh black truffles from the Périgord region are available in December for a short season each year through Williams-Sonoma (see page 298). Beware of truffles sold as fresh in gourmet stores; they may have been out on display too long. Better to look for a good brand of tinned truffles.*

❋ *Fresh foie gras from France is now being shipped to America. It is expensive, but fabulous (see page 173). A fine domestic fresh foie gras is produced by D'Artagnan (see page 298), or buy a good brand like Rougié of canned French foie gras.*

❋ *Accompany this with a fine, young, dry chardonnay from Burgundy or a glass of a rich, full-bodied champagne like Non-Vintage Brut by Veuve Clicquot or Pol Roger Non-Vintage.*

3 ounces fresh foie gras, cut in irregular slices

4 cups strong, clear chicken consommé, defatted (see page 282)

Flaky pastry topping

8 ounces Flaky Pastry (see page 286)

4 egg yolks, beaten

Four 8-ounce ovenproof soup bowls

Margaridou's Soup

Le Potage Margaridou

**Margaridou,
Auvergne**

ONE AUTUMN EVENING IN 1934, *in the village of Saint-Simond, deep in the Auvergne hills, the home of the Cantal cheese, the writer Suzanne Robiglia heard a knock at her door. Margaridou, a country-woman from the next village, came in and placed a large basketful of papers on the table.*

"Take them. They are recipes I have written down from my grandmother," Margaridou told her. "You might find a use for them."

Margaridou, Journal and Recipes of an Auvergne Cook *was published a year later and a new edition came out in 1977 with recipe notes by Jean and Pierre Troisgros. "This is the finest book of French regional recipes that I know," said Jean when he gave me a copy, and added, echoing Margaridou, "You might find a use for them one day." Many chefs have not heard of her, but ask Pierre Grison, former food writer of Lyon's newspaper* Le Progrès, *or ask Paula Wolfert, author of* The Cooking of Southwest France, *and they will confirm Margaridou as a key figure in France's regional cuisine. Margaridou was finally listed in the bibliography of the 1984 edition of* Larousse Gastronomique.

SERVES 4

5 tomatoes (see note)

1 teaspoon olive oil

1 1/2 quarts veal stock or bouillon (see page 282)

2 tablespoons tapioca (see note)

1 cup heavy cream or crème fraîche

2 egg yolks, lightly beaten

1 slice fresh ham

Pinch freshly grated nutmeg

12 buttered slices of french bread (*croutons*)

Peel, core, seed, and quarter the tomatoes. Put the olive oil into a large skillet and add the tomatoes. Cook the tomatoes on medium heat until done. Put the veal bouillon into a large stock pot. Remove the tomatoes from the skillet and press them through a sieve into the stock pot.

Add the tapioca, stir, and cook the mixture over medium heat for 30 minutes, or until tender.

Just before serving, reduce the heat to low. Mix the egg yolks with the cream and stir into the soup. Dice the ham and drop the dice into the pot. Add the nutmeg and cook for a few minutes, still on low heat.

Add the buttered croutons to the soup and serve.

❀ *Depending on your taste, you can increase the number of tomatoes.*

❀ *Size of tomatoes: Medium size unless otherwise indicated by the chefs in this book. However, if young, small, ripe, and tastier tomatoes are in season, never hesitate to buy them if they are listed as one of your ingredients. You will need more in number. It's up to the cook and what is available on the market. Same as for other vegetables: medium unless you see riper and tastier. Our chefs too decide quality first, then size and quantity depending on what's at the market.*

❀ *The soup can be made with beef bouillon, even beef bouillon cubes, if you do not have any bouillon in your refrigerator and are pressed for time.*

❀ *For a change, when adding the croutons, cover them with a layer of grated cheese—in this case do not use cream, just add the 2 lightly beaten egg yolks alone.*

❀ *"This soup is beautiful, extremely refined, and worthy of being classed la très grande cuisine," said Jean and Pierre Troisgros in their notes on this recipe in Margaridou's book. "You should use preferably raw ham, and the tapioca should be replaced by vermicelli which has a more distinct, clear taste. Chicken stock can also be used as the liquid for cooking. A word of warning after making the liaison with the eggs: Do not boil any more."*

❀ *Margaridou added powdered spices, but Jean and Pierre advise, "Use powdered spices discreetly, with the exception of the nutmeg that has to be grated, and when used here, adds a great elegance to the dish."*

❀ *Olive oil: French cooks and chefs naturally cook with good French olive oil.*

❀ *Tapioca: In Margaridou's days, seventy years ago, there was only the real thing, true tapioca imported from the French West Indies.*

Leek and Potato Soup

Soupe aux Poireaux et Pommes de Terre

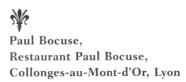

Paul Bocuse,
Restaurant Paul Bocuse,
Collonges-au-Mont-d'Or, Lyon

At dawn one day, Paul took a group of us—Roger Vergé, Jean-Pierre Haeberlin, Pierre Troisgros, Stern magazine photographer Émile Perrauer, the painter Roger Muhl, and his wife, Lynne—to the annual Bresse chicken fair. We came back so late for lunch at Collonges, that the restaurant was deserted.

Paul wanted to serve something special for his table of friends. As the leek and potato soup was being served, he emerged from the kitchen carrying a basket of Périgord truffles. He passed the basket round with his Opinel clasp knife. We shaved off fine slices of truffle into our soup. I will never forget that room filled with the heady aroma from the truffles. It was the smell one finds walking in the underground wine cellars under the town of Saint Emilion in the Bordeaux wine country. Truffles, like fine wine, have their roots below ground.

SERVES 4

4 leeks, white part only
2 tablespoons butter
1 pound Idaho potatoes
1 quart natural spring water
1 1/2 teaspoons coarse salt
6 tablespoons *crème fraîche*
    or heavy cream
2 tablespoons butter, cut in pats
    for garnish
Pinch chervil

Speaking to students at the French Culinary Institute in New York as they prepared a traditional French dinner, Paul Bocuse recommended potato and leek soup for a winter menu. He had these tips: "Wash the leeks well to remove the earth. Cut them in strips not too thin and sautée them well in 2 tablespoons of butter, without letting them turn brown. Peel the potatoes, dry without washing them, so that they keep the starch, cut them in very thin slices, and mix them in with the leeks. The mealy Idaho potato is the best in the world for this soup. Simmer the butter until the leeks and potatoes have softened, then pour in 1 quart of boiling water.

"Add salt, using coarse salt. As we chefs say, a good cook salts his soup once only, at the beginning and that's it! He should never have to touch it, salt it afterward. It should be right from the start.

"For me the soup, uncovered over a moderate heat, is cooked in 15 or 16 minutes. Add the cream. Butter it, dropping the pats one by one into the soup and lightly whisking each time. Add a pinch of chervil, and there! Your soup's ready for serving.

"The secret of a good leek and potato soup is never to let it cook too long. As soon as it's cooked, it should be served. We call it a truly Parisian soup. Quickly cooked, quickly eaten."

※ *The quality of water used in these recipes is important. In Margaridou's village, villagers used water drawn from the spring. In New York, I use Evian or Volvic.*

OPINEL, A CHEF'S KNIFE

"Naturally, every French chef has his Opinel," says André Soltner, chef de cuisine for thirty-four years at Lutèce Restaurant in New York, "though it's not a knife we use professionally in the kitchen." Since his early days with his father, Paul Bocuse has had his Opinel—for going to the market, hunting, fishing, at home and abroad. Dining with him one day at the fashionable Le Cirque, I was surprised to see him pull the knife from his trouser's back pocket, open it up, and lay it alongside the plate in front of him. "It's really our pocket knife," says Roger Vergé, "but you know Paul."

The Opinel family have been making knives for more than 100 years in a valley of the Savoy region in the French Alps. For the first knives, the steel came from local mines and the handles from the nearby forests of oak, chestnut, and pine. The river torrents were harnessed to produce energy. Today, in a modern factory, the carbon steel of each knife is heated to 900°F, chilled, and heated again to 300°F.

Paul gave me a box of Opinels twenty years ago. I have used my Opinel every day since then.

The Opinel is on display at The Museum of Modern Art in New York, and the Victoria & Albert Museum in London classed it among the world's 100 best-designed objects. I cannot find it mentioned in any cookbooks. The chefs have their secret. Finally, I hunted them down, and tell you where they are on sale in America (see page 299).

Cucumber Vichyssoise

Vichyssoise aux Concombres

Roger Vergé,
Restaurant Le Moulin de Mougins,
Côte d'Azur

I HAVE KNOWN ROGER VERGÉ *almost as long as I have known Paul Bocuse. With Jean Troisgros they made a dazzling trio of flying chefs, knowing no frontiers. Working as consultant for Pan Am when the airline launched its flagship route, Nice to New York, in 1984, I asked chairman Ed Acker, a big Texan from Dallas who loved fine food and wines, to give me the task of creating a special first class menu. With fewer than three months to be ready, I called Paul, who sent me to Roger in the hillside village of Mougins overlooking the Mediterranean. We trained the airport chefs to cook with the best-quality produce. Passengers, flight attendants, and pilots were unanimous that it was the finest luncheon they had ever tasted in the air. One of Roger's dishes was this cucumber soup.*

SERVES 4

2 tablespoons butter

1 shallot, peeled and chopped

1 cucumber, peeled and chopped

1 quart cold chicken stock,
(page 282)

1 medium-sized potato,
peeled and quartered

6 tablespoons heavy cream or
crème fleurette

6 finely chopped mint leaves

Heat the butter in a skillet over medium heat and cook the shallot for 1 to 2 minutes. Add the cucumber and the chicken stock. Raise the heat to high, bring to a boil, add the potatoes, and cook for about 20 minutes.

Put the vegetables through a fine-mesh sieve and set aside to chill.

Stir in the cream and mint leaves and serve.

❊ *Crème fleurette is the light cream in France for making Chantilly cream, used in patisserie, meringues, and sundaes. Hervé Riou recommends you use heavy cream here. Chantilly in France is so light that on top of hot coffee or hot chocolate it just sits there. "It has the taste of butter," adds Hervé. "In fact, whip French heavy cream too far and you get butter."*

Fish Soup

Soupe aux Poissons

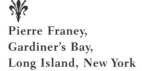

Pierre Franey,
Gardiner's Bay,
Long Island, New York

PIERRE WAS BORN IN BURGUNDY. *He came to America as sauce chef under maitre d' Henri Soulé at the French Restaurant of the 1938 World Fair. He stayed on, becoming executive chef of Soulé's celebrated Le Pavillon Restaurant in New York. Later, he worked as food writer with Craig Claiborne at* The New York Times, *wrote numerous cookbooks, and hosted a series of television cooking programs. He was every chef's good friend. We lost him to a heart attack while giving a cooking demonstration aboard the Queen Elizabeth 2 sailing to England in 1996.*

In my first year in America, one summer's day in the Hamptons, he and Craig barbecued chicken and I served the wine at a couple of dollars a serving to aid a local charity. We raised nearly $1000 in a few hours. "You're invited back whenever you like," Pierre told me. He was my good friend ever since.

"One of the joys of his life in his younger days in East Hampton," Betty, his wife, wrote me, "was to fish from his fast boat in Gardiner's Bay near our home. He would delight in bringing back the catch and then proceed to clean and prepare a delicious seafood recipe for the family. The following is one of many he created."

SERVES 10 TO 12

1/4 cup olive oil

2 cups finely chopped onions

3 cloves garlic, finely chopped

1 green pepper, cored, seeded, and chopped

6 ripe plum tomatoes, quartered and seeded

3 1/2 pounds fresh fish, cleaned and gills removed

2 leeks, split, well-washed, and cut into 1/2-inch pieces

continued

Heat the oil in a large saucepan on medium heat and add the onions. Cook, stirring until the onions are golden. Add the garlic and green pepper and stir briefly. Add the tomatoes and simmer for 10 minutes, stirring frequently.

Cut the fish into 1-inch lengths and add to the vegetables. Stir well and cook for 5 minutes on medium heat, continuing to stir.

Add the bouquet garni and water to the soup. Increase the heat to bring to a boil, and cook for 45 minutes, skimming the surface, as needed.

1 bouquet garni: 2 sprigs fresh
      thyme or 1/2 teaspoon dried,
      1 bay leaf, and 4 sprigs
      parsley, tied together

4 quarts water

2 tablespoons Ricard, or an
      anise-flavored liquor

12 slices of fried french bread
      (*croutons*)

Strain and force much of the solid matter through a food mill. Return to the saucepan and simmer 15 minutes longer. Add the Ricard.

When ready to serve, place a crouton in the bottom of each hot soup bowl. Ladle the soup on top and serve immediately.

THE BOUQUET GARNI

Each chef has his own concept of a bouquet garni, depending on his family's tradition and his restaurant. When Pierre Franey, in the last recipe, wanted a bouquet garni, he walked out into his garden on Long Island to gather the thyme, bay leaf, and parsley, just as he did as a child in Burgundy. Roger Vergé picks his tarragon, basil, and coriander from his garden in that paradise called Provence in the south of France, where herbs run wild over hill and dale.

"To make a bouquet garni," recommends Chef Hervé Riou, "take a piece of the white of a leek, three or four inches long, washed. Slit it open with a sharp knife and inside lay a sprig or two of thyme, tarragon, and parsley. Tie it up with some kitchen string. Still simpler, just tie up the herbs you need with some kitchen string." Hervé does not recommend wrapping the bouquet garni in cheesecloth. "Too expensive." He laughs. "Unless you are working in one of the great chef's kitchens."

The variations of bouquet garni from these chefs are worth trying. They are made on the spur of the moment with, unless indicated otherwise, fresh herbs.

Pumpkin Soup with Porcini Mushrooms, Juniper Custard, and a Spiced Cranberry Coulis

Velouté de Potirons et Flans de Cèpes au Genevièvre,
Coulis d'Airelles Epicé

**Daniel Boulud,
Restaurant Daniel,
New York**

DANIEL WAS BORN NEAR LYON *on the family farm where children ran happily among cows, pigs, goats, chickens, geese, ducks, rabbits, and turkeys. "My parents went every week to sell their produce at the Lyon farmers' market. Every year we loaded twenty tons of garlic on the truck and sold it at the big garlic fair near Grenoble."*

His apprenticeship included three years at Nandron, one of the fine restaurants of Lyon, and a year in each of three 3-stars: La Mère Blanc in Vonnas, Michel Guerard's in Eugenie-Les-Bains, and Roger Vergé's in Mougins.

He came to work in America in the early eighties, and in 1986 was invited by Sirio Maccioni to be executive chef at Le Cirque in New York City. Six years later, he decided to leave and open his own restaurant. "A tapestry of flavors," wrote Patricia Wells in the International Herald Tribune, rating Restaurant Daniel Top Table in the United States. "His menu offers food with a homespun quality sparked with glimmers of classic French."

Today, Daniel has two restaurants—Restaurant Daniel, surely the most elegant and brilliantly inspired French cooking in town, built on the old site of Sirio Maccioni's Le Cirque; and Café Daniel where once stood the first Restaurant Daniel. Great French cuisine never forgets its roots. When I dined chez Daniel one day with Alain and Dominique Vavro, he served us a menu dégustation that opened with six soups.

In his Lyonnais region, cooks make gratins and purées with pumpkin and a soup called gourd soup.

"I cannot remember a day at home," Daniel recalled, "that we did not have a meal with soup, and pumpkin soup was a favorite."

SERVES 8

Soup

3 tablespoons butter

1 cup sliced leeks, white part only, well-washed

1 cup peeled and sliced onion

2 celery stalks, sliced

1 bouquet garni: 2 parsley stems, 1 sprig thyme, 1 garlic clove, peeled, 1 stick cinnamon, and 3 whole cloves wrapped in a sachet

Pinch ground ginger

Salt and freshly ground pepper to taste

4 butternut squash, peeled, seeded, and cut into 1-inch dice

2¹/2 quarts chicken or vegetable stock (see page 282)

3/4 cup heavy cream or *crème fraîche*

Porcini and juniper custard

1/2 cup whole milk

2 juniper berries

1 tablespoon olive oil

4 ounces porcini mushrooms, cleaned and sliced 1/2 inch thick

1 garlic clove, peeled

1 sprig fresh thyme

Salt and freshly ground pepper to taste

1/2 cup heavy cream or *crème fraîche*

1 large egg

1 egg yolk

Preheat the oven to 325°F.

To make the soup, heat the butter in a large skillet over medium to low heat and add the leek, onion, celery, the sachet of herbs, ginger, salt, and pepper. Cover the skillet and sweat the vegetables for 7 to 8 minutes, or until the vegetables are translucent and tender. Add the squash. Cook for 5 minutes more, and add the chicken stock and cream. Simmer for 30 minutes, adjust seasonings, discard the sachet, and blend the soup in a blender. Pass the soup through a fine-meshed sieve and set aside; keep warm.

To make the porcini and juniper custard, while the soup is simmering, bring the milk and juniper berries to a boil in a small saucepan. Remove from the heat, and let steep 5 minutes.

Meanwhile, heat the olive oil in a sauté pan over medium to high heat and add the porcini, garlic, thyme, salt, and pepper. Sauté the porcini until they release their liquid and are tender. Remove the porcini from the pan, and discard the garlic and thyme.

Place the warm milk and porcini in a blender or food processor and blend until smooth. Pass through a fine-meshed sieve and set aside to cool.

Whisk together the heavy cream, egg, and egg yolk in a medium-sized bowl. Whisk in the cooled milk and adjust the seasonings, if necessary.

Fill eight 2-ounce ramekins or aluminium baking cups one-half to two-thirds full with the custard mixture. Place the ramekins in a shallow pan, such as a roasting pan or ovenproof glass baking pan. Place the pan in the oven and fill it with water, like a bain marie, until the water reaches two-thirds of the way up the sides of the ramekins. Be sure to add the water carefully so no water overflows into the ramekins.

Bake for 30 to 40 minutes, carefully rotating the tray halfway through the baking time. When firm but not fully set, remove the custards from the oven and the baking pan and let them cool completely. To unmold, run a paring knife around the inside of each ramekin and invert, tapping lightly.

To make the spiced cranberry coulis, heat the grapeseed oil in a sauté pan over high heat and add the cranberries. Sauté, tossing frequently, until the cranberries become wrinkly and burst.

Add the water, sugar, and spices, stirring quickly to combine, and pass the cranberries immediately through a fine-meshed sieve. Set aside to cool. Adjust the consistency, if necessary, by adding a dash of water or vegetable stock when cool.

When ready to serve, ladle the hot soup into warm bowls, place the porcini custards in the center, and drizzle with cranberry coulis.

Spiced cranberry coulis

1 teaspoon grapeseed oil or other light cooking oil
3 cups cranberries
1/2 cup water
1 teaspoon sugar
Pinch ground cinnamon
Pinch ground nutmeg
Pinch ground ginger
Pinch ground cloves

❋ *Mushrooms today are largely imported and available the year round. They are also sold dried. The field mushroom, flat mushroom, oyster mushroom, even the shiitake, are cultivated, but the porcini is not. (Cèpes and porcinis— see note, page 56). In France, the villagers still bring their baskets of wild mushrooms, wet with the morning dew, to the kitchen door of these chefs.*

❋ *Daniel uses 1 1/2 eggs and 1 yolk. We simplified to 1 egg and 1 yolk.*

❋ *For the bouquet garni, note that he uses parsley, cinnamon, thyme, garlic, and cloves, wrapped in a sachet. Tomorrow, he may decide to add another herb to these. There will never be only one bouquet garni as long as these chefs are around.*

Frogs' Legs Soup

Soupe de Grenouilles

Jean Fleury,
Restaurant Paul Bocuse,
Collonges-au-Mont-d'Or, Lyon

LIKE FERNAND POINT, *the Mère Brazier, and so many of our chefs, Jean Fleury was born in Bresse chicken country. At age sixteen, he began his seven-year apprenticeship, first at the Auberge Bressane in his hometown, Bourg-en-Bresse, then at the Hotel Royal in Evian. After five years as sauce chef, sous-chef, and chef de cuisine at the Brussels Hilton, he came to Lyon as chef de cuisine at the Arc-en-Ciel Restaurant in 1978. The following year, judged by a jury including Jean Troisgros, Paul Bocuse, Alain Chapel, Roger Vergé, and Michel Guerard, he won the coveted chef's medal, Meilleur Ouvrier de France (MOF).*

Then in 1985, Paul Bocuse offered Jean his present post, director of the Paul Bocuse Restaurant at Collonges. Twenty years in the kitchen made Jean the ideal second-in-command, especially during Paul's travels.

The restaurant at Collonges is the house that Paul built, open 364 days a year, with five MOFs, recently celebrating thirty years as a Michelin 3-star restaurant.

I asked Paul for a recipe from each of his MOF chef de cuisine: Roger Jaloux (page 71), Christian Bouvarel (page 170), and this one from Jean Fleury.

SERVES 4

4½ pounds frogs' legs

1½ quarts white stock
(see page 282)

1 cup chopped shallots

1 clove garlic, peeled and
chopped

½ small bunch of watercress,
stemmed

4 tablespoons (½ stick) butter

3 cups dry white wine,
Macon-style

2 tablespoons all-purpose flour

1 quart heavy cream or
crème fraîche

Put the frogs' legs in a large saucepan and add the white stock. Cook over low heat, poaching the legs for 10 minutes without letting them boil. Remove the legs from the poaching liquid and bone them. Set aside the meat and the poaching liquid.

Combine the bones, shallots, garlic, watercress, and 2 tablespoons butter in a saucepan and cook over medium heat for a few minutes. Add the white wine and cook gently on low heat for 10 minutes. Add the poaching liquid and pass through a fine-mesh sieve. Set aside.

Melt 1 ounce butter in a saucepan over low heat and cook until it is clarified—that is, until the milk solids separate and a clear liquid remains. Blend in the flour with a wooden spoon or spatula. Gently cook for 3 to 4 minutes, stirring frequently, until the roux turns light blond. Bring the cream to a boil in a small saucepan and slowly add it to the roux, stirring until smooth.

Add the liquid from the frogs' legs to the roux, stirring continuously, and simmer. Pass this soup through a fine-mesh sieve into a saucepan, discarding the solids, and simmer for 5 minutes.

Bring some salted water to boil in a small saucepan and blanch the leeks and carrots for 10 seconds.

To serve, place some meat in the center of each soup bowl and spoon some carrots and leeks around it. Pour in some warm soup and sprinkle with the chervil.

Salt and freshly ground pepper to taste

3 leeks, white part only, washed and cut in julienne strips

3 carrots, peeled and cut in julienne strips

1 tablespoon finely chopped chervil

❋ *Frogs' legs are not easy to find, but a good gourmet store may be able to order them for you.*

BEST WORKER OF FRANCE AWARD— MEILLEUR OUVRIER DE FRANCE

The most glorious award a chef in France can attain in his professional life is the *Meilleur Ouvrier de France (MOF)* medal. Since its creation in 1924, in 75 years only 131 MOF medals have been awarded. The exam is held every three years. Out of 100 candidates, 36 reach the finals and some years only four or five chefs win the medal.

"We were told the recipes a week before the exam," recalled André Soltner. "Always they are recipes by Auguste Escoffier. I remember the tension in the kitchen was enormous."

On the day of suspense, chef follows chef, sending out his dishes to be tasted and judged by a jury drawn from the leading chefs of France.

Ten of the chefs in this book are Meilleurs Ouvriers de France: Paul Bocuse (1961); Jean Troisgros (1965); André Soltner (1968); Alain Chapel, Pierre Orsi, Roger Vergé (1972); Roger Jaloux (1976); Jean Fleury (1979); Michel Roth (1990); and Christian Bouvarel (1993).

In 1974 Madame Mado Point, widow of the great Fernand Point, was made Honorary MOF, as was Paul Haeberlin in 1993.

"*Meilleur Ouvrier de France* has been the most important event in my professional career," said Paul Bocuse, who became an MOF the year he bought back his family's restaurant at Collonges. Today, he is president of the jury.

Cheese Gratinée

La Soupe au Fromage et au Pain Bis

**Margaridou,
Auvergne**

I REMEMBER LATE NIGHTS IN PARIS, *walking home after the theater, stopping off at a bistrot in Les Halles vegetable and fruit market, the Covent Garden of Paris, for the onion gratinée soup that Parisians call theirs.*

Margaridou made this cheese gratinée on cold days, serving it at midday, followed by a roast chicken on a bed of watercress or endives and a compote of fruit.

"To sit there enjoying this dish while a winter storm rages outside," she wrote in her journal, "knowing that you are safe under the roof of your house, and pour out a small liqueur with your coffee. You will be ready to go out again to work."

SERVES 4

7 tablespoons butter

6 yellow onions, peeled and
    sliced

1/4 cup whole wheat flour

2 quarts natural spring water,
    boiling

A pinch of salt

3/4 pound Cantal cheese, some
    freshly grated, some sliced

4 thin slices brown loaf bread
    (*pain bis*), lightly toasted

Melt 5 tablespoons butter in a deep pot or Dutch oven over low heat. Add the onions and sweat them, stirring often with a wooden spoon.

Raise the heat to medium and cook the onions until lightly browned, stir in the flour and cook a few minutes more. Slowly pour in 2 quarts boiling water, stirring continuously. Add a pinch of salt. Cook the onion soup over medium heat for 30 minutes.

Put the remaining butter and some grated Cantal cheese on the bottom of an ovenproof soup tureen. Add a layer of the *pain bis* and pour some hot soup on the bread to soak. Layer sliced Cantal, and more toasted bread with more soup to moisten the bread. Alternate layers of sliced or grated Cantal with the bread and additional hot soup until you fill the tureen one to two inches below the top. The final layer should be slices of Cantal.

Preheat the broiler.

Place the tureen under the broiler for 3 or 4 minutes and cook until the cheese melts and forms a golden crust.

Serve very hot. Margaridou liked to see the serving spoon stand up in the soup. But for those who would like more soup in their bowl pass some hot onion soup in a sauceboat on the side.

❋ *Hervé explains that when sweating onions, salt them afterwards. (Salting them first would bring out the water in the onions, and they will not brown.)*

❋ *Cantal is to be found these days in good cheese departments, at stores like Zabar's and Citerella in New York. In Lyon, Paul Bocuse's gratinée lyonnaise has Gruyère or another similar style cow's milk cheese. He also adds a little cognac and just before serving, whisks in an egg yolk, and then some port. The Mère Brazier would add 3 or 4 eggs. Paul uses beef stock, the Mère Brazier used chicken stock, and Margaridou, you notice, used spring water. I use Evian and drink it, too.*

❋ *Pain bis: a country bread made from bran. Use whole wheat bread.*

Gascony Garbure Stew

Le Garbure

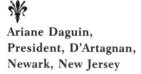

**Ariane Daguin,
President, D'Artagnan,
Newark, New Jersey**

ARIANE GREW UP IN GASCONY *in the Hotel de France at Auch where her father, André Daguin, was renowned for his specialities of duck and foie gras. Today, she lives in America with her own company that specializes in domestic foie gras, poultry, game, and other produce. She still has her warm, heavy Gascony accent.*

"For my daughter Aline on Sundays," said Ariane, "I cook a garbure, the one dish that every family cooks in our Gascony, in the southwest of France. It has everything in it—pieces of poultry, necks, legs, thighs, cabbage, leeks, beans, smoked bacon, a lot of garlic. An extraordinary meal in itself.

"On Sunday, we have the soup, and then every morning of the week some goes in Aline's lunchbox and a little in mine. Monday, we fight over who gets the duck thigh. Tuesday, I add some vermicelli. Wednesday, I take some of the soup and add a purée of vegetables. Thursday, I add duck giblets and a couple of legs of confit. That's our week of garbure."

SERVES 2 FOR SEVERAL DAYS

3 (7 oz.) tubs D'Artagnan duck
    demi-glace (see note)

1½ quarts water

6 carrots, peeled and
    quartered

6 medium turnips,
    peeled and quartered

1 bouquet garni: 1 sprig thyme,
    1 sprig parsley, and 1 bay
    leaf, tied together

1 savoy cabbage,
    cleaned and halved

3 duck legs confits (see note)

1 pound duck gizzards
    confits

3 smoked duck wings

Pour the demi-glace into a large casserole and add the water, carrots, turnips, and bouquet garni. Cook for 20 minutes over medium heat. Blanch the cabbage and put the pieces into the casserole. After 15 minutes, add the meat, beans, and salt and pepper. Cook for 10 minutes.

Remove the bouquet garni.

Serve the very hot pieces of confit on a serving platter and arrange the vegetable around them. The broth is served as a sauce in a sauceboat.

❋ *Confit: A centuries-old recipe that was developed when there was no refrigeration, explains Ariane. The duck legs*

are marinated overnight with garlic and spices, then
slowly stewed in their own juices until they are succulent
and tender.

2 cups Great Northern or
   Tarbais beans, cooked

Salt and freshly ground pepper
   to taste

❊ *Duck legs, wings, gizzards, and demi-glace are some*
D'Artagnan products that are available in quality gourmet
stores. They can also be shipped directly overnight from
D'Artagnan (see page 298).

❊ *If you wish to replace D'Artagnan duck demi-glace with*
3 cups of your own duck stock, follow the recipe for veal
demi-glace (see page 283), adding duck bones instead of
veal bones, and 2 quarts of water, and cook for no longer
than 3 hours. If you do not have duck bones or veal
demi-glace, you can use chicken stock (see page 282).

ANTICIPATING THE TASTE OF A STEW

Returning from the market in Lyon one morning, Paul Bocuse found two journalists from Switzerland waiting for him in the dining room. They had come for an interview on the latest from the Great Chef. Paul talked for an hour about taste.

"Taste is to be found in a leg of lamb, in a fish with a bone," Paul began. "If we don't teach our children to eat and eat well, all is lost."

Paul first learned about taste in the family kitchen while his mother was cooking. "Already from the smells of the cooking pot, the marmite, and from the oven, we've an impression of what we're going to eat."

Food gives a sense of security. "When we're seated with friends around a table and you place the marmite in the center of the table,

it's smoking hot and smells so good when you raise the lid that you will have two helpings."

The stews in this book, each in its respective category, have for centuries given that sense of security. They are hearty stews, like the Garbure soup from Gascony (page 20), the bouillabaisse from the Mediterranean (page 85), the matelote fish stew from Alsace (page 45) and river Saone (page 43), beef bourguignon (page 117), coq au vin from Beaujolais (page 174), navarin of lamb (page 138), and a civet of rabbit (page 190). They all improve by simmering slowly, releasing new depths of flavor well married in the stewpot. "It's marvelous, *c'est formidable!*" Roger Vergé exclaims, as he lifts the lid.

Wooden Leg Soup

Soupe à la Jambe de Bois

Paul Bocuse,
a truly Rabelaisian Pot-au-Feu—
dedicated to Henri Clos-Jouve, president
of the Academie Rabelais, Lyon

HENRI CLOS-JOUVE WAS PRESIDENT OF THE ACADEMIE RABELAIS, *founded in the thirties by the legendary Curnonsky and a group of fellow gastronomes and writers with their headquarters in the restaurants and bistrots of Lyon.*

A larger-than-life figure, he lived in a village down the river from Paul Bocuse and dined regularly at Collonges until his death in 1981.

"He told me this recipe, which like him, was a big, old favorite in Lyon," Paul said. "It's really one immense pot-au-feu. I still serve it."

This larger-than-life recipe, with its truly Rabelaisian list of ingredients, makes a good story to tell while dining on a more traditional Pot-Au-Feu (page 119), and it provides many servings. Neither Paul nor you should take it too seriously. Just keep adding whatever you have at hand into the largest pot you can find. As for the measurements, feel free, as Paul does. Or simply enjoy reading the recipe.

1 loin of beef

6 onions

1 bouquet garni: 1 sprig thyme,
    2 sprigs parsley, and 1 bay
    leaf, tied together

6 leeks

6 turnips

4 celery stalks

3 veal shins

1 pork shoulder

Game (see note)

1 turkey, cut into pieces

1 leg of lamb

1 rump of beef

2 large chickens,
    cut into pieces

6 pork sausages

Soak the loin of beef in cold water to cover in a very large cast-iron, copper, or earthenware stock pot, or *marmite* on the stove. Add the onions, bouquet garni, salt, and anything else on hand to give flavor. Cook, allow to simmer, skimming until the soup is clear.

Add the leeks, turnips, celery, veal shins, pork shoulder, game, pieces of turkey, leg of lamb, and rump of beef. Like all good stews, the longer the cooking, the better the flavor.

One hour before serving, add a couple of large chickens, followed a few minutes later by the pork sausages, generously stuffed with truffles and pistachio nuts.

When all the meat is tender, carry in the stew with the veal shin bone laid across the top of the pot, which gives this recipe its name, Soup of the Wooden Leg.

Truffles
Pistachio nuts
1 veal shin bone

❄ *More than half a century ago, whoever cooked this simply added whatever was at hand. Game means whatever is hanging in the larder, shot last week. Instead of a turkey, add a goose. Only a veal shin bone is a required ingredient. Order it a month before from your butcher.*

❄ *Paul gives the ingredients in this order but as Roger Vergé once told me, there is no one like Paul for adding to a recipe as the moment pleases him. As Clos-Jouve before him, Paul is Rabelaisian at heart.*

❄ *Serve with a good supply of bottles of Beaujolais from your cellar. This could be the dish to serve when celebrating the arrival of the Beaujolais Nouveau on the third Thursday in November.*

❄ *The Wooden Leg Soup, as its name indicates, is a soup. A gargantuan soup totally in keeping with the menus drawn up in the days of the great Rabelais when he was living and working in Lyon. It should be clear after reading this book and learning more about Paul Bocuse that the great chef gives us the grand finale of soups. What goes into the soup depends on your larder (or fridge), on your market, on the size of the biggest pot you can find and how many guests you invite. More or less sausages, 10 or 20 carrots, game or no game—you decide. All Paul and the president of the Academie Rabelais ask is: Have fun when cooking and dining. Moments in cooking like these bring back to me the words of the late Jean Troisgros when he gave me his first cookbook. It's worth repeating: "A cookbook is not just something you copy. If a cook at home who is not a professional takes a cookbook and it gives her ideas, that means the book is good. If she copies the recipes just as they are, then she has understood nothing. Elle a rien compris, rien!" Jean was serious, though he had Paul's sense of humor. They'd make this soup together. You too can make it a group event. Call some friends to join you in the kitchen when you make* La Grande Soupe.

Chapter Two

Eggs

**POACHED EGGS
À LA BEAUJOLAIS,
PAUL BOCUSE**

MELVYN MASTERS,
DENVER

**EGGS MEURETTE
POACHED IN
RED WINE SAUCE**

JEAN DUCLOUX,
TOURNUS

**EGGS POACHED
IN OPUS ONE
WITH TRUFFLES
AND FOIE GRAS**

PAUL BOCUSE,
NAPA VALLEY

**SCRAMBLED EGG
IN THE SHELL
WITH CAVIAR**

ROGER VERGÉ,
CÔTE D'AZUR

**OMELET,
LYON-STYLE**

PAUL BOCUSE,
HYDE PARK, NEW YORK

**BACON AND EGGS
ON A DISH**

GARE DE LYON,
PARIS

Seek out the freshest possible eggs, if you do not have chickens laying eggs in your backyard. One of the joys of living in the country is using a freshly laid egg just gathered by the farmer's wife next door for enjoying the simple boiled egg. In town, no chickens in sight, your best bet is a farmers' market or a gourmet store with a dairy section that has rapid turnover.

To know if eggs are fresh before you start cooking, hold an egg next to your ear and shake the egg. A fresh egg makes no sound.

If it is less than fresh, the egg may make little noises, because the air chamber in an egg grows larger every day.

Another way to test for freshness is to place the egg in water: A fresh egg sinks, less fresh eggs float. Or cook yourself a boiled egg for breakfast. One taste and you will know.

Poached Eggs à la Beaujolaise
Paul Bocuse

Oeufs Pochés à la Beaujolaise Paul Bocuse

**Melvyn Masters,
Mel's Restaurant,
Denver**

IN THE LATE SIXTIES, *a young English wine shipper and his wife stopped for lunch at Collonges-au-Mont-d'Or, and suggested that Paul come to America to sell the Paul Bocuse Beaujolais wines served in his restaurant.*

"They were extraordinary times travelling with Paul," recalls the wine shipper, Melvyn Masters, who today is the owner of a restaurant in Denver.

"Taking him from city to city, with Paul cooking private dinners in big homes. A favorite he liked to serve was his eggs in Beaujolais.

"Paul was the first to introduce Duboeuf wines to America. They had to carry the Bocuse label as Georges Duboeuf was under contract to Alexis Lichine then to bottle the Lichine wines only and not ship any of his own wines to the States. Paul poured a good bottle of Beaujolais Fleurie or Morgon into the sauce and served the same wine with the eggs. After eighty or ninety dinners, I know that recipe by heart."

SERVES 6

6 cold large eggs from the
    refrigerator

Wine sauce

4 tablespoons butter

1 small Spanish onion or
    6 shallots, peeled and
    chopped

1 bottle Beaujolais

2 garlic cloves, 1 peeled and
    chopped, 1 peeled

1 bouquet garni: 1 celery stalk,
    1 small leek, trimmed,
    1 sprig thyme, 1 strip bay
    leaf, tied together

Take the eggs out of the refrigerator and set them aside to warm up.

Meanwhile, to make the wine sauce, melt 2 tablespoons of butter in a large, heavy saucepan and add the chopped onions or shallots. Cook over low heat until translucent.

Add the Beaujolais, chopped garlic, bouquet garni, and pepper. Increase the heat to medium and bring to a boil. Reduce the heat immediately to low and simmer, uncovered, for about 20 minutes. Strain the wine sauce through a fine-mesh sieve and pour the sauce into the cleaned saucepan. Heat to a simmer.

Cut the slices of bread into triangles, brush with butter on both sides, and fry lightly on both sides. Alternatively, oven-dry the bread until crispy like croutons. Rub them with the cut side of a garlic clove, sprinkle with a pinch of salt, and set aside in a warm oven.

Break an egg into a cup and slide it gently into the simmering wine sauce; poach up to 3 eggs at once, if possible. For eggs with runny centers, cook for 4 minutes; for eggs with soft centers, cook for 6 minutes. Gently remove the eggs with a slotted spoon or spatula and drain. Place them on a warm dish. Cover with aluminum foil while you poach the remaining eggs.

Melt the remaining 2 tablespoons butter in another saucepan. Add the flour, stirring with a wire whisk until the butter foams. Pour in the wine sauce, beating with the whisk until it thickens. Adjust seasonings and add salt to taste.

Place 1 or 2 eggs each in a cereal bowl or deep dish and spoon over the sauce. Serve with the warmed croutons.

"I believe Paul used to add a touch of anchovy paste," said Melvyn.

Salt and freshly ground pepper to taste

6 slices of bread, crusts removed

1 tablespoon butter for buttering

2 tablespoons all-purpose flour

* *Very fresh eggs are the secret of good poached eggs.*

* *"There are two schools of cooking," says Hervé Riou. "Some chefs like their eggs at room temperature, some start with them cold. But always for patisserie, chefs use eggs cold from the refrigerator. And you should never use an egg, taken directly from the fridge to add to a warm dish. Cold to cold, room temperature to warm."*

* *When poaching or frying eggs, add salt afterwards or it will break the eggs.*

* *André Soltner recommends seasoning the egg with salt on its underside, or the salt will mark the yolk with miniscule spots.*

Eggs Meurette Poached in Red Wine Sauce

Oeufs en Meurette

**Jean Ducloux,
Restaurant Greuze,
Tournus-on-the-Saone**

PAUL BOCUSE LIKES TO DRIVE UP THE RIVER *to visit his old friend Jean Ducloux. They dine together and exchange stories.*

Aged fifteen, Ducloux apprenticed in the great Alexandre Dumaine's Hotel de la Côte d'Or in Saulieu on the Paris-Mediterranean road. He worked in the big palace-hotel kitchens in France and Africa. He opened his own restaurant in 1947. Like Paul, he collects fairground pipe organs. He still dreams of one day coming to America.

"Paul's my best friend," declares Ducloux, "but I'm older than him. I'm seventy-eight years old, I'm not rich nor in debt, I get up when I wake up, I go to bed when I'm tired, and my duties are my passions, too. All I ask is another twenty years."

SERVES 4

8 large fresh eggs

Red wine sauce

Giblets of 4 chickens, diced, or
    1 chicken carcass cut into
    pieces
12 tablespoons (1½ sticks)
    butter
1 carrot, peeled and diced
2 onions, peeled and diced
1 teaspoon all-prupose flour
1 bottle good red wine
    (see note) plus 2 cups

Remove the eggs from the refrigerator and set aside.

Melt 4 tablespoons butter in a large saucepan over medium heat. Add the giblets, the carrot, and onions and cook until the giblets or chicken are brown. Stir in the flour, the bottle of wine, and the bouquet garni.

Reduce the heat to low and continue cooking for 30 minutes. Remove from the heat and strain the cooking liquid through a fine sieve.

In a separate saucepan, add 2 cups wine, the shallots, and pepper. Bring this to a boil and cook until it reduces by half. Blend the reduction with the cooking liquid from the saucepan. Season to taste and set aside.

Brush the bread slices on both sides lightly with butter and fry in a skillet over medium heat until golden. Set aside on a hot serving platter.

Fill a saucepan, sauté pan, or skillet with 2 quarts water and the vinegar. Bring the liquid to a simmer over medium heat. Break an egg into a cup and slide it gently into the acidulated water; poach up to 2 eggs at once, if possible. For eggs with runny centers, cook for 4 minutes; for eggs with soft centers, cook for 6 minutes. Gently remove the eggs with a slotted spoon or spatula and drain. Place them on a warm dish.

Place 2 eggs on each slice of bread. Pour the sauce over the eggs, sprinkle with a pinch of salt, and serve immediately.

1 bouquet garni: 2 sprigs fresh thyme, 2 sprigs fresh tarragon, and 2 sprigs fresh parsley, tied together

2 tablespoons shallots, chopped

Freshly ground pepper to taste

4 slices white bread, crusts trimmed

8 tablespoons (1 stick) butter

2 quarts salted water

1 cup red wine vinegar

Pinch salt

* *Jean Ducloux suggests adding chopped mushrooms, sautéed with a little lard.*

* *The Mère Brazier poached her eggs in salted water to which she added a bottle of Sancerre red wine. She cooked her eggs hard-boiled and served them in the red wine sauce along with a carafe of the Sancerre.*

* *The original* Larousse Gastronomique *by Prosper Montagne gave ninety recipes for the poached egg; Paul Bocuse in his* French Cooking *suggests more than two dozen ways of serving poached eggs; Auguste Escoffier in his* Ma Cuisine *offers some eighteen variations on a poached egg; Raymond Oliver, born in the Bordeaux region, in his* La Cuisine *proposes five poached eggs recipes, one of which, Poached Eggs-Haut Brion, uses "1 1/2 cups Chateau Haut-Brion or another good red Bordeaux wine."*

* *While Bocuse chooses a red Beaujolais from Georges Duboeuf, Ducloux calls for a "good, big red wine," like the chef himself, a Beaujolais from his friend, winegrower Gerald Cortembert in Beaujolais.*

Eggs Poached in Opus One with Truffles and Foie Gras

Oeufs Pochés au Vin Rouge, aux Truffes, et au Foie Gras

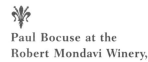

**Paul Bocuse at the
Robert Mondavi Winery,
Napa Valley**

IN THE LATE SEVENTIES, *Bob Mondavi invited the great chefs—Paul Bocuse, Jean Troisgros, and Roger Vergé—to conduct a series of cooking seminars at his winery. The theme: Californian wines go well with French cuisine.*

"One day I was demonstrating a favorite, eggs poached in wine, oeufs pochés au vin," recalled Paul. "I turned to Bob and said, 'We'll need four bottles of your Opus One.'"

"'Oooh,' cried Bob. Opus One, his new baby that he was launching with the Baron de Rothschild of Bordeaux, sold at over $100 a bottle. He was, of course, playing to the gallery and brought me the four bottles of Opus One.

"'Now we need a vegetable,' I said, when I had cooked the onions and poached the eggs. 'We need 500 grams of truffles.'

"'Oooh,', went Bob, giving me the truffles. I sliced them up and added them in.

"'The sauce is looking very clear, Bob,' I said, 'We need something to make a liaison, give it more body. I need 300 grams of foie gras.'

"In came the foie gras and I blended it in and thickened the sauce.

"'There, we have our eggs poached in wine and we need the wine to drink with it,' I said, looking at Bob, 'It must be the same wine as we have in the sauce.'

"We all sat down to eat," Paul concluded, "the most expensive poached eggs in the world."

SERVES 6

3 tablespoons butter

1 Spanish onion or
    6 shallots, chopped

1 bottle red wine,
    Cabernet Sauvignon style

1/4 pound black truffles

2 1/2 ounces fresh or
    tinned foie gras

6 fresh eggs

Salt and freshly ground pepper

"First you prepare your onion," says Hervé, explaining Paul's recipe. "Next, add your wine. Then you add the truffles. Now, poach your eggs and, last of all, you add your foie gras. Most important, you must not put the foie gras in earlier as it must not poach, or the foie gras will totally spoil. That's your order of cooking."

For poaching the eggs in this sauce, see page 27.

✻ If you cannot find Opus One, you might cook and serve
   the second wine of a great Bordeaux chateau like the red
   Pavillon Rouge of Chateau Margaux, or Forts de Latour
   of Chateau Latour—half the price of Opus One and
   very good. Never worry about the vintage of such wines.
   Or choose any other Bordeaux you like.

✻ When cooking for 20 people, increase the quantities on
   your shopping list, making sure you include 20 fresh eggs,
   one per person, tripling the amount of black truffles and
   foie gras, and, in place of the Beaujolais, use at least
   4 bottles of Opus One. You may have to hunt for this wine,
   as annual production is small.

✻ For black truffles, fresh (December through January)
   or in tins, see page 298.

✻ For foie gras, fresh or in tins, see page 298.

Scrambled Egg in the Shell
with Caviar

Coquille de Brouillade d'Oeuf en Caviar

Roger Vergé Cooking School,
Restaurant L'Amandier,
Mougins, Côte d'Azur

"SCRAMBLED EGGS HAVE BEEN MADE AND MASSACRED *for as long as people knew about pots and pans,*" *complained M.F.K. Fisher. In her classic,* The Art of Eating, *she left us the recipe for* Scrambled Eggs for a Shrew:

"Beat eggs angrily until they froth. Add the water. Season without thought...Scrape onto cold plate and slam down on carelessly laid table."

The Mère Brazier seriously considered scrambled eggs to be the most delicate way of cooking eggs. A couple of years ago, I was conducting a tour through the great châeaux of Bordeaux. At Château Cheval Blanc, the meal began with scrambled eggs in the shell with caviar. A young Graves wine was refreshing by its side. The visitors applauded.

Roger Vergé teaches, cooks, and serves scrambled eggs this way in his summer cooking school at his second restaurant, L'Amandier, up on the hill village of Mougins.

SERVES 4

4 large fresh eggs

1 generous tablespoon
    sweet butter

Salt and freshly ground pepper,
    to taste

1 tablespoon heavy cream or
    crème fraîche

8 chives, halved

1 1/2 ounces caviar

2 slices french bread

Using an egg cutter, carefully cut off each shell at the wide end, leaving three-quarters of the shell intact. Pour the contents out into a small bowl.

Delicately wash the shells and dip them in a saucepan of boiling water for one minute. Remove and overturn on a folded towel to dry.

Melt the butter in a small saucepan over low heat. Beat the eggs with salt and pepper and pass through a sieve into the saucepan.

Cook the eggs over low heat, gently stirring with a wooden spoon, until the eggs become creamy. Remove from the heat and stir in the cream. Season to taste.

Place the 4 egg shells in egg cups and, using a teaspoon, fill them with the egg mixture. Arrange four chive halves on top of each egg and place a small portion of caviar in the center.

Toast the bread and cut each slice into quarters to accompany the eggs.

* *Egg cutters are rare and extremely delicate, because they are made of wire. Roger would use an egg cutter, because this dish is often on his menu. Hervé recommends using a small, sharp pair of scissors to make a small hole in the egg, and then to cut off the top of the shell.*

* *Use the freshest eggs possible.*

* *Cooking eggs in a* double boiler *or* bain marie, *stirring constantly, produces creamier eggs.*

* *In season, replace the toast with small bundles of wild asparagus, if desired.*

Omelet, Lyon-Style

Omelette Lyonnaise

**Paul Bocuse at the
Culinary Insitute of America,
Hyde Park, New York**

THE GREAT ALEXANDRE DUMAINE *told a young, aspiring chef visiting him at his 3-star restaurant at the Hotel de la Côte d'Or, "Many people know how to cook. What is important is to know how to teach what you know."*

That same young chef, Paul Bocuse, had just spent four years working in the kitchen of Fernand Point, who believed the best school in the world for chefs was a restaurant. A number of chefs in this book were apprenticed chez Fernand Point: Jean and Pierre Troisgros, Paul Haeberlin, and Paul Bocuse in the fifties, and later, Alain Chapel, Jean Banchet, and Georges Perrier.

Bocuse said, "Point told us it was the duty of a good chef to pass on to the generations that follow what we have learned from our own personal experience."

Forty years on, Paul found himself guest of honor at the Culinary Institute of America, giving the graduation address in the grand hall before some 500 young student chefs.

"This morning, with your President Metz," he began, "I woke up very early. From my bedroom window I saw a river out there and I heard trains. For a moment I thought I was back home in Collonges. For breakfast, I was served a little onion omelette just as we do in Lyon."

Here is the recipe from the Culinary Institute of America.

SERVES 2

3 large eggs
Pinch salt
2 tablespoons plus
  1 teaspoon butter
1 medium onion, peeled
  and finely sliced
Pinch finely chopped parsley

Break the eggs into a bowl, add the salt, and beat lightly with a fork just enough to mix the yolks and whites.

Heat the butter in an omelet pan over medium heat and cook the sliced onion until golden. Increase the heat to high and add the eggs. Sprinkle with the parsley.

Loosen the egg mixture with a fork as it cooks around the edges of the pan. Let the uncooked egg run beneath the cooked egg.

Fold the omelet over fast and cook any egg on the outside that is still runny. Add 1 teaspoon butter to the pan and cook the omelet until lightly brown. Slip it onto a warm serving platter, brush the top with a small knob of butter, and serve immediately.

* *The chefs in this cookbook are most concerned with the quality of what they use in their kitchens. I may repeat myself, but quality confronts us at every recipe in this book. Discover something just arrived at the market in season, ripe, and ready—that is the reason enough to hunt out a recipe and make it. It dawned on me the other day that here I am looking for organic milk and eggs and whatever else I can find organic: When Paul, Jean, and André were youngsters, their parents were cooking with organic food—everything was home grown. Fish swam unpolluted rivers, cows grazed, and hens pecked farmyards safely; harvests of wheat and grapes came in without fear of pesticides or other contamination. Everything was organic but we didn't know it by name. Progress, where are we?*

* *The right consistency of an omelet depends on personal taste. A moment more or less of cooking makes a big difference in texture. An omelette baveuse, as the French generally cook, is firm at the bottom and soft on top.*

Some tips from Paul Bocuse:

* *A plain omelet requires two eggs per person.*

* *Cook a maximum of six eggs at a time.*

* *Use a nonstick omelet pan or vintage cast-iron pan that has never been washed, just scoured with coarse salt and wiped with a paper towel after use.*

Some other words on the omelet:

* *Who cooks the best omelet? "If I want to to be annoying,"
  declared Paul Bocuse one day, and no one can accuse him
  of false modesty, "I say that I am the best, but I don't think
  I am. There is at least one who is better than I am: Jean
  Troisgros. I like all the dishes he cooks for me. He is the
  only one who can make a successful omelette."*

* *"Some might call it banal to offer a recipe for an omelette,
  since we all believe we know how," wrote Ali-Bab, one of
  France's great amateurs of the kitchen, in his culinary
  masterpiece,* Practical Gastronomy, *"but the truth is,
  many people have never eaten a truly good omelette."*

* *"As everyone knows," wrote the English food writer
  Elizabeth David in the fifties, "there is only one infallible
  recipe for the perfect omelette, your own."*

EGGS IN WAR AND PEACE

In the English countryside, as in France, all through World War II, the hens went on laying their eggs. Our eggs were collected from us each week by the Ministry of Food van for distribution under food rationing. So eggs and milk for cooking came in powdered form, out of cardboard boxes or tins. We were fed puddings soaking in a tired, dull yellow sauce that they told us children was a custard. From a little cookbook that my wife Jeannie's mother had in her kitchen, I copied this wartime custard.

serves 4

2 powdered eggs
2 tablespoons flour
1 tablespoon sugar
5 tablespoons household milk (dry)
1 pint water

Mix all the ingredients. Mix to a smooth cream with cold water. Boil remainder of water and pour over mixture. Return to pan and boil 1 to 2 minutes, stirring well. Flavor and serve.

In those same dark years, during the occupation of Paris, the great French writer Colette, author of *Cheri* and *Gigi*, retired to her appartment in the rue de Beaujolais, looking out over the gardens of the Palais-Royal, and wrote in her *Paris From My Window*:

Someone is reading aloud, trying to make us laugh, a recipe of better days, I mean from 1939, "Take eight or ten eggs."

"Take them where," asks the young girl, who did not laugh.

She is a young girl of these days, nearing adolescence, thin, bright and misses nothing. She lives our life and her own. With her folding stool, shopping bag, her knitting and school book, her socks rolled round her ankles, she is off to queue when school is over. Her thoughts, her desires while she waits outside a big grocery shop, she keeps to herself. But in one word she has just shown us that she has her own opinion on what is permitted, what is forbidden, and some personal thoughts on "Take eight eggs."

She knows that eight eggs cannot be bought anywhere. Her nostrils, her sharp look, she is like a fox cub. She seems to have a dream of a hen run, of a hen as well as the egg. Like many children, she has her own little world. She pulls tight the buckle of her raincoat, pockets her bus tickets, listens to some complaint from her mother, and is off to win a slice of cheese, a kilo of chestnuts, and some Brussel sprouts. All of which, nicely cooked, will make an excellent dinner."

Paul Bocuse was a young soldier in the Free French Army, fighting in the Alsace of his colleagues, the Haeberlin brothers, in the last years of World War II. At the Liberation, he marched in the Victory Parade down the Avenue of the Champs-Elysées in Paris, returned to Lyon, and went to work in the Mère Brazier's kitchen.

Bacon and Eggs on a Dish

Oeufs au Bacon sur le Plat

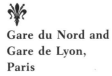

**Gare du Nord and
Gare de Lyon,
Paris**

THE WAR IS OVER. *France is free. All of fourteen years old, I took my younger brother and, landing at Dieppe, we cycled across Normandy. The countryside looked war-scarred, desolate, but the patronne of the small inns smiled kindly on us, serving bowls of café au lait, croissants, and fresh farmhouse butter. Our midday meal was a picnic of country pâté, ham, tomatoes, and fruit. We had enough francs leftover for dinner at the inns. Two young boys from across the English Channel were tasting for the first time family cooking in these small country restaurants in a land barely recovered from four years of occupation.*

Reaching Chartres, we took the train back to Paris. On the platform of the Gare du Nord waiting for the boat train, we ordered a last taste of France: eggs and bacon in a dish, oeufs au bacon sur le plat.

I learned from Paul Bocuse many years later, this was the dish by which both the Mère Brazier and Fernand Point would judge a new chef. You can still order it at the Gare de Lyon station buffet in Paris, before boarding the 10:00 A.M. TGV train named the Paul Bocuse. Destination: Lyon.

SERVES 2

2 tablespoons butter
4 thin slices bacon
4 large eggs

Heat 1 tablespoon of butter in each of two individual enameled cast-iron pans. Place 2 pieces of bacon in each pan and, over medium heat, brown lightly on both sides.

Break 2 eggs into a small bowl and slide carefully into one pan; repeat with the remaining eggs. Reduce the heat to low and cook for 3 minutes or until the whites are partially cooked. Increase the heat to medium and cook for another 3 minutes. Or place the pans in a preheated 350°F oven for the final 3 minutes and serve immediately.

THE FAMILY OF CHEFS

While this young boy was on his first trip to France, American soldiers were returning to the States and would be back with their families and friends to taste again this France they had just seen liberated.

Eleven of the thirty-eight chefs featured in this book were actively part of that first stage in rebuilding France and her cuisine after the war: Bocuse, the Troisgros and Haeberlins, Soltner, Franey, Ducloux, Vergnes, Bernachon, Vergé, together with their elders, Bocuse *père*, Troisgros *père*, Lacombe *père*, Boyer *père*, Blanc *père*, Fernand Point, and the Mère Brazier.

Many of those chefs of subsequent generations whom I've included were apprenticed in the kitchens of Point, Bocuse, Troisgros, Vergè, and company. This is part of the story of a large family of chefs, *une grande famille nombreuse des chefs*

Chapter Three

Fish

FRESHWATER FISH

**MATELOTE, A STEW
OF EEL AND OTHER
FRESHWATER FISH**

THE MÈRE BRAZIER,
LYON

**MATELOTE,
FISH STEW WITH
RIESLING WINE**

PAUL HAEBERLIN,
ILLHAEUSERN, ALSACE

**SALMON SOUFFLÉ
AUBERGE DE L'ILL**

PAUL HAEBERLIN,
ILLHAEUSERN, ALSACE

**SALMON ESCALOPES
WITH SORREL SAUCE**

JEAN AND PIERRE
TROISGROS, ROANNE

**SALMON TROUT
WITH WILD LEEKS**

ANDRÉ SOLTNER,
NEW YORK

**LOIRE RIVER
PIKE-PERCH IN ITS
PURÉE AND SAUCE**

REGIS MARCON,
HAUTE-LOIRE

BLUE TROUT

PAUL BOCUSE
AT HIS LAKE
IN THE DOMBES

**CARP STUFFED
AND ROASTED**

PAUL BOCUSE,
COLLONGES-AU-MONT-
D'OR, LYON

SALTWATER FISH

**FRESH HERRINGS
MARINATED IN
WHITE WINE**

THE MÈRE BRAZIER,
LYON

**SOLE MEUNIÈRE
WITH MUSHROOMS
MÈRE BRAZIER**

THE MÈRE BRAZIER,
LYON

**FILLET OF SOLE
WITH FRESH
NOODLES,
JEAN VIGNARD**

PIERRE ORSI,
LYON

**DOVER SOLE
RIVIERA**

JEAN BANCHET,
ATLANTA

Sole, Crayfish, and Oysters with Fava Beans and Baby Onions

Michel Chabran,
Pont de l'Isère, Rhône

Red Mullet in Potato Scales

Roger Jaloux,
Collonges-au-Mont-d'Or, Lyon

Pavé of Codfish with Red Wine and Fried Shallots

Gilbert Le Coze,
New York

Roasted Fillet of Sea Bass or Codfish in Red Wine Sauce

André Soltner,
New York

Alsace Fish Tart in Beer Custard

André Soltner,
New York

Baked Chilean Bass with Coco Beans, Carrots, Leeks, Celery, and Roasted Tomatoes

Jean-Louis Palladin,
Washington, D.C.

Sea Bream, Oven-Cooked à la Provençale

Paul Bocuse,
Collonges-au-Mont-d'Or, Lyon

Mediterranean Fish Stew

Etienne Sordello,
Cap d'Antibes,
Côte d'Azur

Turbot with Seaweed, Shellfish, and Demi-Sel Butter Chips

Alain Ducasse,
Monte Carlo and Paris

SHELLFISH

Mussels Marinière in White Wine

The Mère Brazier,
Lyon

Soft-Shell Crabs Sautéed with Lemon Juice and Cognac

Jean Troisgros, Roanne
and Georges Troisgros,
New York

Scallops in a Half-Moon with Chicory and Truffles

Gerard Boyer,
Reims, Champagne

Lobster and Macaroni Gratin

Roger Vergé,
Côte d'Azur

Lobsters Oh! Marcoco

Claude Troisgros,
Miami Beach

Gratin of Freshwater Crayfish, Fernand Point

Patrick Henriroux,
Vienne, Rhône Valley

Wading in the river with the village children, I learned early (and long since forgot) how to tickle for fish with my hand underwater. I cannot recall if we caught much, but it was more fun than sitting in the rain on the river bank with an adult's rod, waiting for trout to bite.

In the upper reaches of the Auvergne where the rivers run down the mountains, the home of the trout, Margaridou wrote in her journal, "Under every man's blue serge jacket lies the soul of a fisherman and hunter. They know where to find the trout with the elegant head and shiny body with its rock marks that look hand-painted." When she was a child, her mother would always put aside from the catch two small trout weighing about three-and-one-half ounces each, for her and her sister for dinner.

"Paul Bocuse had the good fortune to be brought up on the banks of a river," recalled his colleague, Alain Chapel. Indeed, Paul learned fishing—and poaching—by night with his father on the River Saone while his best friend, Jean Troisgros, learned on the Loire. Their training as chefs in Fernand Point's La Pyramide was at Vienne on the River Rhône.

Under every chef's jacket, too, lies the soul of a fisherman and hunter.

Matelote, a Stew of Eel and Other Freshwater Fish

Le Matelote

**The Mère Brazier,
Restaurant Mère Brazier,
Lyon**

ALONG THE BANKS OF THE RIVER SAONE *outside Lyon were small restaurants with menus of fish freshly caught in the river. Paul Bocuse's family has had a restaurant on the banks of the Saone since the 1650s. These riverside restaurants, called* guinguettes, *were favorite haunts of the nineteenth-century painters Manet, Degas, and Renoir. The film* La Partie de Campagne (A Trip to the Country), *directed in the late thirties by the painter's son, Jean Renoir, retelling the Maupassant romance of a summer's day by the river, is one of Paul's favorite films. In the film, the family arrives for their Sunday lunch of a* matelote, *the traditional fish stew that Paul's family served at their restaurant-mill on the river for decades, that he still brings back to his menu from time to time.*

Here are two versions of the matelote *first by the Mère Brazier in Lyon; the second from Alsace, an old family recipe given me by Jean-Pierre Haeberlin and made by his brother Paul from fish out of the River Ill that runs past their restaurant. Both eel and fish must be very fresh—if possible, caught the same day.*

SERVES 6

1¹/2 pounds eel, skinned, cleaned, and washed

1 pound pike or carp, filleted

1 garlic clove, crushed, plus 1 garlic clove, peeled

1 sprig thyme, chopped

1 sprig tarragon, chopped

Salt and freshly ground pepper to taste

1 bottle dry white wine, Macon-style

2 tablespooons (¹/4 stick) kneaded butter (*beurre manié*) (see note) plus 4 ounces unsalted butter

6 thin, round croutons, cut from half baguette

Cut the eel and fish into small slices. Place the eel in the bottom of a heavy, enamelled cast-iron pan. Add the crushed garlic and sprigs of thyme and tarragon. Place the fish on top and season with salt and pepper. Add enough wine to cover the fish.

Cook over high heat until it boils. Thicken by stirring in the kneaded butter. Reduce heat to medium and cook for 30 minutes, stirring the mixture from time to time.

Rub the croutons with the peeled garlic. Heat the remaining 4 ounces butter in a skillet and sauté the croutons until golden brown. Place the croutons on the bottom of a heated large, deep serving dish, layer the fish on the croutons, and pour the sauce through a fine-mesh sieve over the fish. Serve hot.

* *Kneaded butter, beurre manié, is equal parts softened butter and flour. Use a fork to soften the butter and mix the flour into it. Add in small knobs to boiling liquid.*

* *The Mère Brazier, cooking her matelote, scales, empties, and washes the eel and fish, cuts them into slices, then puts them straight into the pot.*

* *We have listed the fish here as filleted. "Fillets were for the rich or for feast days," Hervé tells me. "In the old days, there was nothing wrong in finding some bones or some skin in a cooked dish. Bones and skin give more taste to food. Nothing wrong either in taking up a good piece of meat from the table in your fingers and eating it. Today we have lost touch with so much of taste."*

* *This dish is usually called a matelote when cooked with red wine, and a pochouse when using white wine. Paul Haeberlin in his recipe (see below), likes to use and to serve a white Alsace wine and calls his recipe matelote. The word is possibly derived from a 'sailor's dish,' plat de matelot.*

* *The Mère Brazier cooked her pochouse with a dry white Macon or Pouilly-Fuissé–style wine. Paul Bocuse uses a red wine, Beaujolais. Fernand Point, further down river, served his matelote with a sturdy red Côtes du Rhône. In the days of Maupassant, when Parisians dined on the banks of the Seine at a guinguette, the matelote was cooked in red Bordeaux, so they would usually ask for the same wine to drink with it. About that time, across the English Channel, Mrs. Beeton in her matelote used a half pint of port and her fish included a tench, a dozen oysters, and two anchovies. The Haeberlins naturally recommend the dry, fruity Alsace Riesling.*

Matelote, Fish Stew with Riesling Wine

Matelote d'Illhaeusern au Riesling

**Paul Haeberlin,
Auberge de l'Ill,
Illhaeusern, Alsace**

ASK THE FISHMONGER *to gut and bone the eel and fish and to give you the bones, fins, and tails to use in the court bouillon. If you want the heads, have the gills and eyes removed and any blood washed off. Paul Haeberlin likes to serve this dish with fresh noodles (see page 232).*

SERVES 6 OR 8

Court bouillon

1 leek, well washed

1 carrot, trimmed, peeled, and washed

1 onion, peeled

1 1/2 quarts water

Tails and bones from the fish

1 sprig thyme

1/4 leaf basil

1 sprig tarragon

1/4 clove garlic

Matelote stew

One 2-pound eel

One 1-pound pike

One 7-ounce perch

Two 14-ounce trout

4 shallots, peeled, chopped

1 bottle Alsace Riesling or other dry white wine

Salt and freshly ground pepper to taste

continued

To prepare the court bouillon, cut the vegetables in pieces and soak them in the 1 1/2 quarts water. Add the fish bones and tails, thyme, basil, tarragon, and garlic. Bring to a boil over medium heat and cook for 30 minutes. Pour the liquid through a fine-meshed sieve and set aside.

To prepare the *matelote*, chop the fish into pieces. Set aside. Put 3 1/2 tablespoons butter in a large saucepan and heat over medium heat. Add the shallots and cook until sweated and lightly brown. Add the wine and 1 quart court bouillon. Season with salt and pepper, and bring to a boil. Add fish in the following order: the eel, and after 5 minutes, add the pike, the perch, and the trout. Reduce the heat to low and cook and for 15 minutes more.

Meanwhile, heat the remaining 2 tablespoons butter in a small skillet over medium heat and cook the mushrooms until lightly brown and tender.

To prepare the sauce, put 3 1/2 tablespoons butter in a saucepan and melt over medium heat. Stir in the flour to make a roux, stirring constantly. Add some liquid from the poached fish, reduce the heat to low and cook 5 minutes. Pour through a fine-mesh sieve.

5 1/2 tablespoons butter

2 1/2 pounds fresh small white mushrooms

Sauce

3 1/2 tablespoons butter

5 1/2 tablespoons flour

2 egg yolks, chilled in refrigerator for at least 1 hour

1 cup heavy cream, chilled in refrigerator for at least 1 hour

Juice 1/4 lemon

Pinch freshly grated nutmeg

1 tablespoon chopped parsley

Remove the egg yolks and cream from the refrigerator and mix them together in a small bowl. Stir gradually into the sauce and reduce the heat immediately to low. Season to taste, and add the lemon juice, nutmeg, sautéed mushrooms, and chopped parsley.

Place the fish on a warm serving dish and pour the sauce over top.

❊ *The great taste here is the eel. Paul and Jean-Pierre say the eel is* indispensable. *The Alsace wine for them, too, is* indispensable!

❊ *You can substitute other white fish, such as sea bass, pompano, red snapper, monkfish, and John Dory.*

❊ *Paul likes to cut some pastry* fleurons *from Flaky Pastry (see page 286) and cook them in a 200°F oven. He decorates the fish on the serving platter with these fleurons.*

❊ *Ask the fishmonger to cut and bone the fish, reserving the bones and tails and discarding the head; use these for the court bouillon.*

❊ *The art of finishing a* roux *is simple: Whenever you mix in the flour or other starch, you must always cook the roux slowly over low heat. This takes away the taste of the starch. How long do you cook it? The taste will tell you.*

❊ *"One of the secrets of good cooking," says Hervé Riou, "is to taste all your preparations. Taste. Add a little of an ingredient at a time, taste, add some more, taste, add more if it needs it. Remember, you cannot take it away once it is added. Taste regularly what you're cooking and trust your taste."*

THE RIESLING WINE OF ALSACE

I only drink red wines, some say. But have you tasted the dry white wine from the hillsides in that northeastern corner of France called Alsace, so often handed over to Germany after peace treaties in centuries of wars? I have a friend, winemaker Hubert Trimbach, whose grandmother changed her nationality—French to German—five times in her lifetime.

The wines of Alsace are named after the grape varieties of Riesling, Muscat, Sylvaner, Pinot Blanc, and Gewürtztraminer. Rieslings are made in the Rhine and Moselle valleys of Germany, in California, and in Chile, often by winemakers with German roots, and all these wines have a certain sweetness.

The Riesling is Alsace's Grand Vin. "It offers something much more elusive," wrote Hugh Johnson in his *World Atlas of Wines &*
Spirits, "a balance of hard and gentle, flowery and strong, which leads you on and never surfeits."

In the courts of the Czars in the last century, the finest Alsace wines were priced higher than the Bordeaux.

Among the old wine families making these Rieslings, I recommend the houses of Trimbach, Preiss-Zimmer, Hugel, Beyer, and Ingelbrecht.

To understand their past, in Alphonse Daudet's *Les Contes du Lundi* (*Tales of Monday*), read the first chapter entitled *La Derniere Classe* (The Last Lesson). It is 1873, the defeat of France, with the Prussian army at the gates of Paris. In a small Alsace village school, the children are being given their last lesson in French. Tomorrow they must speak German only.

Salmon Soufflé Auberge de l'Ill

Saumon Soufflé Auberge de l'Ill

**Paul Haeberlin,
Auberge de l'Ill,
Illhaeusern, Alsace**

THE GREAT CHEFS *enjoy many of the same things. Ask Paul Bocuse which is one of his favorite dishes: foie gras and a fine Sauternes. At Christmas time in Alsace, the great treat of the Haeberlin family is to open a bottle of Chateau Yquem and enjoy this greatest of Sauternes wines with their homemade fresh Alsace foie gras, followed by Paul Haeberlin's salmon soufflé.*

SERVES 8

2 pounds salmon fillets, cut into eight 4-ounce medallions, free of bones, set aside in the refrigerator (see note)

2 shallots, peeled and finely chopped

3/4 cup Alsace Riesling wine

1/2 cup fish stock *Fish Fumet* (see page 284)

Soufflé mousse

9 ounces white fish or yellow pike, skinned and boned

2 large eggs

2 egg yolks

Salt and freshly ground pepper to taste

Pinch freshly grated nutmeg

1/2 cup heavy cream or *crème fraîche*

2 egg whites

Preheat the oven to 375°F. Butter and salt a large ovenproof baking dish.

Keep the salmon fillets in the refrigerator until ready to use. Combine the shallots, wine, and fish stock in a small bowl, cover, and refrigerate until ready to use.

To prepare the soufflé mousse, using a fine blade of a meat grinder or food processor, grind the white fish for 30 seconds. Add 2 whole eggs, 2 egg yolks, salt, pepper, and nutmeg and start the food processor again. Slowly add 1/2 cup cream and process briefly until smooth. Do not overblend.

Scoop the mousse into a small bowl standing in a bowl of ice cubes and refrigerate for 15 minutes. When it is cold, beat 2 egg whites until a soft peak forms, and gently fold the whites into the cold mixture. Refrigerate again.

To prepare the salmon, place the fish in a baking dish and sprinkle chopped shallots over each piece. Using a pastry spatula, cover each piece with the fish paste, forming a dome shape.

Pour the stock and Riesling around the fish, no higher than $1/2$ inch; the fish will release water during cooking. Set aside in the refrigerator for 15 minutes.

Remove the salmon from the refrigerator and place in the oven. Bake for 15 to 20 minutes. Remove and put the fish on a warm serving platter; keep warm.

To prepare the sauce, pour all the cooking liquid into a saucepan, and over medium heat, bring it to a boil to reduce by half. Add the cream and reduce by half. Add the cold butter, vigorously whisking. The sauce should become light and creamy. Add the lemon juice, and salt and pepper to taste. Pass through a fine-mesh sieve into a warm serving jug.

Serve 1 piece of fish on each warm plate and surround with the sauce.

❁ *Before cooking, check the fillets for small bones and, if found, remove them with small tweezers.*

❁ *The Alsace Riesling is Jean-Pierre's recommendation. A salmon soufflé is worth the search for its ideal partner, the exquisite Trimbach family's Riesling St. Hune. There are not many bottles made in a vintage, so call up the best wine merchant you know—and a table of your best friends.*

❁ *For the record, Collonges, Paul's village on the Saone river, is twinned with the Haeberlin's Illhaeusern, on the banks of the little stream called the Ill. In the days when rivers were not polluted, André Soltner recalls, salmon was fished in the River Rhine that runs through Germany, past Alsace at Strasbourg and on to Switzerland.*

Sauce

1 cup heavy cream or
    créme fraîche
4 tablespoons ($1/2$ stick) very
    cold butter, cut into pieces
Juice $1/2$ lemon
Salt and freshly ground white
    pepper to taste

Salmon Escalopes with Sorrel Sauce

Escalope de Saumon à l'Oseille

Jean and Pierre Troisgros,
Restaurant Les Frères Troisgros,
Roanne

IT WAS THE SEVENTIES AND THE CHEFS *were flying in to America in full force. Paul Bocuse, the leader, had already taken New York by storm. Sitting at the round table with the brothers Troisgros in the kitchen in Roanne, I invited them to come, their first time to Texas, for a gala dinner in a new restaurant, Oz, in Dallas. As we planned the menu around ribs of Texas beef with marrow, preceded by their navarin of lobster and escalopes of salmon with sorrel sauce, I knew they had visions of cowboys driving herds of cattle into the sunset.*

I left the restaurant late in the afternoon, on my way to see Paul Bocuse, whom Jean had already called to announce my arrival. "You must invite Paul. He should be the first," Jean told me. I thanked them for their hospitality. Pierre smiled, "No, no, please, no need for thanks. Even if we don't ever go to Texas, we'll always remain friends."

Paul had gone to bed when I reached Collonges, but he had my table waiting for me. Jean and Pierre, Alain Chapel, and Jean-Pierre Haeberlin did come to Dallas that year, but I had to wait another year before I could meet Paul.

SERVES 4

2 pounds fresh salmon, filleted,
    or 2 salmon fillets
Salt and freshly ground pepper
    to taste

Sorrel sauce

1/2 tablespoon butter
1 quart natural spring water
2 pounds backbones of fresh sole
    or white fish
1 carrot, trimmed, peeled,
    and sliced
1 onion, peeled and sliced

To prepare the salmon, cut each salmon fillet across the width into 2 escalopes or thin slices. Remove any bones in the center of the flesh with a pair of tweezers. Place the escalopes between two sheets of parchment or well-oiled greaseproof paper and flatten each piece gently with a saucepan or rolling pin to equal thickness. Season the escalopes on their underside with salt and pepper. Set aside.

To prepare the sorrel sauce, heat the 1 quart of water in a large saucepan or stockpot over medium heat until it boils, then add the fish bones, carrot, onion, and bouquet garni. Reduce the heat to low and cook for 30 minutes. Strain through a fine-mesh sieve into another saucepan. Add the white wine, vermouth, and shallots to the fish stock and cook over low heat until reduced by half. When the liquid thickens slightly, strain again.

Add the cream, increase the heat to medium, and bring to a boil. When the sauce thickens, add the sorrel and simmer for 20 seconds. Remove from the heat and whisk in the butter. Season with salt, pepper, and add some drops of lemon juice.

To cook the fish, heat 1 tablespoon peanut oil—just enough oil to coat the bottom of a large sauté pan—and sauté 2 escalopes for 30 seconds on each side. Set aside on a warm serving platter and repeat with the remaining escalopes.

When ready to serve, fill the center of each warm plate with the sorrel sauce. Wipe any excess fat from the fish and place, seasoned side down, on the sauce on each plate.

1 bouquet garni: 1 sprig parsley and tarragon, bay leaf, tied together

1 cup dry white wine, chardonnay style

1/2 cup dry white vermouth

2 shallots, chopped

2 cups heavy cream or *crème fraîche*

2 3/4 ounces sorrel, stemmed and torn in small pieces

2 tablespoons butter, cut into small pieces

Salt and freshly ground pepper to taste

1/2 teaspoon fresh lemon juice

2 tablespoons peanut oil

❆ *In the early days of the recipe, boiling the sorrel in water was necessary as Jean and Pierre used home-grown sorrel that had a fairly dominant flavor. Sorrel in the stores today does not have such a strong character, so this step has been omitted.*

❆ *Sauté the salmon escalopes quickly, only a few seconds on each side so that, slightly undercooked, the flesh remains moist. If using a nonstick sauté pan, no oil is required. In the early days of this recipe, Jean and Pierre advised, "Cook 25 seconds and then turn carefully to the second side and cook 15 seconds longer."*

❆ *Finally, their excellent advice, "This dish suffers if left waiting, so it should be prepared at the last moment."*

❆ *For this dinner, Jean asked his friend Madame Lalou Bize-Leroy, co-owner then of Domaine de la Romanée-Conti in Burgundy, to join us with her wines. She gave us a fine white Burgundy.*

Salmon Trout with Wild Leeks

Truite Saumonée aux Poireaux Sauvages

**André Soltner,
Lutèce Restaurant,
New York**

I HAVE KNOWN ANDRÉ *for more than twenty-five years, and it seems as if he has not changed. André was born to be a chef, first in Paris and then New York.*

After thirty-four years at the ovens of Lutèce, fourteen to sixteen hours a day, six days a week, he retired in 1995.

"I cook the way I feel," says André. "Like the weather; one day you like the fine weather and the next day, it's raining and you like the rain.

"I used to finish at Lutèce after midnight on Saturdays, clear up, and leave for the country by about one or two in the morning and Simone and I would get there about five. Then I'd be up at 10:00 A.M. to look for the wild leeks in the valley. I've a friend who's a fisherman and some days he'd catch us a couple of trout."

For the recipe that follows, André has used fresh salmon trout from the North Atlantic waters or flown in from the North Sea or the Norwegian fjords.

SERVES 4

Julienne of vegetables

2 tablespoons butter

1 carrot, peeled, washed, and cut in julienne strips

2 leeks (wild, if possible), rinsed well and cut in julienne strips

2 sticks celery, peeled and cut in julienne strips

Salt and freshly ground pepper to taste

Preheat the oven to 325°F. Set a fire in a barbecue for grilling. Butter an ovenproof baking dish.

Melt the butter in a skillet over medium heat and add the vegetables. Cover and cook for 10 to 12 minutes, stirring occasionally to prevent browning. Season with salt and pepper. Set aside and keep warm.

To prepare the fish, sprinkle the skin and cavity with salt and pepper. Rub the skin with the oil and grill on both sides. When grilling, mark the skin strongly to impart a smoky taste to the sauce. Alternatively, broil the fish, cook in a grill pan, or in a skillet.

Place the fish in the baking dish and add the white wine, cream, salt, and pepper. Cover the baking dish with buttered parchment paper.

Bake in the oven for about 25 minutes. Carefully remove the fish to a warm serving dish and arrange the vegetables around the fish. Heat the vegetable cooking liquid over medium heat to reduce and thicken slightly. Put through a fine-mesh sieve and pour over the fish. Serve hot.

Fish

1 salmon trout, about 3 pounds, cleaned and gutted

Salt and freshly ground pepper to taste

1 tablespoon olive oil

1/2 cup dry white wine

1 1/2 cups heavy cream

1 tablespoon butter

❄ *Dry white wine. Naturally, André recommends a young Alsace Sylvaner or Pinot Blanc. He would agree there are excellent California and Washington State dry whites, maybe one or two years old. I recall the most beautiful, young Napa Valley dry white wine from a prestigious winery at a press tasting. "Marvellous," I told the representative serving it. "When will it be in wine stores?" "We have to age it a little more," he told me. That said, only buy a young Alsace Sylvaner or Pinot Blanc; older than two years, they lose all signs of youth and fade away.*

Two other dry white French wines that are at their best when young include Muscadet, delightfully fresh when the new vintage arrives in Paris around New Beaujolais time, and Entre-Deux-Mers, from some of the poorest land of Bordeaux, where once the Atlantic Ocean reached and has left shells in the soil, lighter than the white Graves across the river, delicious with shellfish.

❄ *When his neighbor drops by with river trout, André cooks the fish on his outdoor grill.*

Loire River Pike-Perch in its Purée and Sauce

Sandre de Loire Grillé aux Cèpes,
avec sa Purée et son Jus de Poisson

Regis Marcon, Auberge des Cimes,
St.-Bonnet-le-Froid,
Haute-Loire

WINTER IS LONG AND THE SNOW IS DEEP *at 14,400 feet where Regis Marcon has his restaurant, Auberge des Cimes, the inn on the mountain peaks, in the village of St.-Bonnet-Le-Froid, population 128.*

In 1994, Regis entered the international chef's competition, the Bocuse d'Or in Lyon, cooking a dish inspired by Margaridou of the neighboring Auvergne region, and won the gold medal. "He's out there, one of the leaders of the pack of French cuisine," says Paul Bocuse. "His cooking is authentic. He's as solid as a mountain."

From the Auberge des Cimes, Regis looks down on one side to the River Rhône's valley, on the other to the River Loire. His recipe evokes the pike and the trout in the rivers, the fresh mushrooms from the hillsides—morels in springtime, cèpes *in autumn.*

SERVES 4

1¼ cups dried mushrooms, morels and cèpes, if possible

1½ quarts natural spring water

4 fresh porcini mushrooms, cleaned

2 tablespoons clarified butter

2 small, young onions, peeled and sliced to make twelve ¼-inch-thick slices

1 pound potatoes, peeled and thinly sliced

3 tablespoons heavy cream or *crème fraîche*

Soak the dried mushrooms in 1½ quarts of water for about 1 hour. Drain, pour the soaking water through a fine-mesh sieve, and reserve.

Preheat the oven to 375°F. Set a fire in a barbecue for grilling.

Slice the porcini. Heat 1 tablespoon clarified butter in a skillet over medium heat and cook the mushrooms until lightly brown and tender. Remove and set aside. Heat the remaining butter over medium heat and cook the onions until completely sweated. Set aside.

Using 2 cups of the mushroom's water, cook the potatoes over medium heat until tender, drain, and sieve the potatoes.

Add the soaked mushrooms, the cream, and 2 tablespoons butter to make a potato purée. Season with salt and pepper to taste. Set aside in a warm double boiler—the heat of the potatoes will finish cooking the mushrooms.

To prepare the fish fumet, heat 1 tablespoon butter in a saucepan over medium heat and brown the fish bones. Add enough water to cover the bones and cook for 5 minutes. Strain through a fine-mesh sieve into another saucepan. Cook over medium heat and reduce by half for $3/4$ cup. Do not reduce too much, or the fish taste will be too strong. Cook again for 2 minutes, whisking in 1 teaspoon of butter. Season. Set aside in a double boiler over simmering water to keep warm.

Season the fillets and cook them on a hot grill a minute on each side. Alternatively, heat the olive oil in a nonstick skillet and cook the fish on both sides. Then finish cooking them in the oven for about 4 to 5 minutes. Serve immediately, placing a serving of fish on each plate with sliced porcini alongside. Add three onion slices and two small quenelle-shaped mounds of potato purée (see note). Make a well in the potatoes and add some fish juice, pouring extra over the fish. For decoration, sprinkle mushroom powder in small circles on each fish.

※ *Some alternative fish include sea bass, monkfish, or John Dory.*

※ *Chefs like the small, young onions because, like young wines, they have a fresh, young taste, which makes them more delicate in the dish than older, larger onions. When not available, buy medium onions.*

※ *Quenelles are small dumplings of spiced meat or fish presented in the form of a sausage or egg. To form the potato purée into a quenelle, the chef suggests using two tablespoons to scoop up potato purée and press them together to form an oval dumpling.*

Fish fumet

$1/2$ pound white fish bones

1 tablespoon plus
    1 teaspoon butter

4 fillets of pike-perch,
    about 8 ounces each

Salt and freshly ground pepper
    to taste

1 teaspoon olive oil

Poudre sauvage—dried
    coulemelle mushroom
    powder (optional for
    decoration)

❋ *There are more than one dozen varieties of* cèpe *mushrooms in France, but the finest is the* cèpe *from Bordeaux, picked in the woods and fields in September and cooked the same day. Delicious. Alsace is known for its* cèpes *in October. Here, Regis uses dried* cèpes *and morels. His porcini mushrooms would come from Italy, unless grown commercially in France as they are in America. Because of the differences in the soil, climate, and farmers, a specific type of mushroom, like other produce, tastes differently when grown in another country or even in another province or region.*

In the same way, a wine labelled St. Emilion, Margaux, or even Beaujolais will taste differently depending in which part of the region lies the vineyard. In the case of the truly great Chateau Margaux, it can be a matter of acres of vineyard so precisely situated with soils that only nature understands, which we call microclimates. And of course, there is man. That is why it is impossible to generalize about vintages; good winemakers make good wines even in lesser years.

Great chefs are about the man, too. The prestigious Guide Michelin *has just given three stars to the chef, Michel Bras, whose restaurant stands out alone in the hills, way off the beaten track, south of Margaridou country, the Auvergne. "A great chef," Paul announced some years ago.*

Blue Trout

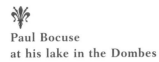

Paul Bocuse
at his lake in the Dombes

ON THE CHEF'S DAY OFF, *Paul Bocuse goes to his lake in the Dombes region.*

"I love to fish or hunt there with a few friends like Bobosse my gardener, Marius, a retired blacksmith, and Alain Vavro, my menu designer," said Paul. Alain also provided the artwork for this cookbook's cover.

"Some days, even as soon as the midday service is over, I jump in my car and can be there to hunt and back at the restaurant before the first dinner customers arrive for their glass of champagne. Those thirty-five acres of lake I bought fifteen years ago are like my little Caribbean."

The catch may be trout, pike, or carp.

"Even though it's the chef's day off, it's usually Paul who cooks," says Alain Vavro, "on a stove in a corner of the one-room cabin he has built at the edge of the lake."

Paul's great advantage is that he has his lake and the trout at hand. The fish could not be fresher or more delicious. Everyone is seated in the cabin, a glass of Beaujolais in hand, waiting for the chef to serve.

SERVES 4

4 quarts spring water

1 1/2 cups vinegar

4 live trout, about 6 to 8 ounces
each (see note)

4 tablespoons butter

Juice of 1 lemon

Salt and freshly ground pepper
to taste

Put the water and vinegar in a large saucepan and bring to a boil over medium heat.

Stun the live trout by hitting its head with a block of wood or something solid. Remove the gills and intestines of each fish, using your Opinel knife or another very sharp knife. Do not wash or dry the trout in order to maintain its blue color.

Plunge them immediately into the boiling water for about 8 minutes. They will take on a bluish color. Drain the trout and lay them out on a napkin on a warm serving platter and bring to the table. Place a trout on each plate, dotting each fish with a knob of butter, a few drops of lemon juice, and salt and pepper.

✴ *For those of us who don't have a lake with trout, the fresh trout at your fish store is an alternative. Head removed, gutted, well-rinsed. Of course, it will not be* truite au bleu, *but trout is delicious. Farm-raised domestic trout in fish stores here (not live) are about the same size so cooking time is the same.*

✴ *Paul serves the trout with boiled potatoes and a salad. Sometimes he adds a mayonnaise sauce (page 286). Afterwards, he serves cheeses that he has brought from his friend, Mère Richard at the Lyon market, and the morning's bread from his baker, Philipe Jocteur, at the Boulangerie de l'Ile on the island a little downstream from his restaurant.*

✴ *Two cups of Beaujolais or white Macon can be added to the court bouillon giving a simpler, fast version of the* matelote *for only one type of fish.*

✴ *On other days, Paul may cook his trout* meunière *(see Sole Meunière with Mushrooms Mère Brazier, page 62).*

Carp Stuffed and Roasted

Carpe Farci et Roti

Paul Bocuse,
Restaurant Paul Bocuse,
Collonges-au-Mont-d'Or, Lyon

BACK AT THE RESTAURANT *with a real kitchen and oven, Paul offers on his menu stuffed carp from his lake. This recipe can also be used for striped bass.*

SERVES 4

8 tablespoons (1 stick) butter

2 large shallots, peeled and chopped

1 chicken liver, optional

1/4 pound boiled ham, minced

1 sprig parsley, chopped

2 cups fresh breadcrumbs

1 cup whole milk

1 garlic clove, crushed

Salt and freshly ground pepper

1 large egg

4 whole carp, cleaned and ready for stuffing

2 large shallots, peeled and chopped

1/4 pound white mushrooms, peeled and chopped

2 tablespoons parsley, chopped

1 1/2 cups dry white wine

Salt and freshly ground pepper

5 tablespoons heavy cream or *crème fraîche*

Preheat the oven to 350°F. Generously butter an ovenproof baking dish.

To prepare the stuffing, heat 1 tablespoon of the butter in the skillet over medium heat. Add the shallots and cook for 5 to 6 minutes. Add the chicken liver and cook until light brown, then mash the liver with a fork. Add the ham, parsley, breadcrumbs, milk, garlic, and salt and pepper. Stir to combine. Remove from the heat and stir in the egg. Scoop the mixture into a small bowl standing in a bowl of ice cubes and refrigerate for 15 minutes. Remove from the refrigerator and stuff into the cavity of each fish. Set the fish aside.

To cook the fish, cut into small pieces the 7 tablespoons remaining butter and dot on the bottom of the baking dish. Add the shallots, mushrooms, parsley, and wine. Place the stuffed fish in the baking dish and season with salt and pepper.

Bake for about 45 minutes to 1 hour until cooked. Remove the fish from the oven, place on a warm serving platter, and slice into individual portions. Stir the cream into the cooking liquids, blending well. Pour the sauce into a warm sauceboat. Serve.

❄ *Carp has a firm, compact flesh, so it may need the full hour cooking.*

Fresh Herrings Marinated in White Wine

Harengs Frais Marinés au Vin Blanc

The Mère Brazier,
Restaurant Mère Brazier,
Lyon

I GREW UP WITH IMAGES OF THE HERRING FLEETS *moving south each year through the North Sea ports of Scotland and England, my wife Jeannie's country, with the fisherwomen in their waterproof gear working on the dockside in all "weather when the ships came in. I see them every time I hear Jean Redpath sing* Caller Herrin'—"Who'll buy my caller herrin'? They're bonnie fish and wholesome farin, buy my fresh herrin' new pulled in from the sea. When ye were sleepin on yer pillows... they're naw brought here without great daring, hauled through wind and rain...Caller herrin! Caller herrin!"

When I was in my teens in London, my grandmother in Covent Garden would have me buy her two herrings or mackerel at the market, lay them in an ovenproof glass terrine with a bay leaf and a couple of slices of lemon, then pour half a bottle of Guinness beer over the fish. Cooked for 30 minutes in a medium oven of her Aga cooker, cooled in the refrigerator overnight, they were a meal in themselves.

Paul Bocuse told the student chefs at the French Culinary Institute in New York, when I took him there when it opened in the early eighties, "You can have as much satisfaction cooking a herring as cooking a lobster. You can do très grande cuisine *with herrings if you do it well. Just as you can do bad cooking with a lobster."*

SERVES 4

Four 4-ounce herrings, gutted, scaled, and heads and tails removed

1/2 bottle (12 1/2 ounces) good dry white wine

Salt and freshly ground pepper

1 lemon, peeled and sliced

1 stalk celery, sliced

2 small carrots, sliced

2 small onions, finely chopped

Sprinkle the herrings with salt and set aside for about 1 hour. Meanwhile, put the wine, salt, and pepper in a saucepan and bring to a boil over high heat. Add the lemon, celery, carrots, and onions to the wine. Put the herrings in the saucepan, reduce the heat to medium, and cook for 15 minutes.

Remove the fish, place them in an earthenware dish, and cover them with the warm bouillon and some slices of lemon. Cover the dish and refrigerate for at least 6 hours. The herrings will cook in their marinade.

Serve one herring on each plate. Remove the lemon slices and spoon some of the cold marinade sauce around each fish.

❄ *This is delicious accompanied by a salad of spring lettuce and arugula with a salad of new potatoes.*

❄ *The Mère Brazier would set the herring aside in her cold room for two months. A marinade of vinegar kept in the cold would not spoil in that time, says Hervé. In those days, people liked their cooking with a bigger taste, just as there was a clientele—there still is in England—for aged champagne.*

❄ *Mackerel can be used as an alternative. Jean Ducloux serves as one of his appetizers small mackerel in white wine vinegar with herbs (thyme, tarragon, and parsley) and lemon juice. Cook for 20 minutes and then set aside in the cooler overnight to marinate in the vinegar and herbs. Sometimes he starts by laying the fish in a bed of crushed tomatoes. This little appetizer of marinated mackerel seems to be on the menu of every Paris bistrot. I yearn for it this side of the Atlantic.*

❄ *Alfred Guerot cut herring fillets that had been marinated in olive oil, in thick strips, laying them in a garnish of chopped potato, quartered hard-boiled eggs, capers, chervil, and onion slices and sprinkled with a vinaigrette.*

❄ *My grandmother placed unpeeled slices of lemons on the herring, but Paul Bocuse prefers the lemon peeled, so as to remove the bitterness under the lemon skin—as in his Tajine of Chicken (page 186). She would add a spring salad that, too, came from the Covent Garden market downstairs.*

❄ *For sauces with a base of wine, bring the wine to a boil and then reduce the heat to medium to cook. Never do a reduction over high heat because this will bring out the acidity in the wine.*

❄ *The Mère Brazier recommended a glass of Chardonnay to drink with this dish.*

Sole Meunière with Mushrooms
Mère Brazier

Sole Meunière aux Cèpes

The Mère Brazier,
Restaurant Mère Brazier,
Lyon

IN THE FIFTIES, *an English foodwriter was revealing to her countrymen that good food was close at hand across the Channel. Visiting France to write her* French Provincial Cooking, *Elizabeth David found in Lyon, "what I do truly believe to be the most delicious and deliciously cooked* sole meunière *I have ever eaten. Ah, if the clients of one or two of those London restaurants specializing in fish dishes could eat a* sole meunière *as cooked at Mère Brazier's, they would certainly wonder what it was that had been served them under the same name in London."*

SERVES 2

2 whole sole, about 14 ounces
    each
Salt and freshly ground pepper
    to taste
All-purpose flour for dredging
6 tablespoons butter
24 small white mushrooms,
    peeled and sliced
Juice of 1 lemon
2 sprigs of parsley,
    finely chopped

Preheat the oven to 325°F.

Ask the fishmonger to remove the black skin and fins, to scrape the white side, and to gut and clean the fish. Rinse the sole under running water and dry. Season with salt and pepper, then dredge each fish in the flour, shaking off the excess.

Put 1 tablespoon butter in each of 2 medium-sized skillets. Heat the butter over high heat. When the butter is very hot but not sizzling, place one fish, white side down, into each skillet. Cook for 5 minutes until light brown, turn each fish over carefully with a spatula, and cook the other side until light brown.

Place both fish in one large skillet, if possible, and place in the oven for about 5 minutes. Using a spatula, gently lift the fish; when the fillets come away from the skin, the sole is cooked.

Meanwhile, heat 2 tablespoons butter in a large skillet. Sauté the chopped mushrooms.

Melt 1 teaspoon butter on a long, hot serving platter. Remove the skillet from the oven and, with a spatula, slide the fillets onto the platter. Spoon the mushrooms over the fish. Sprinkle each fish with lemon juice and some chopped parsely. Melt the remaining butter in the skillet, stir in the remaining chopped parsley, and pour over the fish. Serve.

❋ *A whole sole should weigh from 12 to 16 ounces. If you buy the fish filleted, there will be 4 fillets, 2 fillets per person, the 2 back fillets weighing slightly less than the 2 front ones.*

❋ *For the last cooking stage, chef Alfred Guerot, past president of the jury of the Meilleur Ouvriers de France and mentor to Paul Bocuse when Paul was compiling his first cookbook, advised, "Sprinkle the fish with a few drops of lemon juice and a teaspoon of chopped parsley blanched in boiling water at the last moment. Add 3 tablespoons of butter to the pan in which the sole was cooked, heat until it acquires a light brown color, and pour over the sole. The contact of very hot butter and moist parsley makes the sauce very frothy."*

❋ *Elizabeth David warned that unless you have the right size pan, it is wisest to not try to cook sole meunière or similar dishes for more than two people at a time. Paul works with a pan the same size as the sole.*

Fillet of Sole with Fresh Noodles
Jean Vignard

Filet de Sole aux Nouilles Fraîches—
Homage to Jean Vignard, Grand Chef de Lyon

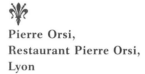

Pierre Orsi,
Restaurant Pierre Orsi,
Lyon

HAVING APPRENTICED AT PAUL BOCUSE *in Collonges-au-Mont-d'Or, Lucas-Carton in Paris, and the Café Royal in London, Pierre is an honorary citizen of Chicago where in 1967 he opened a Maxim's, and in 1971, the Ninety-Fifth Restaurant on top of a skyscraper where we first met. "A fabulous city, a fabulous time," he recalled.*

Winning his Meilleur Ouvrier de France medal, Pierre returned to Lyon in 1975 and opened his own restaurant with his wife Geneviève. His son, Jean-Louis, is already in the kitchen with his father.

This recipe is dedicated to one of the great chefs of Lyon, Jean Vignard. It shows the chef at work in his kitchen. "Everything is prepared in advance," says Hervè Riou, "cooked stage by stage. Except for the sole. At the last minute, the sole is cooked and the sole, the sauce, and everything is finished together in the oven. It looks complicated, but prepared in advance professionally, it's ready—has to be ready—in minutes. And delicious."

SERVES 4

2 whole sole, filleted, 4 fillets
    from each sole

Fish stock

Bones from the sole or
    other white fish

3 shallots, chopped

1 cup dry white wine,
    Macon-style

1 bouquet garni: 1 sprig each
    thyme, tarragon, parsley,
    tied together

1 1/2 ounces white mushrooms,
    stemmed, peeled (set aside
    peel), and thinly sliced

Flatten the sole slightly with a large flat knife or cleaver and put the fish in a bowl of iced—not merely cold—water for 10 minutes to bring out any impurities. Drain.

To make the fish stock, clean the fish bones, crush them, and wash them. Put them in a large saucepan with the shallots, white wine, bouquet garni, and the peel from the mushrooms. Cook for 10 minutes, strain, and set aside in a second saucepan.

Cook the mussels like *moules marinières* (see page 92) until they open, and then remove them from their shells and set aside. Pour the cooking liquid through a fine-mesh sieve and set aside.

Steam the crawfish in a covered pan for 2 minutes, remove their tails and set aside.

Poach the scallops for 2 minutes in the fish stock, remove and cut them into small, thin slices, escalopes.

Place equal serving of the mussels, crayfish, and scallops onto 4 warm, ovenproof plates. Set aside.

Bring lightly salted water to a boil and cook the noodles until al dente; fresh noodles cook quickly. Drain. Season with salt and pepper. Cut 2 tablespoons butter onto the noodles. Place a portion of noodles over each serving of shellfish.

Place the fillets in a large saucepan, season lightly with salt and pepper, and brush with butter. Cover with a sheet of aluminum foil and cook in the oven for several minutes. Drain and place 2 fillets on each serving of noodles. Set aside.

Heat 1 teaspoon butter in a saucepan over low heat and sweat the shallots. Increase the heat to medium and add the white wine, fish stock, and 1 cup of the mussels' cooking liquid. Reduce by two-thirds. Add 1 tablespoon cream and cook for 5 minutes more. Thicken the liquid with the cornstarch. Add the mushrooms and tomatoes and remove from the heat.

Preheat the oven to 425°F.

Whisk the remaining cream until it thickens like a Chantilly cream, and add it little by little to the sauce. Add the parsley and chives. Season to taste. Pour the sauce over the sole.

Place the 4 plates in the oven and cook until golden brown on top. Serve immediately.

7 ounces mussels, well-scrubbed

12 crayfish, cleaned

2 large scallops, meat only

10 1/2 ounces fresh noodles (see page 232) or dried noodles

Salt and freshly ground pepper to taste

6 tablespoons butter

3/4 cup dry white wine, Macon-style

2 tablespoons heavy cream, (crème fleurette)

1 teaspoon cornstarch

2 medium-sized tomatoes, peeled, seeded, sliced, and diced

1 sprig parsley, chopped

Small bunch chives, chopped

※ *A note from Pierre Orsi: The beauty of this recipe is that all the ingredients start off as lightly cooked as possible, so that they can finish their cooking in the oven.*

* *The chef in his kitchen can* gratinée *four plates at a time.*

* *Crème fleurette, used by Pierre Orsi, is the light cream used in France for making chantilly cream, for pastries,* fromage frais, *and in coffee. To make this in America, says Hervé, the light cream available is too light to whip into a chantilly so he recommends using heavy cream.*

* *Wine: Try to find a Macon-style chardonnay as used in the cooking.*

SOLE

Sole plays a leading role among saltwater fish in the kitchen. The great French chef Antonin Carème, who cooked for the Prince of Wales and the Duke of Wellington when he visited England, wrote in his *The Art of French Cuisine* in 1854, "The sole is one of the most highly esteemed saltwater fish, especially those fished off the Normandy coast, called the Dieppe sole. Look for the ones with a beautiful grey skin, rather than a black skin..."

Auguste Escoffier, who directed the kitchens of the Savoy and Carlton hotels in London at the turn of the century, gave 95 ways to cook sole in his *Escoffier Cookbook*. Madame Prunier with her restaurant on St. James Street in London and also her family's legendary fish restaurant Prunier's in Paris, describes 162 recipes for Dover sole in her *Fish Cook Book*. The legendary gastronome and foodwriter Ali-Bab called sole the queen of all saltwater fish.

"Fernand Point was fond of fillet of sole with pasta," Paul Bocuse recalls, talking to student chefs in America of his apprentice days. "Point would make a little sauce of white wine and tomato purée. Or he would cook the fillet of sole entirely in a mousse of butter, or after poaching the sole, he would pour over it a sauce, like a *sabayon*, of egg yolks and cream.

"A good fillet of sole should be seasoned at the table at the last moment. That is, on the fish itself. One does not season the sauce that you serve it with. You season the fish on the table so that it takes on the salt, though I know today people are taking less and less salt."

Paul's *chef de cuisine* Roger Jaloux, as soon as dinner is over at Collonges, is on the phone calling his order in to Dieppe, where the day's catch is arriving and will be shipped in refrigerated trucks overnight to Lyon. French chefs often prefer the more delicate taste of sole fished on the line, *sole de ligne*, as it is indicated on the menu. Fish from the line being much finer than fish gathered in the nets.

* *A sabayon is the chef's classic sauce, hot or cold, as an accompaniment. Using egg yolks or egg whites, heavy cream, sugar, and a flavoring, such as wine, liqueur, or fruit. It is beaten up until fluffy with a whisk or in an electric blender and then heated in a double boiler until it becomes a light cream, like a custard.*

Dover Sole Riviera

**Jean Banchet,
Restaurant Le Riviera,
Atlanta**

JEAN BANCHET IS FROM ROANNE *and began as chef in the kitchens of the Troisgros and Bocuse. "Jean and Paul called up La Pyramide, where they had been chefs under Fernand Point, for me to work there. Point had died the year before, but his chef Mercier was still in the kitchen, a perfectionist, never satisfied. Paul and Jean had warned me it would be a tough school.*

On days that the restaurant was closed, Madame Point would ask me to cook for her. 'I've a guest coming, Jean, do something simple like a roast chicken or a Dover sole.'"

SERVES 4

1/4 cup olive oil

2 bulbs fennel, chopped

2 large fresh Dover sole,
    18 ounces each, cleaned
    and filleted

Salt and freshly ground pepper
    to taste

2 tablespoons olive oil

4 toothpicks

Greaseproof parchment paper
    or wax paper

Sauce

1 pound fresh mussels

1/4 cup fish stock (page 284)

1/4 cup dry white wine

1/4 cup dry vermouth

1 tablespoon chopped shallots

1 tablespoon chopped parsley

1 teaspoon saffron

continued

Preheat the oven to 400°F. Generously oil a large ovenproof baking dish with olive oil.

Heat the 1/4 cup olive oil in a small saucepan over medium heat, add the chopped fennel, and slowly cook until the fennel softens. Strain and set aside.

Season the fish with salt and pepper and place them in the baking dish. Sprinkle with the fennel. Roll up each fillet with the fennel on the inside and hold together with a toothpick. Cover the fish with parchment paper and set aside.

To prepare the sauce, clean the mussels thoroughly. Discard any that are open or remain open after tapping on the shell. Scrape off any barnacles and beard protruding from the mussel. Wash in running water.

Combine the fish stock, white wine, vermouth, shallots, parsley, and saffron, in a large saucepan and heat over medium heat. Add the mussels and cook until they open. Strain the mussel juice into a bowl or another saucepan and cover the fillets of sole with some of this juice (reserve the rest of the juice). Open the mussels, discard the shells and any mussels that do not open, and set aside in a warm covered pan.

Garnish

8 cups medium mushrooms,
  cut and shaped

8 leaves from fennel bulbs,
  chopped

2 medium tomatoes, peeled,
  seeded, and diced

1/4 cup heavy cream or *crème
  fraîche*

1/4 cup olive oil

Salt and freshly ground pepper
  to taste

Pasta

2 quarts water with 1 tablespoon
  salt

8 ounces fresh black linguini
  pasta

8 tablespoons (1 stick) butter

Salt and freshly ground pepper
  to taste

To make the garnish, blanch the mushrooms for 2 minutes in boiling salted water. Blanch the fennel in salted water for 30 seconds. Blanch the tomatoes for 30 seconds in salted water. Drain and set aside on a warm platter.

To cook the pasta, bring the 2 quarts water to a boil in a large saucepan over high heat and add the pasta. Remove from the high heat, cover, and poach without boiling for 12 to 15 minutes, or until al dente. Drain, but do not rinse. Stir in the butter. Set aside and keep warm.

Meanwhile, cook the fish, covered, for 10 minutes. Remove fillets from the oven and place on a platter, cover, and set aside. Keep warm.

Return the remaining mussel juice to a saucepan and over medium-high heat reduce by three-quarters. Add the cream and reduce by half. Pour the mixture into a blender, add the olive oil, salt, and pepper and process until well combined.

To serve, place a portion of pasta in the center of the plate, then place 2 fennel leaves on the side and top with 1 sole fillet. Repeat with each plate.

Garnish each plate with mussels and spoon sauce over the mussels and sole. Spoon the mushrooms and diced tomatoes on each piece of fish. Serve hot.

❋ *If you need to reheat the noodles after they have been cooked a little less than al dente, drop them into a colander of boiling salted water with a little olive oil for just 1 minute, or until al dente.*

❋ *Our chefs insist to cook slowly. These more relaxed recipes were evolved in the kitchen slowly, gently, sometimes taking much of the day. For many of them, part of the preparation is the day before. Even the produce depends on when the season is ready.*

Sole, Crayfish, and Oysters with Fava Beans and Baby Onions

La Nage de Sole, Langoustines, aux Creuses de Bretagne,
aux Fèves et Petits Oignons Nouveaux

Michel Chabran,
Restaurant Michel Chabran,
Pont de l'Isère, Rhône

TWENTY YEARS AGO, *tasting wines in the Rhône valley with Jean Troisgros on his day off, we looked in on Michel Chabran, who had apprenticed in the Troisgros kitchen at Roanne. The autoroute Paris-Mediterranean had bypassed Michel's restaurant, which was empty. He wanted us to stay for lunch, but Jean had planned a late lunch at Collonges for me to meet Paul Bocuse. Michel graciously opened a bottle of champagne for us. In the years that followed, he came to America, including an exciting venture with two chefs of his generation, Michel Richard of Citrus in Los Angeles and Michel Rostang from Paris. Today, his restaurant just off the autoroute thrives as a popular, refreshing stop for fine food lovers. As Jean used to do, today Paul Bocuse regularly drops in. Michel Richard now also has his Restaurant Citronelle in Washington, D.C.*

SERVES 4

2³/4 pounds fresh fava beans in pods

2 cups water

12 small, young onions, peeled and cut

1¹/4 cups (2¹/2 sticks) butter, softened

12 oysters, unopened

2 tablespoons dry white wine, Rhône style

2 gray shallots, chopped

Salt and freshly ground pepper to taste

8 fillets of sole

8 crayfish tails

Preheat the oven to 400°F.

Shell the fava beans. To remove the skins, blanch the beans in salted water and then drop them in ice water. The skins should easily rub off. Set aside.

Bring 2 cups water to the boil over medium heat, add the onions and 1 teaspoon butter, cover the pan, and cook until tender. Set aside.

Open the oysters, carefully catching the juices and water. Put the oysters in a bowl and refrigerate.

Cut the remaining butter, except for 1 tablespoon, into small pieces. Heat the wine in a skillet over medium heat and add the shallots. Cook until the liquid has almost evaporated. Remove the skillet from the heat and add the butter, piece by piece, returning the skillet to the heat after each addition.

Stir the mixture when the skillet is off the heat. When all the butter has been added, beat the sauce with a wire whisk until it becomes foamy. Season the sauce with salt and pepper to taste.

Sprinkle the fish fillets with pepper but not with salt and place them on an ovenproof baking pan. Bake them without butter or oil in the oven under the grill for no more than 3 minutes.

Heat the remaining 1 tablespoon butter in a large skillet over medium heat and sauté the crayfish tails for 2 minutes on each side.

In each of four soup bowls, arrange equal portions of the onions. Add 2 fillets, 3 oysters, 2 crayfish tails, and portions of fava beans around the onions. Pour the liquid from the oysters into each bowl and spoon the sauce over top.

* *Oysters: Michel Chabran orders his favorite Brittany oysters,* les creuses de Bretagne. *Differing from oysters with shells that are flat, or* plat, *their shells are hollowed out, or* creuses.

* *By "small, young onions," Michel means those first little onions of the season, white or yellow, and young. Pearl onions can be substituted but these do not have the freshness and youth the chefs consider so vital for their cooking. If you use pearl onions, soak them for 15 minutes so that they can be peeled easily.*

* *When Michel tells us he prefers grey shallots, my editor rightly notes that most of us must take our shallots as we find them in the local store. Sometimes I suggest alternatives. When in doubt, follow that good advice: Take the best to be found in the local store.*

* *Saint Peray, a dry white wine from the Rhone valley, is the chef's choice.*

Red Mullet in Potato Scales

Rouget Barbet en Ecailles de Pommes de Terre

Roger Jaloux,
Restaurant Paul Bocuse,
Collonges-au-Mont-d'Or, Lyon

ROGER JALOUX HAS BEEN BRIGADE COMMANDER, chef de cuisine, *in the Paul Bocuse kitchen at Collonges since 1976, since the day he won his Meilleur Ouvrier de France diploma. Aged fifteen in 1957, he began a ten-year apprenticeship under Paul, followed by ten years as chef de cuisine in restaurants in Bordeaux, Nantes, and the Landes.*

"Paul is almost a father to me." Says Roger. "I've known him all my life, since I was two or three years old. We're both from Collonges. I was born next door. From seeing him as chef, I wanted to be chef, too. I began here at fourteen.

"The cuisine is the cooking he likes: cream, butter, cuisine that demands to be worked—the good cuisine that he likes. We do what he likes." On his chef's whites, Roger touches his heart. "It comes from the heart, Monsieur Michel. The cuisine we don't like, we don't do."

SERVES 4

8 fillets of red mullet

Brunoise

1 tablespoon butter

4 small carrots, finely diced

4 zucchini, finely diced

1 pound potatoes

4 tablespoons (1/2 stick) butter, melted

2 egg yolks, lightly beaten

1 cup dry white wine, Macon-style

1 cup vermouth

1/2 cup chopped shallots

continued

Clean and wipe the fish dry with paper towels. Set aside.

To prepare the *brunoise,* melt the butter in a small skillet over low heat. Add the diced carrots and zucchini. Cover and cook for 10 minutes. Set aside.

Peel and cut the potatoes into thin round slices about 8 inches in diameter. Blanch the slices, remove from the water, dry, and coat them with melted butter. Set aside.

Brush the fillets on the skin side with the egg yolks. Place the potato slices over the surface of the fillets, overlapping like fish scales. Trim the potatoes to the shape of the fish.

Combine the white wine, vermouth, and shallots in a saucepan and cook over medium heat until it reduces by two-thirds. Add the heavy cream and cook until it reduces by half.

2 cups heavy cream or
    créme fraîche
Salt and freshly ground pepper
    to taste
4 tablespoons finely chopped
    fresh basil
1/2 cup olive oil

Add the salt, pepper, and basil. Process the wine sauce in a blender. Add 2 tablespoons vegetable mixture.

Heat the olive oil in a nonstick skillet over medium heat. Place the fillets, scales side down, in the skillet and cook for 6 to 8 minutes. Using a spatula, carefully remove from the skillet and arrange on plates. Pour the sauce over them and serve immediately.

❋ *Hervé warns: Warm the plates, but do not overheat them or the sauce will separate.*

❋ *A secret to the success of this recipe, says Hervé, is to make sure the fish with its scales has been well-refrigerated before cooking. And be sure the nonstick pan is hot. This way, the scales should not stick and should brown well.*

Pavé of Codfish with Red Wine and Fried Shallots

Pavé de Codfish, Sauce Vin Rouge et Echalottes Sautées

**Gilbert Le Coze,
Le Bernardin Restaurant,
New York**

GILBERT AND HIS SISTER, MAGUY, *born in Brittany, once ran the most successful fish restaurant, Le Bernardin, in Paris. Young and adventurous in the eighties, they accepted an invitation to open a restaurant in New York. With a contract that required so much of their time overseas, they closed the Paris restaurant.*

Built like a rugby player, plainspoken Gilbert believed in buying the fish himself at the Fulton Street fish market. "They've grown to trust me," he said, slapping his wallet pocket, "seeing me coming, they know I always pay cash on the spot."

At that time, I was flying in the châteaux owners of the twelve great châteaux, Premiers Grands Crus, of Saint Emilion, their first official visit to America. Gilbert came to me and said, "My kitchen is too small to do anything for their gala reception, but I have a small upstairs room with one round table that seats fourteen. I would like to invite your chateau owners as my personal guests for lunch next day. I will join you for the lunch as I'd like to get to know them and their wines. It would be good for me." A fine example of generous gestures of time and hospitality one experiences among the great chefs.

We lost Gilbert in 1990 from a heart attack. Le Bernardin in New York goes on. Maguy and her chef de cuisine Eric Rippert sent me one of Gilbert's recipes.

For the wine, I suggest a Saint Emilion for cooking, and at the table a recent year from Chateau Belair, Chateau Magdelaine, Chateau Monbousquet, or if you can find it, the second wine of Chateau Cheval Blanc—Chateau Petit Cheval, literally the little white horse. Or use any other St. Emilion you like.

SERVES 4

Marinade

1/2 carrot, thickly sliced

1/3 medium onion, thinly sliced

1/4 celery stalk, thinly sliced

1 fennel leaf, thinly sliced

2 cloves garlic, lightly crushed

5 sprigs parsley, chopped

1 ounce smoked slab bacon

1 strip orange peel

1 whole clove

1 teaspoon coriander seeds

1/4 stick cinnamon

1 bay leaf

1 sprig thyme

1 bottle red wine, preferably
    Saint Emilion

4 pieces, (pavés) of cod, 6 to
    7 ounces each, cut from
    thickest part of the fish,
    scaled

Sauce

2 tablespoons olive oil

1 pound fish bones from
    snapper, bass, or monkfish

1 tablespoon cornstarch
    (optional)

Garlic butter

10 tablespoons sweet butter

1 large garlic clove, chopped
    and crushed

1 small bunch parsley leaves,
    minced

1/2 teaspoon ground white
    pepper

1 tablespoon cognac, to taste

To make the marinade, one or two days ahead, put all the marinade ingredients, except the fish, in a nonreactive container and refrigerate.

Two hours before cooking, put the fish in the marinade and set aside.

To make the sauce, strain the marinade, separating and reserving the vegetables and liquid. Heat 1 tablespoon olive oil in a heavy saucepan over medium heat and sauté the vegetables to caramelize slightly. Add the fish bones, reduce the heat to low, and cook for several minutes. Add the marinade liquid, increase the heat to medium, and bring just to a boil—do not let it boil—and hold at this temperature for 45 minutes to 1 hour. Strain without pressing on the solids. Discard the solids and continue cooking until the sauce reduces to about 1 cup. If the sauce still does not have the proper consistency, make a wash with a little cornstarch and red wine and stir into the sauce. Cook a few minutes more, check the seasonings, and strain again.

Preheat the oven to 450°F.

To make the garlic butter, 45 minutes before serving, gently heat the butter in a small saucepan over medium-low heat and stir in the garlic, parsley, white pepper, and cognac.

Thirty minutes before serving, heat 6 tablespoons olive oil in a large skillet over medium heat. Place the codfish, seasoned skin side down, in the oil. Finish cooking the fish in the oven for 2 to 3 minutes. Remove when slightly under-done and set aside.

Reheat the sauce and stir in 1 to 2 tablespoons garlic butter. Add the red wine vinegar, salt, and pepper. Taste. Add the chives.

Dredge the shallot rings in flour. Heat the remaining olive oil in a skillet over medium-high heat and fry the shallots. Remove with a slotted spoon and drain well on paper towels. Season lightly with salt.

Reheat the fish briefly in the oven, then place one in the center of each dinner plate. Surround with the sauce and garnish with fried shallots.

8 tablespoons olive oil

1 tablespoon red wine vinegar

Salt and freshly ground pepper to taste

2 tablespoons chives, minced

3/4 cup all-purpose flour

12 large shallots, thinly sliced, large outer rings only

❋ *Cognac, to taste: The recipe calls for 1 tablespoon of cognac. Taste. If you don't taste enough of the cognac, add another tablespoon and taste. If your bottle of cognac has been open a week or a month, the cognac will have lost some of its taste.*

❋ *For cooking times (see page 290), professional chefs know that it is impossible to be too precise. All depends on so many elements, including freshness, size, and age of the produce being cooked, and the kitchen utensils, capabilities of the oven, even the altitude, not forgetting the chef and for whom the chef cooks.*

❋ *Fennel is sold as a bulb, but the feathery leaves growing above the bulb, with their anise taste, are used by chefs as garnish.*

Roasted Fillet of Sea Bass or Codfish in Red Wine Sauce

Filet de Bass Roti ou Codfish, Sauce Vin Rouge

**André Soltner,
Lutèce Restaurant,
New York**

"When I was at Lutèce, *I bought my fish from one supplier," André Soltner explained. "I worked with him over twenty years. We talked by phone every morning. He used to have a fish store in London and retired. Walking around Fulton Street market, if he saw anything he liked he called me up, 'André, there's some beautiful blowfish.' He would tell me how the fish was and if it was fresh, the way I like it, I took it. He never sent me junk. If he didn't have it, we had an understanding and he called me, 'André, I don't have it.' Why should I get up at five o'clock in the morning to go to the market and lose my time for nothing? You gained nothing in quality, only in price."*

SERVES 4

4 fillets sea bass or codfish,
about 1¹/2 pounds

3 tablespoons olive oil

3 carrots, trimmed, peeled,
washed, and cut in ¹/2-inch
pieces

1 onion, peeled and cut in
¹/2-inch pieces

1 leek, well washed and cut
in ¹/2-inch pieces

2 ribs celery, washed and cut
in ¹/2-inch pieces

1 tablespoon cognac

2 cups red wine

2 cups water

1 small head garlic, halved

1 bouquet garni: a sprig each of
rosemary, tarragon, parsley,
and a bay leaf tied together

Ask the fishmonger to cut each fillet in half and to reserve and rinse the bones and heads.

Heat 2 tablespoons olive oil in a saucepan over medium heat. Add the carrots, onion, leek, celery, and fish bones and heads. Cook for about 8 minutes, stirring constantly. Deglaze the saucepan with cognac. Add the wine, water, garlic, bouquet garni, salt, and pepper. Stir well and bring to a boil. Reduce the heat to low and cook for 45 minutes.

Strain the simmered stock through a fine-mesh sieve, pressing hard on the solids to extract all liquid. Return the stock to the heat and cook until it reduces to 1 cup, skimming as necessary. Add the vinegar and set aside.

Rinse the fillets under cold water and pat dry with a paper towel. Season both sides with salt and pepper and dredge in flour. Heat the remaining olive oil in a skillet over medium heat and cook the fish about 4 minutes each side, or until golden brown.

Transfer the fish to 4 warm plates. Bring the sauce to a boil over high heat. Remove from the heat and whisk in the butter, one tablespoon at a time. Pour the sauce around the fish and sprinkle it with parsley.

A pinch of salt and coarsely cracked pepper

2 tablespoons balsamic vinegar

All-purpose flour to dredge

2 tablespoons cold butter

Sprig fresh parsley, chopped

❊ *Deglaze:* déglacer *and* mouillir. *There is confusion about the term deglaze. Shouldn't one remove everything from the pan before deglazing? Here, no. The French term here is* mouillir, *pour in, a liquid (in this case cognac). In his salmon soufflé, he poured in (*mouillir*) some Alsace wine, and deglazed.*

❊ *Cognac: Whenever a French chef indicates using cognac in cooking, he means a French cognac, such as one by Hennessy, Courvoisier, Martell, or the like. Every chef has his favorite cognac and would never use a "cooking cognac."*

Alsace Fish Tart in Beer Custard

Tourte de Poisson à la Bière

André Soltner,
Lutèce Restaurant,
New York

As well as its Riesling and Gewürztraminer white wines, *Alsace brews over half the beer consumed in France. When André Soltner was a child, there was a brewery in every village in Alsace.*
Microbreweries have sprung up across America in recent years. A large wine store offers dozens of different brews by the bottle. The beer used for this fish tart, says André, should be as light as a draft beer.

SERVES 6 TO 8

Pastry

4 ounces all-purpose flour
4 tablespoons (¹/2 stick) butter
¹/2 teaspoon salt
1 large egg
1 tablespoon water

Filling

One 12-ounce can beer
1 pound sole fillets
1 pound salmon fillets
3 large eggs
Pinch freshly grated nutmeg
¹/2 cup (4 ounces) heavy cream
    or *crème fraîche*
Salt and freshly ground pepper
    to taste
1 teaspoon chopped fresh
    parsley
1 teaspoon chopped fresh
    tarragon

To make the short pastry, two hours ahead, mound the flour on a flat work surface, making a well in the center. Put the butter and salt in the well and using the fingertips, work into a crumbly dough. Add the egg and water, kneading continuously into a ball. Cover the dough in plastic wrap and refrigerate.

Preheat the oven to 325°F.

After 1 hour, unwrap the dough and roll it out on a floured board or other flat work surface into a 10¹/2-inch circle. Carefully place it into a 10-inch pie tin. Refrigerate the dough for another 10 minutes. Then line the dough with parchment paper, weighting it down with dried beans or pie weights. Bake for 10 to 12 minutes. Remove from the oven and discard the beans and parchment paper. Leave the oven on.

To make the filling, pour half the beer into a skillet and bring to a boil over medium heat. Salt and pepper the fish fillets and put them in the boiling beer. Bring to a boil again, then remove from the heat and set aside.

Beat together the eggs, nutmeg, cream, salt, pepper, and remaining beer and herbs in a mixing bowl. Pour into a saucepan and over medium heat, bring almost to a boil.

Drain the fillets well and place them carefully in the prebaked tart shell. Pour the cream mixture over the fish. Bake the tart for about 25 minutes. Remove and allow to rest 5 minutes before serving hot.

Baked Chilean Bass with Coco Beans, Carrots, Leeks, Celery and Roasted Tomatoes

Basse de Chile avec Cocos, Carottes, Poireaux,
Celeri et Tomatoes Roties

Jean-Louis Palladin,
Jean-Louis at The Watergate,
Washington, D.C.

IN THE EARLY EIGHTIES, *Jean-Louis left France, where he had been one of twenty-five young chefs that Gault-Millau magazine ranked as the "Paul Bocuses of Tomorrow." From chef at the Le Logis des Cordeliers restaurant in Condom, deep in Gascony country, he went to be chef de cuisine and man behind the name of the finest restaurant in Washington, D.C., Jean-Louis at The Watergate Hotel.*

Whenever I had winemakers visiting Washington, we held our wine gala dinners chez Jean-Louis. He greeted us in his thick, warm Gascon accent, which must sound real "country" in Las Vegas, where he is at present, chef de cuisine *at The Napa Suite while waiting to open in New York. Stop the presses: While waiting for his big New York restaurant, Jean-Louis has just opened Palladin, a "techno-bistro with sass and style," as* The New York Times *describes it.*

SERVES 4

1 pound coco beans (see note)

4 quarts water

2 carrots

2 sticks celery

1 turnip, peeled

1 leek, trimmed

1 ham hock

8 ounces smoked Parma
    prosciuto rind

1/2 pound smoked Parma
    prosciutto

1 medium onion, peeled

4 garlic cloves, peeled

2 sprigs thyme

To make the coco beans, put them in a large saucepan with 4 quarts water to soak for 24 hours.

The next day, using ample cheesecloth for a bag, wrap the carrots, celery, turnip, leek, hock of ham, prosciutto, onion, garlic, thyme, rosemary, and bay leaves in the cheesecloth and knot it closed.

Drain the coco beans and put them in a large stockpot with the wrapped vegetables. Add enough water to well cover the beans and cook over very low heat for 2 to 2 1/2 hours.

Remove the cheesecloth bag and discard. Strain the beans, reserving the cooking liquid, and put the beans into a baking dish. Cover with a damp towl and set aside. Strain the bean liquid through a fine-mesh sieve into a large saucepan and cook over medium heat to reduce by half. Set aside.

Preheat the oven to 150°F.

To make the clarification, combine the ground Parma prosciutto, chopped leek, celery, and egg whites in a saucepan. Slowly pour in the hot bean liquid, whisking continously as you pour, and over medium heat, bring to a boil. Reduce the heat to low and cook for 1 hour. Taking care not to break the skin that has formed on the surface, strain only the liquid through a cheesecloth. It is now a consommé.

To make the garnish, 2 hours before serving, season the tomatoes with garlic, thyme, salt, and pepper and put them on a baking sheet. Roast for 2 hours, remove from the oven, and set aside.

Increase the oven temperature to 450°F.

Ladle 1 quart consommé into a large skillet or ovenproof baking pan. Add the carrots and put them in the oven. After 15 minutes, add the celery sticks. After 20 minutes, add the leeks. At the end of 30 minutes, remove the vegetables and put them into a bowlful of ice cubes to chill. Once cold, cut them into chunks and set aside. Pour the consommé into a large saucepan.

Season the fillets with salt and white pepper. Put the fish and butter in a large skillet and roast for about 8 minutes. Remove and set aside in the warm, covered skillet.

Reheat the consommé. Arrange some coco beans, celery, tomatoes, carrots, leeks and garlic in 4 warm soup bowls. Into each bowl, put a fillet and pour in some consommé. Add some lemon juice and about 1 teaspoon of olive oil into each bowl, too. Serve immediately.

1 sprig rosemary

2 bay leaves

Clarification—*consommé*

1 pound smoked Parma prosciutto, ground

1 leek, chopped

2 stalks celery, chopped

10 egg whites

Garnish

4 whole medium tomatoes, preferably ripe

1/2 garlic clove, peeled and chopped finely

1 sprig fresh thyme, chopped, or 1 teaspoon dried thyme

Salt and freshly ground black pepper to taste

3 carrots, whole, peeled

3 sticks celery, trimmed

1 leek, whole, trimmed, and well-rinsed

2 pounds Chilean bass (four 8-ounce fillets)

Salt and freshly ground white pepper to taste

2 tablespoons butter

Juice of 1 lemon

2 tablespoons extra-virgin olive oil

✳ *Coco beans*, les cocos, *are large, white beans, not at all floury, grown in Brittany, that are excellent for stews. Jean-Louis tells me he would bring them over with him to make this stew for friends. In America, he says, use cranberry beans.*

✳ *Chilean sea bass: Four fillets are easier to handle than one 2-pound piece of fish that would take a little longer to cook. Jean-Louis knows his fish—I used to see him travelling to visit the fishermen where the fish came in when he was chef at Jean-Louis at The Watergate. He knows Chilean sea bass is marvelous for this dish. Alternatives, without the same strong character, could be monkfish, John Dory, or sea bass.*

✳ *The heady smell of country ham throughout this recipe evokes home for Jean-Louis, with* jambon de Bayonne *from the Basque country to the southwest and Dordogne's farm-cured hams to the north.*

✳ *Parma prosciutto: Try to find smoked prosciutto with an earthy taste.*

✳ *Olive oil should be the finest olive oil you can find, Jean-Louis insists—real extra-virgin.*

✳ *For the wine, Jean-Louis typically suggests a young, ready-to-drink, full-bodied red from neighboring Bordeaux, or a young thirst-quenching chianti—not an aged chianti. Chilean sea bass might call for a Chilean wine, such as a young red Concho Y Toro, lightly cooled.*

Sea Bream, Oven-Cooked à la Provençale

Dorade Provençale au Four

Paul Bocuse,
Restaurant Paul Bocuse,
Collonges-au-Mont-d'Or, Lyon

SERVES 4

7 ounces tomatoes

7 ounces white mushrooms

1 whole sea bream, about 2½ pounds, scaled, gutted, and backbone removed

2 tablespoons olive oil

1 bouquet garni: 1 sprig each thyme, tarragon, and parsley, and a bay leaf, tied together

1¾ ounces onions, peeled and thinly sliced

1¾ ounces shallots, peeled and thinly sliced

Salt and freshly ground pepper to taste

½ cup dry white wine, Macon-style

1 lemon, sliced

Preheat the oven to 360°F. Pour olive oil into a large ovenproof baking dish.

Plunge the tomatoes into boiling water for 10 seconds, remove with a slotted spoon, and rinse under cold water to peel more easily, and then quarter. Cut the stems off the mushrooms, then clean, wash, drain, and wipe dry. Set aside.

Rinse the bream under water—preferably not tap water—and dry with a paper towel. Brush the inside and outside of the fish with olive oil.

Stuff the fish with the bouquet garni and put it on the baking dish. Surround the fish with the sliced onions, shallots, and tomatoes. At the last minute, chop and add the mushrooms. Season with salt and pepper. Pour the white wine over the fish.

Bake for 20 minutes, then turn the oven off and let the fish rest for 5 to 7 minutes. Garnish the fish with lemon slices at the last minute and serve in the baking dish.

※ *Sea bream: when not available, look for a good, fresh sea bass.*

※ *Bring the codfish to the table and serve your guests from the serving dish, so they can smell the herbs of the bouquet garni emerging as the fish is portioned out.*

❋ Rinse under cold water—preferably not tap water. Paul remembers, from his traveling the United States over thirty years, there are still places where he found tapwater with a taste, often of chlorine. Personally, I notice that the ice used around oysters and prawn cocktails or ice in a drink too often has a taste of chlorine in the background. Understandably, when cooking in America, Paul prefers to use Evian or American bottled water.

The water is important, even in France. I lived four years in Bordeaux and the oysters from beds in the bay of Arcachon tasted quite different just gathered and served in an Arcachon restaurant. Arcachon oysters that travel thirty miles sitting on ice and served in a restaurant in Bordeaux arrive with their rich flavor of sea water diluted by the ice.

❋ A young, light dry rosé wine would be delicious to accompany this fish.

Mediterranean Fish Stew

La Bouillabaisse de la Côte d'Azur

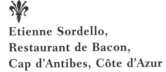

Etienne Sordello,
Restaurant de Bacon,
Cap d'Antibes, Côte d'Azur

DURING MY SECOND YEAR IN PARIS, *a friend invited me on a vacation. We took the fast train, the Train Bleu, overnight from the Gare de Lyon in Paris south to Le Rayol, a small halt on the line within smelling distance of the sea. We found an apartment over a fish store with a view from the living room balcony of the Mediterranean, at ten old francs—about two dollars—a day.*

It was late September in the fifties, some years before the hordes, busloads, and caravans from Northern Europe made their annual descent on the Cote d'Azur. Not a soul on the beach. Every Wednesday a small hotel down the road served bouillabaisse with rouille sauce that I knew even then was out of this world.

Thirty years later, I flew Roger Vergé and his colleague, Etienne Sordello, in to New York for the first-night gala dinner of Martha Graham's dance company at Lincoln Center. They brought with them containers of Etienne's bouillabaisse from his Restaurant Le Bacon in Antibes, the best fish restaurant on the Cote d'Azur.

As an example of the great camaraderie among these chefs, in the middle of preparing this gala dinner, Paul Bocuse arrived. He greeted us, "I just stopped off in New York to see if my friend Roger needed a hand."

SERVES 4

6 pounds fish for the soup and
    8 pounds fish for poaching
    in the soup, such as sea
    bass, John Dory, monkfish,
    and red mullet

Soup

¹/4 cup virgin olive oil
2 medium-sized onions, peeled
    and chopped

continued

Ask the fishmonger to fillet and cut the fish into 4-ounce slices. Wash and drain the fish and refrigerate.

To prepare the soup, in an extra-large stockpot, mix together ¹/4 cup olive oil, onions, garlic, celery, leeks, pepper, and tarragon and sweat over high heat for 7 minutes. Add the tomato paste and cook for another 4 minutes. Add the chopped tomatoes, the 6 pounds fish for the soup, and the herbs. Stir well to combine. Stir in 4 quarts salted water, bring to a boil, and cook for 10 minutes.

1 head garlic, halved

1 stalk celery, washed and sliced

2 leeks, white part only, washed and sliced

1 sweet red pepper, sliced

Pinch tarragon

4 tablespoons tomato paste

4 ripe medium-sized tomatoes, cut into pieces

2 sprigs each thyme and fennel

2 bay leaves

Pinch fresh thyme

4 quarts water, salted with sea salt

Pinch best-quality saffron

Sea salt and freshly ground pepper to taste

4 medium-sized potatoes, cut in 1/4-inch-thich slices

Rouille

1 sweet red pepper

2 or 3 garlic cloves

Generous pinch coarse sea salt

4 large egg yolks

1/4 cup olive oil

Pinch best-quality saffron

1 day-old *baguette*

Remove the pot from the heat and process the soup ingredients in a blender for 1 minute. Put the processed ingredients through a vegetable mill with first a big blade and then with a small blade. Then put the soup through a fine-mesh sieve, pressing down heavily with a ladle to extract all fish flavors. Season the soup with saffron, salt, and pepper. Taste.

Pour the soup into the stockpot and add the potatoes and 8 pounds of fish. Cook over medium heat for 5 minutes.

To prepare the *rouille*, using a mortar and pestle, crush the red pepper with the garlic cloves and coarse salt, in a bowl. Add the egg yolks, and like making a mayonnaise (see page 286), slowly pour in the olive oil, stirring all the time with a wooden spoon. When the sauce is made, add the remaining saffron to give it the beautiful golden *rouille* color. Set aside.

Preheat the broiler. Cut the baguette into 8 or 12 thin slices and rub each slice on both sides with garlic. Put the slices on a baking sheet and broil till golden. Remove from the sheet and line the bottom of a soup tureen with them. Pour in the hot soup and pass warm soup bowls. Pass the *rouille* in a separate serving dish.

❋ *When buying fish for the soup and for poaching, Etienne buys his fish whole, straight off the fishing boats in the port of Cannes. When the heads are removed and the fish filleted, there is a loss of between 30 percent to 40 percent. He is then left with about 4 pounds for the soup and about 6 pounds for the poaching. This is a great soup. There may be some leftovers for the next day, but with a good* bouillabaisse, *we had second helpings. And a chef who flies 3,000 miles with his* bouillabaisse *is a generous chef, indeed.*

❋ *Some like it with grated Gruyère-style cheese on the side. Etienne at his Le Bacon prefers his bouillabaisse without grated cheese.*

❋ *In Marseille, further west along France's Mediterranean coast, the fish, cut in large slices, is cooked separately.*

❋ *Etienne Sordello's* bouillabaisse *contains small Mediterranean rockfish* (rascasses, girolles, rouquiers, blaviers, *and* sarans) *for the soup, and larger, firmer fish for the poaching* (St. Pierre, baudroie, vives, galinettes, chapon, *and* murene)—*names that reflect the azur of the Côte d'Azur.*

❋ *All round the coast of France—from the English Channel to the Atlantic and Mediterranean—cooks make* bouilla-baisse *with their local fish. Memories of the* bouillabaisse *in his native Brittany—called a* cotriade, *made with conger eel and lobster—brings tears to Hervé Riou's eyes.*

Turbot with Seaweed, Shellfish, and Demi-Sel Butter Chips

Turbot de Bretagne aux Algues,
Coquillages et Copeaux de Beurre Demi-sel

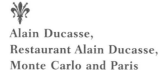

Alain Ducasse,
Restaurant Alain Ducasse,
Monte Carlo and Paris

ALAIN DUCASSE AND CLAUDE TROISGROS *are two chefs who stand out as perhaps the most adventurous among the young ones today.*

Alain Ducasse is today's French chef who has climbed so far so fast and defied the odds, aiming for two Michelin three-star restaurants, not seen since the Mère Brazier reigned in Lyon in the thirties. Finally, in 1997, Michelin awarded three stars to the Alain Ducasse Restaurant in Paris and, in 1998, to his Louis XV Alain Ducasse Restaurant in the splendid old Hotel de Paris in Monte Carlo.

One of the dozen chefs who began in Roger Vergé's kitchen, Alain is today his own master on the high wire of exciting performances by the great chefs.

It is tough at the top, exceedingly demanding to succeed night after night, year after year.

The recipe Alain gave me, and the one from Claude Troisgros in Rio de Janeiro (see page 103), are here to make good reading. Monte Carlo and Rio have always had a touch of dream about them.

SERVES 1

One 7-ounce slice turbot or
    fresh halibut
4 tablespoons (1/2 stick) salted
    butter (*demi-sel*) (see note)
Coarse sea salt

Seaweeds

1 sheet wakame
1 sheet dulse
1 sheet sea lettuce
1 sheet each royal kombu,
    varec, kelp

Ask the fishmonger to gut the fish and reserve and clean the head. Brush the slice of turbot or halibut with softened butter in a *pommade* (see below) and season with coarse sea salt.

Wrap the slice of turbot very tightly in the wakame, dulse, sea lettuce, and royal kombu. Set on a steamer rack in a saucepan over boiling water and cook over low or medium-low heat for 15 to 20 minutes.

Remove from the steamer and unwrap the turbot. Clean off any impurities.

Brush the fish again with more softened butter. Place in a deep cast-iron skillet with a cover on top of the kelp and other seaweeds.

To make the fish bouillon, blanch the calf's foot in salted water and set aside to cool. Put the 2 quarts water in a large saucepan and add the vegetables and bouquet garni. Cover with parchment paper and set aside to bubble for 3 hours. Occasionally, skim off any foam. Then put the bouillon through a fine-mesh sieve and set aside.

Put the turbot head and 3/4 cup fish bouillon in a casserole. Add the chicken bouillon, and put through a fine-mesh sieve. Strain off any impurities. Add the crushed peppercorns, thyme, and sea salt. Cover the pan again with a sheet of parchment paper, and leave on a medium heat to simmer for 1 hour. Then add the nori and infuse for 10 minutes. Pass through a clean cheesecloth and set aside to cool.

To prepare the shellfish and seaweed, clean and cook each of the shellfish separately in its own juice by washing each in cold water, drain, and put a large skillet with 1 tablespoon of boiling water. Repeat the procedure with each shellfish and discard any that do not open.

Pass each of the juices from the shellfish through a fine cheesecloth and set aside each juice in separate pans. Starting with the clams, remove the shellfish from their shells, rinsing each one thoroughly under running water to eliminate any grains of sand, and set aside each shellfish in its own juice.

Blanch the seaweed in salted water. Cook the shellfish separately for 3 to 4 minutes in their juices by placing on a low heat. Pour the shellfish liquid through a cheesecloth and set aside.

Preheat the oven to 350°F.

Fish bouillon

1 calf's foot, halved

2 quarts water

1 teaspoon coarse sea salt plus coarse sea salt to taste

3 1/2 ounce peeled and sliced carrots

1 ounce sliced onion

1 ounce sliced celery

1 small bouquet garni: 1 sprig each of tarragon, thyme, and parsley, and a bay leaf (tied together)

1 turbot head, gills removed and cleaned

6 tablespoons chicken stock or bouillon (see page 282)

5 white peppercorns, crushed

1 sprig thyme

1 sheet nori

Shellfish

5 clams, *palourdes*

4 clams, *praires*

6 cockles, *coques*

6 periwinkles, *bigorneaux*

2 knife-edge clams, *praires "knife edge"*

2 tablespoons kneaded butter, (*beurre manié*) (see page 44)

Lemon juice

Cook 3 tablespoons fish bouillon in a small saucepan over high heat and reduce by half. Season with the clam juice only, and thicken by blending in some kneaded butter. Add a squeeze of lemon juice and freshly ground pepper.

Heat the fish in the oven. Arrange the seaweed in the center of a platter and surround with the shellfish. Place the slice of turbot on the seaweed and cover the plate with shavings of demi-sel butter. Serve a small dish of the sauce on the side.

❀ *Ingredient measures: In ounces, these are the precise measures from one of the most brilliant chefs in the world. Take a young carrot, 2 if necessary, then peel and slice them for 3 1/2 ounces. No more. From a young peeled and sliced onion, you need 1 ounce. Later, 5 white peppercorns, 5 palourdes, 4 prairies, and so on. I know Alain. A dish like this is what makes him so highly respected by his profession and by those who dine in France's Michelin three-star restaurants, of which Alain directs two such kitchens.*

❀ *Remember that this recipe is for one person. Hence the fine measures.*

❀ *Fresh halibut is an alternative to turbot, if it is unavailable.*

❀ *Ask the butcher to chop the calf's foot in half.*

❀ *Sea salt is usually available in gourmet stores. Buy the coarse, not the fine, sea salt, says Hervé, who has worked on a sea salt farm.*

❋ Demi-sel *butter: In France, chefs cook with lightly salted, demi-sel, butter all the time, says Hervé. In America recipes more often call for unsalted butter, since salt is considered not so healthy. Since this is a book of recipes given directly by the French chefs as they cook in France, I have indicated "butter." American salted butter is readily available; imported French demi-sel is in some stores. Try it. The difference in taste is enormous. For this recipe, you make a* pommade—*that is, soften the butter to spreadable consistency and beat it with a spoon to the desired consistency.*

❋ *Seaweed: Alain Ducasse has fresh seaweed shipped to him directly from the Atlantic shores of Brittany. In the United States, use Maine or Japanese seaweeds dried in sheets. These are sold in packets at Japanese or other Asian markets and at health food stores.*

Mussels Marinières in White Wine

Moules Marinières au Vin Blanc

The Mère Brazier,
Restaurant Mère Brazier,
Lyon

DEMONSTRATING *oeufs à la neige* TO SOME STUDENT CHEFS IN MIAMI, *Paul Bocuse was asked how to beat eggs for 100 people. "Take a hundred eggs," he replied.*

So in the fifties, when I was invited to manage and cook for a young summer repertory theater company for their season in Cornwall, I multiplied the food for every meal by fifteen and I was getting close.

Each Wednesday I left the company their dinner and hurried back to the theater to help the stage designers Valerios Caloutsis and Monica Stirling strike the set and build and paint the new one. We paused at dawn to run down to the beach for a swim and pick the mussels off the rocks. The best seat on first nights, the local drama critic knew, was next to the door to the kitchen, from where the smell of Monica's mussels cooking in white wine and garlic wafted across Noel Coward's Blithe Spirit.

The season over, the designers took their recipe for mussels soup and happiness back to their home in Paris and invited me to stay with them for a couple of weeks. I did. I stayed and worked and ate and drank in France for more than a dozen years. But it all began with the call of those mussels à la marinière, *literally "mussels by the beach."*

SERVES 4

4 pounds fresh mussels
  in the shell

Freshly ground pepper to taste

4 sprigs parsley, chopped

4 sprigs thyme, chopped

6 shallots, peeled and sliced

2 cups dry white wine,
  preferably a young
  Muscadet or Sancerre

5 tablespoons butter

Inspect the mussels. If any are open, or do not tightly close when scraping with your Opinel or another sharp knife to remove the "beard" on each shell, throw those away. Wash under cold running water. Do not set aside in water or they will open.

Place the mussels in a large saucepan. Add the pepper, half the chopped parsley, thyme, sliced shallots, and wine. Do not add salt. Cover and cook over high heat until the mussels have opened. Check by shaking the pan several times.

Remove the mussels with a slotted spoon and put into a deep serving dish. Cook the cooking liquid over medium heat to reduce by half. Pour through a fine sieve over the mussels.

Add knobs of butter on top and serve immediately in warm bowls, garnished with parsley.

* *Paul Bocuse likes to add the juice of half a lemon and 2 stalks of celery, diced, to the cooking mussels. He uses a young white Beaujolais, Macon, or Muscadet. The Haeberlin brothers in Alsace would use their Pinot Blanc or Sylvaner.*

* *When the Romans occupied the north of England, they enjoyed the mussels from the rocky shores. They added milk to the dry white wine that the mussels cooked in, and cream at the moment of seasoning. Cream sounds even more French than the French style of cooking them.*

* *The most spectacular cooking of mussels is in the Charente-Maritime region, on the Atlantic coast above Bordeaux, where my St. Emilion winemaker, Alain Querre, goes to his friends for an éclade—the mussels are laid out on a bed of dry pine needles that are set ablaze and the mussels are cooked in a couple of minutes. They are washed down by a young, dry white Graves wine. The winemaker brings the wine.*

Soft-Shell Crabs Sautéed with Lemon Juice and Cognac

**Jean Troisgros,
Restaurant Troisgros, Roanne
and Georges Troisgros,
New York**

"When you come to France," *Jean Troisgros would say, "you don't come here to eat American food. In Morocco, I eat Moroccan food. In England, I eat English food. In Italy, I eat their pasta. In America, I prefer to eat a good American hamburger rather than a bad French steak. And if I were going to France, I would go to Paul Bocuse and eat his cuisine."*

Traveling to America several times a year through the seventies and early eighties, Jean found much more than hamburgers. He discovered soft-shell crabs and ordered them whenever he saw them on a menu. "They're one of the best things I've found in America," he told me.

Georges, his son, has been chef at New York's Lutèce Restaurant these past fifteen years, first under André Soltner and then, when André retired in 1995, under Eberhard Mueller. He gave me his father's recipe for soft-shell crabs.

SERVES 4

12 small, young soft-shell crabs

Salt and freshly ground pepper to taste

6 tablespoons (3/4 stick) butter

3 tablespoons cognac

1/4 cup lemon juice

3/4 cup chicken stock (page 282)

Buy soft-shells crabs during the first 6 weeks of their spring season. Be sure they are live and eat them the same day you buy them.

Season the crabs with salt and pepper.

Heat the butter in a large skillet over medium heat. Add the crabs and sauté them 3 minutes on each side, or until crispy brown,

Without a large skillet, cook the crabs in batches of 6 and using a spatula, transfer them to a warm platter at the back of the warm stove.

Add the cognac to the skillet and cook over high heat, stirring for 1 minute. Add the lemon juice and chicken stock and continue cooking over high heat, until the liquid has reduced to 1/2 cup.

Allow 3 crabs per serving. Arrange them on the plates and spoon the sauce over them.

※ *André Soltner, when he came to America in the sixties, also discovered the joy of cooking soft-shell crabs and offers this variation—sprinkle the crabs with chopped parsley and with slivered almonds that have been sauteed in butter until golden brown.*

※ *Cognac: Jean Troisgros was a collector and lover of fine old cognacs. The late Alexis Lichine called cognac "The most wonderful spirit ever devised by the genius of man," but you can cook the crabs in a cup of heavy cream and replace the cognac with 3/4 cup of dry white wine.*

※ *Soft-shell crabs can also be enjoyed sautéed without wine or cognac.*

Scallops in a Half-Moon with Chicory and Truffles

Papillote de Coquilles St. Jacques aux Endives et aux Truffes

Gerard Boyer, Hotel and Restaurant Les Crayères, Reims, Champagne

GERARD AND ELYANE BOYER RUN THE GRANDEST HOTEL AND RESTAURANT *in Champagne country. Owners of the great Champagne houses take their distinguished guests from abroad there, when not entertaining them in their own homes.*

The elegant salons and dining rooms of Les Crayères offer a perfect setting and ambiance for champagne.

The host at our table, Christian Pol Roger, welcomed a colleague—and competitor—from the house of Veuve Clicquot, who had just arrived at a table across the room with a party of four who were clearly British. Christian graciously ordered for us a bottle of Veuve Clicquot, saying, "You will see, my colleague will be ordering a bottle of Pol Roger for his table."

This is the way of the world where Scallops on the Half-Moon are served with a glass of your colleague's champagne.

SERVES 4

1¹/4 pounds endive

16 to 20 scallops, depending on size, opened and in their shells (see note)

10 tablespoons (1¹/4 stick) butter

Juice of ¹/2 lemon

2 teaspoons acacia honey

2 shallots, finely chopped

¹/4 cup port

4 tablespoons truffle juice from the can

6 ounces truffles, preferably canned, cut in julienne

Salt and cayenne pepper to taste

8 sprigs chervil

Cut the endives in half lengthwise and chop in small ¹/8-inch-wide strips. Wash them quickly, drain, wipe dry, and set aside.

Remove the scallops from the shell. Remove the outer grey fringe, or beard, and separate the muscle from the flesh and coral. Wash thoroughly in several changes of water to remove any sand and dry on a clean towel.

Put the beards in a large saucepan, cover with water, and bring to the boil over medium heat. Cook for 15 minutes. Pour this liquid through a fine-mesh sieve and set aside.

Heat 1¹/2 tablespoons butter in a large skillet and before it browns, add the endive and lemon juice. Cook for

3 minutes, stirring constantly. Add the honey and cook for
30 seconds. Using a slotted spoon, remove the endives.

Heat 1 teaspoon butter in a small casserole and sweat
the shallots. Deglaze with port wine, 2/3 cup of scallop stock,
and the truffle juice. Cook over medium heat and reduce by
three-quarters. Reduce the heat to low and add *most* of the
remaining butter, whipping it until emulsified. Season with
salt and cayenne pepper. Put through a fine-mesh sieve into
a serving bowl, pressing hard. Add the truffles and set aside.

Preheat the oven to 500°F.

Using heavy-duty aluminum foil, take 4 sheets the size
of the dinner plates. Take one sheet and place on top of
another for two separate squares. Fold the doubled sheets
into half-moon shapes the diameter of the dinner plate.
Lightly butter the half-moons on both sides, and place some
endives on each. Place 8 or 10 scallops on each portion of
endive, taking care that the scallops do not touch the foil.
Fold and close each aluminum packet, crimping the edges
to seal tightly.

Put the packets in the oven on a sheet pan and cook
for no longer than 4 minutes. Using tongs or a slotted spoon,
remove the endives and scallops from the packets and place
the endive surrounded by 4 or 5 scallops on 4 warm plates.
Garnish each plate with two sprigs of chervil.

❄ *Scallops must be fresh and come from a good fish store.*
They are gathered off the shores on both sides of the
Atlantic. French scallops are exported to America, so ask
local fish stores and buy only fresh arrivals. Scallops are
sold in their shells, closed, like oysters. Put them in a low-
heat oven for a few minutes and then open with your
Opinel or other strong knife. If your fishmonger opens
them for you, take them straight home and refrigerate them
until you cook them—the same day.

❋ *Acacia honey—a very pale, very fine honey—comes from the Auvergne, Rhône Valley, and Provence and it is also produced in Canada. Many honeys are too strong for this dish, but one alternative would be a good clover honey from California or France. Beware of honeys that are not 100-percent produced from their place of origin as stated on the label.*

❋ *Port for cooking: Use a good port from Portugal—Sandeman, Taylor Fladgate, Warre, Croft, Quinta da Noval, and Graham are some of the old port houses. Discover port. Half-bottles are available in some stores—a glass for the cook and your sous-chef. No "cooking" port, please.*

❋ *For truffle juice, use the juice from the can. Set ^{1}/2 teaspoon truffle juice aside to add to the sauce before serving, if you like a stronger truffle flavor.*

❋ *Truffles: Last winter, I spent a weekend with Gerard and Elyane at Les Crayères and dinner on my first night was composed entirely—from appetizer to dessert—of Gerard's brilliant creations with truffles. It was late January; truffles were just in season and at their most exquisite. An aroma of truffles was drifting through the candlelit dining room. After a glass of champagne, I recall I was served a ravioli of scallops and black truffles; truffles in pastry with a périgueux sauce; escalopes of cod with artichokes and truffles; a milk-fed veal in truffle juice; truffled lamb; a small, delicate salad with truffles; and finally, a dessert of truffled chocolates. No other chef in France celebrates the truffle season with such elegance and imagination as Gerard at Les Crayères.*

He uses the finest, the black truffle from the Périgord or the grey truffle from the forests around Champagne. They grow underground near the roots of certain trees such as oak, hazel, and chestnut, hunted out late autumn by farmers with trained, muzzled pigs. Deforestation has reduced the land where truffles might be found. There are also white truffles from Piedmont and Tuscany that are popular in Italian cooking.

Since truffles are seasonal and expensive, Gerard advises us to use canned truffles for his recipe. Fresh truffles in season, when we do find them in a store, may not be so fresh after sitting on a shelf. For good quality fresh truffles in season, see page 297.

❋ For this dinner with truffles in the winter garden at Les Crayères, I was served the Veuve Clicquot Brut and stayed with it through the evening.

Lobster and Macaroni Gratin

Gratin d'Hommard aux Macaroni

Roger Vergé,
Restaurant Le Moulin de Mougins,
Côte d'Azur

WORKING WITH ROGER IN 1984 *to produce the first-class menu on Pan Am's new flagship route, Nice to New York, we had only ten weeks to be ready for the first flight. Everything went well, except one main course dish. Patiently, Roger welcomed the chef from the airport kitchens and carefully showed him step by step. The chef returned to the airport, cooked, and had the lobster loaded aboard. Flight after flight, we tasted, and the quality was not there.*

Finally, we discovered what was amiss. The chef refused to get up early and cook the lobster on the morning of the flight. He cooked it the night before and set it aside in his cooler, so next morning all he had to do was assemble and warm up the lobster.

I requested a meeting with the president of the airport's catering services in Paris. He dined me at Gaston Lenotre's restaurant that they had just bought, and agreed to give me the chef from their Michelin one-star airport restaurant to cook for us. He was glad to please us because he knew Pan Am's daily flights were bringing a colossal upsurge of traffic and business to the Côte d'Azur. (It was Pan Am's highest revenue route, still running today by Delta.) We had freshly cooked lobster every morning from then on.

Those six months working with Roger on the Pan Am menu were my closest to actually working with these great artists, the Great Chefs of France. A fabulous experience, and a fabulous dish.

SERVES 6

One 4^1/2-pound live lobster

2 tablespoons butter

^{1}/2 cup cognac

1 medium carrot, washed and sliced

1 celery stalk, scraped and sliced

3 tablespoons chopped shallots

^{1}/2 cup port

"It is simple," Roger begins. "I prefer the Breton lobster, as it is best for quality, alive, of course. We cook it as if for *à l'americaine*, plunge it live into a large saucepan of boiling water for 2 minutes, remove, and drain.

"In a wide skillet, melt the butter over a high heat and when it starts to foam, add the lobster and move it around with a wooden spoon until is has turned all red. Pour in the cognac and flambé the lobster completely.

"Once flambéed, add the sliced carrots, celery, shallots and the port. Drop in the bouquet garni and stir in 2 cups of the heavy cream. It's the cream that really makes the sauce. Leave the lobster to simmer and soak in this marvelous sauce for about 15 minutes.

"Over another flame, cook the macaroni for 7 or 8 minutes in a saucepan of boiling salted water. In one more saucepan heat the milk and when it is boiling, lift the macaroni out into the boiling milk and finish the cooking in the milk. This way the macaroni will taste so much better.

"Once the lobster is cooked in the sauce, remove it, drain it, and cut it up, setting the sauce aside. Cut the claws off close to the body, crack the shells, and remove the meat. Slice the tail into 5 or 6 sections and cut the body in half lengthways, removing first the sand sacs in the head and the intestinal tract. Set aside the coral. Discard the green tomally. Return the lobster pieces to the sauce, the coral, too, if you wish, and reduce a little.

"The macaroni, now cooked, drain and mix it with the lobster in the sauce and do a *glacage*. That means taking the rest of the heavy cream and whisking it up in a bowl almost as for a *crème chantilly*, adding the egg yolks as you whisk. Put the lobster, its sauce, and the macaroni in a large, deep gratin dish and pour the cream over and place under the salamander or grill of the oven for 2 or 3 minutes until browned. Remove, decorate with lobster body and claws, and serve immediately."

For our Pan Am first-class service, Roger suggested we serve the lobster in individual gratin dishes, each one put under the broiler for 2 or 3 minutes and served hot. A small piece of claw and parsley was placed as decoration on each dish.

1 bouquet garni: 1 sprig each of parsley and thyme, and a bay leaf, tied together

3 cups heavy cream or *crème fraîche*

7 ounces short elbow macaroni

1 quart whole milk

2 egg yolks

4 small sprigs parsley

Salt and freshly ground pepper to taste

* Roger sometimes cuts the live lobster up just before cooking and assembling this dish.

* Coral is optional. Some people like it for the color it gives.

* Port: The chef means using port from one of the fine port houses of Portugal (page 98).

* No flour in the sauce, say Roger, Paul, Jean, Pierre, and André, though some cookbooks recommend thickening a navarin sauce with flour. Ugh! say my chefs.

* "It's the cream that really makes the sauce," are Roger's own words. Just as in Georges Blanc's Chicken in Cream (page 171), in Paul Bocuse's Custard (page 279), it is the quality and richness of the cream—ideally, crème fraîche—that makes this dish—an echo of the old days of French cuisine when so much was cooked in cream. Notice how Roger is back with the rest of the cream for the macaroni gratin that goes with the lobster. Cream, cream, always cream, Paul says.

* Cream: Crème fraîche avaliable from Vermont Butter & Cheese Co. (page 301).

Lobsters Oh! Marcoco

Claude Troisgros,
Blue Door Restaurant,
Miami Beach

CLAUDE TROISGROS BEGAN IN THE TROISGROS FAMILY KITCHEN *in Roanne and apprenticed chez Paul Bocuse, who sent him to work in Rio de Janiero. Claude fell in love, married, and opened his own place in Rio. Roanne, he called his restaurant, not wishing to use the family name in case he did not succeed. It seated eight, the kitchen was closet space, but he went to the market just as he did in Roanne with his father. He later opened a bigger restaurant, Restaurant Claude Troisgros, in the most fashionable part of the city, rated today the finest restaurant in Brazil.*

In 1994, still keeping his restaurant in Rio, Claude decided to venture north, to New York and open CT Restaurant. He was showered with praise by the press, but finally, after three years, the call of Rio was too strong and he returned to Brazil full time.

Since 1997, he returns regularly as chef consultant to the Blue Door Restaurant in Miami Beach, hence the next recipe.

I have known Claude and his wife, Marlene, at home and in his restaurant from his earliest days in Rio. He brings a constantly refreshing approach with his blend of New and Old World cuisine. Like his uncle, Jean, and Paul Bocuse, Claude does not take himself too seriously. Recipes like Lobsters Oh! Marcoco *show a brilliant young chef at work in his restaurant kitchen. So enjoy the reading, and imagine that he is preparing it for you and your table.*

SERVES 4

3¹/₃ cups white rice
4 live lobsters, about 1¹/₂
    pounds each
1 teaspoon red wine vinegar
Pinch salt

Sauce

6 tablespoons cashew nuts
1 teaspoon chopped
    fresh ginger
2 ounces dried shrimps

continued

Wash the rice in cold water and drain. Then soak it for 2 hours in cold water.

Cook the lobsters for 8 minutes in boiling water with vinegar and salt. Remove the lobster and cool to chill in ice. Remove and discard the lobster shells, keeping only the tail for decoration. Remove and discard the hard stomach sac near the head and the intestinal tract down the middle. Draw the meat from the tail in one piece and cut all the meat from the lobster into large cubes. Cut the meat from the claws horizontally, so as to preserve the claw shape. Remove sinew running through center of the claw.

2 teaspoons palm oil

2 small onions, peeled and chopped

1 clove garlic, chopped

2 tomatoes, peeled and diced

1 teaspoon chopped lemon balm leaves, *citronelle,* or lemongrass.

Freshly ground pepper to taste

2 cups unsweetened coconut milk

1 teaspoon chopped fresh coriander

Sugar to taste

Salt to taste

1²/₃ cups peas, preferably fresh

4 sheets phyllo dough, cut into 3-inch squares

1 egg yolk

To prepare the sauce, process the nuts, ginger, dried shrimp, and 1 teaspoon palm oil in a blender. Heat 1 teaspoon palm oil in a saucepan and sweat the onions and garlic, then add the diced tomatoes, chopped lemon balm or lemongrass, and pepper. Reduce for 5 minutes, then add the cashew nut mixture and sweat for 5 minutes more. Deglaze in coconut milk and bring to a boil. Add the chopped coriander. Season with sugar and salt.

Cook the rice in a saucepan in twice its volume of water over low heat for 25 minutes. Add salt.

Cook the peas quickly—maximum 10 to 15 minutes— in a saucepan of boiling salted water.

Preheat the oven to 370°F.

When ready to serve, what Claude calls the chef's *toque final,* arrange some lobster in each ovenproof soup bowl. Add 2 tablespoons of peas wrapped in a sheet of phyllo, the edges brushed with the paste of egg yolk and sealed. Lay a phyllo packet on top of each lobster.

Place the 4 bowls on a tray in a hot oven for 5 minutes. Remove from the oven and add the lobster tail, standing to attention like a guardsman, as decor.

Serve the rice and the sauce on the side.

❋ *Coconut milk: Claude, working in New York for the first time, told me that he found the Goya brand best for his dish—if you don't have a spare coconut in your kitchen.*

❋ *The cooking time for peas depends on whether the peas are young or fresh or frozen. Thus, the time can vary from 5 to 15 minutes. Taste.*

❋ *Taste, our chefs cannot stress enough, taste, taste what is cooking all along. Paul Bocuse can be heard often saying, if only more chefs tasted what is cooking in their kitchen, if only more chefs themselves dined on what they cook for their customers.*

In his kitchen at Collonges, Paul can be seen tasting what is cooking. Every time I dined with Paul in his small, private dining room behind the main restaurant, his chef de cuisine Roger Jaloux came in with a dish on the menu or a new dish he and Paul are working on for Paul to taste.

Gratin of Freshwater Crayfish, Fernand Point

Gratin de Queues d'Ecrevisses
dans la Tradition Fernand Point

**Patrick Henriroux,
Restaurant La Pyramide,
Vienne, Rhône Valley**

PATRICK HENRIROUX IS THE ASCENDING YOUNG CHEF *who has already his two Michelin stars since taking over this landmark restaurant of France. In the steps of the master, Fernand Point, he creates this dish with the locally fished crayfish.*

Across the River Rhône in Auvergne, home of the red-clawed crayfish, Margaridou advised, "A dozen crayfish will be sufficient, though three dozen for the same quantity of soup could only make it better."

She evoked the smell of crayfish cooking—"If you don't want everyone to know what a delectable dish you're preparing, don't even start"—and the memories of the catch—"the bridge over the river down by the old mill, the pure enchantment along the banks of the streams in your quest for the crayfish, that time you fell in." Happy days.

"Red feet" crayfish are rare even in France today. They can be replaced by unshelled large prawns or a small lobster.

SERVES 4

Court bouillon

2 carrots, trimmed, scraped, and cut in thin rounds

2 onions, peeled and sliced finely

2 cloves garlic, peeled

2 stalks celery, scraped and sliced

1 bouquet garni: 1 sprig each of rosemary, tarragon, and parsley, tied together

continued

To prepare the court bouillon, put the carrots, onions, garlic, celery, bouquet garni, thyme, bay leaf, peppercorns, 2½ cups white wine, and 1 cup water in a casserole or pot with the lid and cook over medium heat for 30 minutes. Remove and press through a fine sieve.

Preheat the oven to 350°F.

To prepare the crayfish, remove the black gut under the central flange of each tail. Plunge the crayfish in boiling water for 2 minutes until the water boils again, then stop the boiling by adding a dash of cold water.

Separate the crayfish heads and tails. Melt 4^1/$_2$ tablespoons butter in a saucepan and quickly sauté the crayfish heads. Add thyme and other herbs, as desired. Deglaze the pan with the liqueur and flambé it. Add ^{1}/$_2$ cup white wine and reduce totally, *à sec,* that is until every drop of water has been evaporated. Be careful not to burn. Pour in 1 cup of water so that it covers the carcasses and cook for 5 minutes over high heat. Add the cream and reduce to a simmer for 10 minutes more.

Remove and press through a fine-mesh sieve, pounding down the carcasses as hard as possible. Set aside the sauce in a bowl, seasoning with salt and cayenne pepper.

Combine the egg yolk and water in a small saucepan and over low heat, whisk the mixture until frothy. Add the remaining butter, whisking this into a rich, smooth sauce with the crayfish liquid.

Remove the crayfish tail shells and set them out in a circle on an ovenproof serving dish. Put the crayfish on a baking sheet and heat in the oven. Remove and preheat the broiler. Pour the sauce over the crayfish and return to the oven to brown lightly under the broiler. Remove from the oven and serve immediately.

✳ *Crayfish may not be easy to find, but more and more freshwater fish are becoming available, sometimes on "special order" from your fishmonger.*

1 teaspoon dried thyme

1 bay leaf

^{1}/$_2$ teaspoon peppercorns

3 cups (1 bottle) dry white wine, chardonnay style

1 cup water

4 pounds freshwater "red feet" crayfish

8 tablespoons (1 stick) butter

^{1}/$_2$ teaspoon fresh thyme or other herbs (optional)

1 cup liqueur *fine* de Château Grillet

1 cup water

^{1}/$_2$ cup heavy cream or *crème fraîche*

Salt and cayenne pepper to taste

1 egg yolk

1 cup water

Salt and peppercorns to taste

Chapter Four

Meat

BEEF

Beef Rib with Marrow and Beaujolais Fleurie

Jean and Pierre Troisgros, Roanne

Filet of Beef on a String with Mushrooms and Chinese Vermicelli

Pierre and Michel Troisgros, Roanne

Beef, Burgundy-Style

Paul Bocuse, Collonges-au-Mont-d'Or, Lyon

Pot-Au-Feu

Paul Bocuse, Brasserie Le Nord, Lyon

Beef Tripe, Lyon-Style

Paul Bocuse, Brasserie Le Nord, Lyon

French Shepherd's Pie

Paul Bocuse, Collonges-au-Mont-d'Or, Lyon

Hamburger with Truffles and Foie Gras

Paul Bocuse and Roger Vergé in Los Angeles

Hungarian Goulash

Paul Bocuse, Brasserie L'Est, Lyon

Steak for the Chef's Day Off: Rib Eye Steak Boned with Three Peppers

Jean Banchet with Paul Bocuse, Orlando

LAMB

Roast Lamb with Potatoes

Margaridou, Auvergne

Roast Leg of Lamb

The Mère Brazier, Lyon

Lea's Lamb Baked in a Galette of Potatoes

Lea Linster, Luxembourg

**NAVARIN OF
SPRING LAMB WITH
BABY VEGETABLES**

ROGER VERGÉ,
CÔTE D'AZUR

**MECHOUI OF LAMB
WITH COUCOUS**

PAUL BOCUSE,
LYON

VEAL

**VEAL KIDNEYS
SAUTÉED IN
MADEIRA**

GEORGES AND
PAUL BOCUSE,
COLLONGES-AU-MONT-
D'OR, LYON

**VEAL SWEETBREADS
IN WHITE WINE**

JEAN TROISGROS, ROANNE
AND GEORGES TROISGROS,
NEW YORK

**RUMP OF VEAL
IN CASSEROLE**

RAYMOND OLIVER,
PARIS, AND
GRANDMÈRE BOCUSE,
COLLONGES-AU-MONT-
D'OR, LYON

PORK

**TO COOK A HAM AND
PEASE PUDDING**

ADAPTED FROM
AUGUSTE ESCOFFIER,
LONDON

**PETIT SALÉ
OF PORK WITH
LENTILS**

PAUL BOCUSE,
BRASSERIE L'EST, LYON

**BRAISED SPICED
PORK BELLY**

DANIEL BOULUD,
NEW YORK

PIG'S TROTTERS

ANDRÉ SOLTNER,
NEW YORK

**SAUERKRAUT
WITH MEATS
AND SAUSAGES**

ANDRÉ SOLTNER,
NEW YORK

The Winemaker and the Chef

MY FRIEND ALAIN QUERRE's father Daniel Querre, ambassador at large of the winemaker's brotherhood, the Jurade of St. Emilion, was a close friend of Fernand Point. A man of large girth, and resembling a cardinal when dressed in his long, red robes of office at harvest festival time, Querre would dine regularly at La Pyramide. Point would visit St. Emilion to dine at Querre's Château Monbousquet and choose his wines.

Alain grew up among such men who knew how to cook a piece of meat. Every year, when the grapes were in, the harvesters gathered in the cellar for the harvest dinner. Alain would be at the fire with his cellar-master watching as each piece of meat cooked on the red-hot embers.

He told me, "Cooking a piece of meat is a tradition, a culture, the art of a region, that I learned from my father. It is something rare that we must hold on to and not let disappear. There are still people, like my cellar-master, who know how to cook meat—meat cooked over a fire. Families still know how to do it, but ask for a steak in many restaurants today, and they'll carbonize it. Even good restaurants with barbecues have lost the way to cook a steak.

"The customer in a restaurant wants to eat well. But if he hurries the kitchen, and shouts to the waiter, 'Quickly, quickly!' then the meat may be taken off the flame before it is ready. Or if the customer is not ready to be served, the meat gets cold or turns into charcoal. I'd treat him like someone seated in my house and be confident enough to say 'Monsieur, it's not ready. Don't you want your meal to be good? Please, wait.' But so many restaurants allow themselves to be walked over. In a family kitchen, everyone waits. In a restaurant, if you're going to offer the best steak, you have to be able to insist 'Please, have another glass of red wine. The steak is coming. It's worth waiting. When it comes, you'll be happy.' If you cannot say that, then there's no hope."

The winemaker who knows how to lay and make a fire, and how to prepare and cook a piece of meat, like the chef at the spit in his restaurant, he, too, is guardian of the magic of the fire.

Beef Rib with Marrow and Beaujolais Fleurie

Côte de Boeuf au Fleurie

Jean and Pierre Troisgros,
Restaurant Troisgros,
Roanne

THIS DISH WAS ON THE MENU *for our Troisgros dinner at Oz Restaurant in Dallas in 1975.*
In Roanne, the beef was choice Charolais, one of the best breeds of cattle originally from the north
of Roanne. Jean had invited the winemaker, Lalou Bize-Leroy, a co-owner of the Romanee-Conti at
the time, to join them in Dallas for the dinners. Lalou was accompanied by her husband, Marcel Bize,
who himself raised a herd of Charolais. Our chef, Jean Laffont, found some Texas-raised Charolais.
The day after the dinner, we took them over to Fort Worth to buy cowboy gear and on the way to visit
a herd of Charolais grazing. Marcel, with all his French elegance, had difficulty hiding his doubts
about the Texas climate for raising Charolais.

SERVES 4

2³/4 pounds rib of beef,
    in one piece
Salt and freshly ground pepper
    to taste
3 tablespoons butter
1/4 pound beef marrow

Beaujolais sauce

2 shallots, peeled and finely
    chopped
1 bottle Beaujolais
1 cup beef stock or demi-glace
    (see page 283)
1¹/2 tablespoons butter,
    cut into small pieces

Season the beef with salt and pepper. Heat the butter
in a cast-iron skillet over medium heat and when it begins to
sizzle, add the beef and cook for 20 to 25 minutes, depending
on its size. Baste often with the pan juices. Remove from the
heat and let the beef rest—on a warm plate covered by
another warm plate—for the 15 to 20 minutes it takes
you to prepare the marrow and the sauce.

Meanwhile, cut the marrow into slices and put them
in a small saucepan filled with salted water to cover.
Lightly poach the marrow over medium heat for 5 minutes.
Remove the marrow with a slotted spoon, put in ice water
for 15 seconds, and set aside.

Preheat the oven to 350°F.

To make the sauce, deglaze the skillet used for the beef rib with some Beaujolais and with some beef stock or demi-glace, raising the heat. Add the chopped shallots and sweat over very low heat, uncovered, until the shallots release their water. Add the wine and beef stock, increase the heat to medium, and bring to a boil. Reduce the heat to low and cook until reduced by half and the mixture is syrupy. Remove from the heat and whip in the butter, a little at a time. Keep the sauce warm, but do not allow it to simmer again or it will separate. Set aside.

Warm the beef again in the oven on an ovenproof platter, reserving any juices rendered while the meat was resting. Serve on warm plates with the slices of marrow alongside, warmed again for 10 seconds in boiling salted water. Pour the sauce over the beef ribs or pass in a separate serving dish.

❋ *For beef stock, says Pierre, you may use 1 bouillon cube and 1 chicken cube.*

❋ *Depending on which brother was in the kitchen, they cooked the rib for 15 minutes on each side over high heat, or 20 to 25 minutes over medium heat.*

❋ *The Troisgros brothers liked to accompany the beef with a potato gratin without cheese, which was how they learned it with Fernand Point.*

❋ *In Bordeaux, cooks make the sauce with the beef marrow including shallots, lemon juice, thyme, bay leaf, beef extract and, of course, Bordeaux wine. They call it a sauce bordelaise.*

❋ *For wines, Jean chose a Beaujolais Fleurie for the cooking; Paul Bocuse likes a Beaujolais Brouilly in his version. Fleurie and Brouilly are villages in the Beaujolais region with wines with slightly different characters. The other*

Beaujolais villages—Chenas, Chiroubles, Julienas, Regnié, and St. Amour—can be excellent alternatives for cooking and serving with this dish.

❋ The Mère Brazier, for her steak entrecôte bordelaise, added slices of marrow to her red Bordeaux sauce while it was cooking and served the steak with a slice of marrow on top. To accompany it, she recommended french fries or fresh noodles and a bottle of light, young red Bordeaux. The Mère Brazier, Fernand Point, and Paul Bocuse used to serve a young vintage of Alain Querre's Château Monbousquet. A few years ago, Alain sold the family château and Monbousquet today is no longer made to drink young. This is a loss since young, fresh Bordeaux is delicious—and rare.

Filet of Beef on a String, with Mushrooms and Chinese Vermicelli

Filet de Boeuf à la ficelle aux cèpes
sèches et Vermicelles Chinoises

Pierre and Michel Troisgros,
Restaurant Troisgros,
Roanne

WHEN JEAN DIED SUDDENLY OF A HEART ATTACK *on a tennis court in 1984, Pierre's young son, Michel, was in the kitchen at Roanne, his other son, Claude, was in Rio, and Jean's son, Georges, was at Lutèce in New York. After the brothers' thirty-year partnership, a new relationship in the kitchen grew up beween father and son, Pierre and Michel. Pierre sent me this one, one of their father-and-son recipes.*

SERVES 4

1½ ounces dried mushrooms

2 cups mountain spring water, such as Evian

1 quart consommé

1½ pounds beef filet

Coarse sea salt and freshly ground pepper to taste

One ½-ounce piece celeriac, peeled and blanched

2 ounces short vermicelli

1 tablespoon strong Dijon-style mustard

Soak the dried mushrooms the water for 15 minutes. Pour the mushroom's soaking water through a cheesecloth and pour it into a large saucepan or cast-iron stockpot. Add the consommé.

Rub the meat all over with the sea salt and pepper. Using kitchen string, tie the meat up as for a roast, leaving a long end of string to secure to the pot handle. Put the meat in the pot and add the celeriac.

Cook over low heat for 24 minutes. Using the string, pull the meat out of the pot and set aside to reset for 20 minutes in a cool place. (See note).

Meanwhile, put vermicelli in a saucepan with half the consommé cook over low heat for 4 minutes. Put the remaining consommé in another saucepan, add the mushrooms, and cook them over medium heat for 5 minutes. Drain the vermicelli and the mushrooms, reserving the consommé, and set them aside.

Remove the celeriac from the stockpot and crush it with a fork, stirring it with the mustard and some consommé until smooth. Add a tablespoon of Dijon mustard and mix in enough consommé for a smooth sauce.

Put the vermicelli and the mushrooms in a large serving bowl, remove and discard the string, and put the meat into the bowl. At the table, in front of the guests, cut the beef into very thin slices. Place some slices on each plate, garnish with the vermicelli and the mushrooms, and season with a sprinkling of sea salt. Serve the bouillon and the sauce in separate serving dishes.

✳ *Cooking for 24 minutes: Pierre Troisgros has a wicked sense of humor. Thirty years ago, Jean and Pierre wrote "Cook 20 to 25 minutes" for this recipe. I hear Pierre saying, "They're still asking us for cooking times, Michel? Surely they can tell when meat is done. Put down 24 minutes!"*

✳ *Consommé is a clarified bouillon (see pages 282, 283). It can be replaced by beef or chicken bouillon cubes.*

✳ *For French chefs, unless their recipes say otherwise, mushrooms mean those from France—for example, cèpes, chanterelles, mousserons, or the Paris mushroom. If none of these is available, of course, there is usually the porcini mushroom, originally from Italy, but now cultivated in many other places. Mushrooms, like all produce, taste best "in season," something we tend to forget with globally cultivated food in the stores today. (See note on mushrooms and seasons on page 56).*

✳ *Sea salt is available from Williams-Sonoma, Sur La Table (see page 297), and many health-food stores.*

Beef, Burgundy-Style

Boeuf Bourguignon

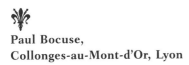

**Paul Bocuse,
Collonges-au-Mont-d'Or, Lyon**

CHEFS ALWAYS EAT *before service starts in the restaurant. One day Paul Bocuse said, "At midday I ate a boeuf bourguignon with fresh noodles and I washed it down with a good Burgundy wine. I made my boeuf bourguignon with some covered ribs because they're a little fatty, and like that it's good. For me, that is the grande cuisine."*

Living near the Beaujolais region, some days Paul likes to use the local wine and call his boeuf bourguignon a boeuf beaujolaise.

"The boeuf beaujolaise can be cooked in several ways," explained Paul Bocuse to student chefs at the French Culinary Institute in New York. "We can marinate it like a stew, or civet, of rabbit or hare, but in the marinating all the sweetness from the meat goes into the wine. Personally, I prefer to make a reduction so that the sweetness stays inside the meat, at the same time forming a coating on the bottom of the casserole so that we can deglaze it with the Beaujolais and it will give us a good taste. Add to that a garniture of little pieces of bacon, little onions, and mushrooms and you have a simple dish that requires produce of good quality."

3 pounds flank steak or
    rump of beef

2 tablespoons all-purpose
    flour

3 tablespoons butter

1 bottle red Burgundy or
    Beaujolais

2 cloves garlic,
    finely chopped

Salt and freshly ground pepper
    to taste

continued

SERVES 4

Preheat the oven to 325°F.

Cut the beef into 1½- to 2-inch cubes and sprinkle with flour. Heat the butter in a large casserole over medium heat and add the meat. Brown on all sides. Add the red wine and garlic. Season with salt and pepper. Add the bouquet garni, sliced carrots, and tomato paste.

Cut the bacon into small strips and fry them in a skillet over medium heat, adding the sliced onions to brown. Add the bacon and onions to the meat. Cover and cook in the oven for 3 hours.

1 bouquet garni: 1 sprig thyme,
   1 sprig tarragon, and 1 bay
   leaf, tied together

2 carrots, peeled and sliced

1 tablespoon tomato paste

1/4 pound lean bacon,
   rind removed

2 medium-sized onions,
   peeled and sliced

12 small mushrooms, peeled,
   washed, and drained

1 sprig fresh parsley,
   chopped

After the 3 hours cooking, remove the bouquet garni, add the mushrooms and, to reduce the sauce in the skillet, return the casserole, reduce the heat to 275°F, and simmer for another hour.

Remove the casserole from the oven. Place the meat on a warm, deep platter and surround it with the vegetables. Pour the sauce over the meat and sprinkle lightly with chopped parsley. Serve hot.

❋ *Chefs have their favorite cuts for* boeuf bourguignon. *Paul recommends covered ribs, eye of round, flank, or rump steak. Mère Brazier would chose neck or rumpsteak. Raymond Oliver liked rump steak, too.*

❋ *Boiled or steamed potatoes can accompany this dish along with croutons sautéed in butter. Mère Brazier liked to serve potato purée or fresh noodles. In spring in the Auvergne, Margaridou recommended a young salad or the first cauliflower of the year.*

❋ *The people of Burgundy believe the best wine for this is a Burgundy. In Beaujolais, they might recommend a Beaujolais Chiroubles or even nearer to the Burgundies, a Moulin-a-Vent or Morgon. Moulin-a-Vent, aged in a barrel, would be a treat. This was for Sunday lunch in Beaujolais homes and they brought out a special bottle from the cellar. Or a guest brought a bottle. I once surprised my friends in Beaujolais and brought them a bottle of Bordeaux—they don't drink much Bordeaux in that part of the world. Bring them a bottle and they are delighted.*

❋ *Marinade: see page 288.*

Pot-au-Feu, an old regional recipe

Pot-au-Feu

**Paul Bocuse,
Brasserie Le Nord,
Lyon**

THE DISTINGUISHED, MUCH-TRAVELED FRENCH FOOD WRITER *Ali-Bab called this "the family recipe" handed down from generation to generation. Paul calls it "one of the simplest and most beautiful creations of French cuisine, and I will naturally claim it is belonging to the category of typical Lyonnais dishes." It is on the menu of one of his three brasseries in downtown Lyon.*

SERVES 6

1 pound, 12 ounces beef
    top ribs
5 quarts water

Ribs

2 carrots
2 onions
4 garlic cloves
2 whole cloves
1 celery stalk
1 bouquet garni: 1 sprig thyme,
    1/2 bunch parsley, and
    1 bay leaf, tied together
2 pounds top round, tied
    by the butcher
2 pounds beef rump, larded
    and tied, by the butcher
1 oxtail, boned and pared
Coarse or sea salt to taste
15 peppercorns

continued

Put the beef ribs in a large stockpot and cover with 5 quarts of cold water. Bring the water to a boil over medium heat and cook for 1 hour. Skim the foam off the liquid from time to time.

Meanwhile, peel the carrots, onions, and garlic. Spike each onion with a clove. Wash and remove the strings from the celery. After 1 hour of cooking, add the vegetables and bouquet garni to the pot, bring to a boil again, and add the top round, beef rump, and oxtail. Add the salt and peppercorns. Reduce the heat to low and cook for 3 hours more; the water should barely move.

To make the garnish, peel and wash the vegetables and tie the leeks into small bunches. When the meat has cooked for a total of 4 hours, remove the meat, and pour the liquid through a fine-mesh sieve. Return the liquid to the pot, add the meat, increase the heat to medium, and bring to a boil. Continue to cook for 30 minutes more. Add the carrots, turnips, celeriac, and parsnips. Ten minutes after the liquid has returned to the boil, add the leeks cook for 20 minutes more.

Garnish

2 1/2 pounds baby carrots

8 turnips

1 small celeriac

2 medium-sized parsnips

3 pounds spring leeks,
    well rinsed

6 new potatoes, peeled

Coarse or sea salt to taste

6 large marrow bones

Condiments such as pickled
    gherkins and cherries

In a separate saucepan, cook the potatoes in boiling salted water.

Fifteen minutes before serving, rub some coarse salt on both ends of the marrow bones and wrap them in cheese-cloth. Pour 2 cups bouillon into another saucepan, bring to a boil over medium heat, reduce the heat to low, and cook the marrow bones for 10 minutes.

Remove the meat and marrow bones and keep warm in a covered pot. Remove the vegetables with a skimmer and keep warm in another covered pot. Skim the bouillon to remove any fat.

Cut the meat into slices and arrange them with the vegetables and marrow bones on a large, warm serving platter. Serve the bouillon on the side with the pickled gherkins, cherries, and coarse salt.

❈ *An easy way to remove the fat is to chill the bouillon. The fat rises to the surface and hardens, making it easy to remove in one piece.*

❈ *There are two kinds of larding in French cooking,* larder *and* entre-larder, *explains Hervé.* Larder *is to wrap and tie a layer of fat around the meat, usually done by the butcher in France, as here.* Entre-larder *is to use a hollow steel larding needle to push strips of fat into the meat.*

❈ *Whatever size oxtail your butcher gives you, throw it in.*

Beef Tripe, Lyon-Style

Tablier de Sapeur

Paul Bocuse,
Brasserie Le Nord,
Lyon

THE SILK WEAVERS OF LYON *lived down narrow, dark streets and one of their dishes was this tripe and wine. "A poor man's dish," Paul Bocuse calls it.*

When I was working with Jacques Esterel—the Paris fashion designer who made his name creating Brigitte Bardot's gingham wedding dress—I would watch the silk houses of Lyon arrive in our store each season, throwing down rolls of their latest silks at Jacques' feet. Such an array of colors I did not see again till walking through the batik markets in Malaysia a few years ago with Jeannie.

Jacques' real name was Martin. He was born in a village near Lyon, Bourg-Argental, where his father ran a small silk-weaving factory. One day Jacques invited me to Bourg-Argental, where we dined in his home and Madame Martin cooked us a beef tripe, Lyon-style.

SERVES 4

½ cup dry white wine, preferably Pouilly Fuissé or another chardonnay wine

Juice of 1 lemon

1¼ cups olive oil plus 1 teaspoon

One 8-ounce jar Dijon-style mustard

Salt and freshly ground pepper to taste

1¾ pounds cooked beef tripe, well-washed, rinsed, trimmed, and cut into 3-inch squares (see note)

1 large egg

1 tablespoon cold water

1 cup fresh bread crumbs

1 cup (2 sticks) butter

Gribiche Sauce (page 286)

Two hours before cooking, marinate the beef tripe: Place in a large mixing bowl the white wine, lemon juice, olive oil, and the mustard. Season with salt and pepper. Mix well with a whisk. Add the pieces of meat and marinate in the refrigerator for 2 hours.

Just before cooking, drain the pieces of beef tripe and set aside. In a second bowl, whisk 1 egg, 1 teaspoon of olive oil, and 1 tablespoon of cold water. Season with salt and pepper. Put the crumbled bread crumbs on a plate.

Dip each piece of tripe in the beaten egg, then in the breadcrumbs, and set aside.

Heat the skillet over medium heat. Add the butter and cook each piece of tripe 5 to 6 minutes on each side, until golden.

Serve the tripe hot on each plate immediately, accompanied by the Sauce Gribiche.

✳ *The beef tripe comes from the thickest part of the animal. Ask your butcher to cut it in triangles of about 5 inches each side.*

✳ *For her wine, I am sure Madame Martin did not use the fairly expensive Pouilly Fuissé, but rather a young, dry white wine like the white Beaujolais from the hills to the northwest of Lyon.*

✳ *French tripe is usually sold partially cooked. If your butcher has only uncooked tripe, proceed as follows: Soak the tripe in cold water, scrub, and wash again. Blanch for 20 minutes in boiling water. Drain and rinse again. Cook in salted water for 6 hours. Remove, cool in its water, drain and refrigerate.*

✳ *Gribiche sauce: Every chef has his own, says Hervé.*

French Shepherd's Pie

Hachis Parmentier

**Paul Bocuse,
Collonges-au-Mont-d'Or,
Lyon**

MONDAY WAS SHEPHERD'S PIE DAY *in our homes in England. The Sunday roast would be minced. This is the recipe from my wife's mother's wartime recipe book from when they lived down South in Essex. The ingredients and the instructions were quite simply:*

> Cooked meat
> Gravy
> Salt and pepper
> Mashed potatoes

Chop or mince the meat, and mix with gravy and seasonings. Put the potatoes, well mashed and seasoned, on top of the meat, and score with a fork. Bake until hot right through and brown.

Up North along the border between England and Scotland, in Newcastle-upon-Tyne and Jarrow, Jeannie's grandmother added carrots and onions that had been browned in a little butter and flour. These were cooked with the meat and then laid out in the baking dish, covered with the mashed potato and put in a hot oven until the top was a light golden brown. I prefer Jeannie's northern version, but I had to wait for it until we met in New York.

For the version Française, *sail or tunnel across the English Channel and you can find it called* hachis parmentier, *or French Shepherd's Pie.*

SERVES 6

Potato topping

5 pounds Idaho potatoes, peeled
1 cup whole milk
10 tablespoons (1¼ stick) butter

continued

Cook the potatoes by boiling or steaming them. Put the milk in a saucepan and cook over medium heat until it boils. Drain the potatoes, mash them, and add the milk and 5 tablespoons butter, cut in small pieces. Beat well and add the nutmeg, garlic, salt, and pepper. Set aside.

Pinch freshly grated nutmeg

1 small garlic clove,
   peeled and crushed

Salt and freshly ground pepper
   to taste

Filling

2 large onions, peeled and finely
   chopped

1 clove garlic, peeled and
   chopped

2 pounds boiled bottom round,
   ground, or chopped beef

10 sprigs parsley, trimmed and
   finely chopped

Pinch dried thyme

1/2 cup grated Gruyère cheese

Preheat the oven to 400°F. Butter a shallow ovenproof baking dish.

Heat 3 tablespoons butter in a small saucepan and cook the onions and garlic over medium heat until lightly brown. Add the ground boiled beef and parsley, and sweat for 2 minutes. Season with thyme, salt, and pepper.

Spoon a layer of mashed potato onto the bottom of the dish and cover with a layer of the beef. Alternate layers of potato and meat, finishing with a layer of mashed potato. Sprinkle with the grated cheese and dot with the remaining butter. Bake for about 20 minutes, or until nicely browned. Serve hot and, Paul recommends, with a green salad.

※ *Paul uses the Bintje potato in France, a floury potato like the Idaho, that he considers excellent for soups and purées.*

※ *Chefs like Bocuse, Loiseau, Blanc, and the late Mère Brazier often steamed their potatoes, that is, cooked them over boiling water. Loiseau created a whole cuisine cooking over water, cuisine à vapeur or cuisine à l'eau (see page 167).*

Hamburger with Truffles and Foie Gras

Steak Haché aux Truffes et Foie Gras

**Paul Bocuse and Roger Vergé
in Los Angeles**

"ONE DAY IN CALIFORNIA *with Roger," Paul recalled, "we made this hamburger for a very important client. It wasn't bad, believe me."*

"Not bad, indeed," exclaimed Roger Vergé. "Ten sous of hamburger and $100 of truffles and foie gras!"

SERVES 4

2 pounds sirloin steak

Salt and freshly ground pepper
    to taste

2 ounces foie gras

1/2 truffle

2 tablespoons butter

1/2 bottle (12 ounces) red wine,
    such as Mondavi Cabernet
    Sauvignon-style

Remove the fat and sinews from the meat and chop finely. Season with salt and freshly ground pepper.

Slice finely and dice the foie gras and the truffle. Mix together with the meat and shape into 4 hamburger patties, about $1^{1}/_{4}$ inches thick.

Heat the 2 tablespoons butter in a large skillet over medium heat and sauté the hamburgers on both sides until a little blood appears on top. The hamburgers are done. Cook 1 minute longer for well-done. Remove the hamburgers to a warm serving platter.

Add the red wine to the skillet and bring to a boil. Cook for 2 minutes to reduce by half. Serve the hamburgers on warm plates and pour the red wine sauce over each burger. The same wine should be served at the table.

❉ *Jean Troisgros told me: For a hamburger, chop the meat yourself with a knife. This way you know the quality of the meat and you keep the juice in the meat that is otherwise lost in meat grinders and mixers. I can still see him in his kitchen, chopping the meat for our hamburgers.*

❉ *Imported fresh French foie gras is now available from D'Artagnan (see page 298) or tinned foie gras (Rougié) from good gourmet stores.*

Hungarian Goulash

Goulasch Hongrois

Paul Bocuse,
Brasserie L'Est,
Lyon

WHEN THE CHEFS AND WINEMAKERS OF FRANCE *were flying in to America in the late sixties and seventies, Paul Kovi at the Four Seasons Restaurant in New York was their host extraordinaire. He and his partner, Tom Margittai, no longer stand at the top of the steps leading into the Pool Room to greet you—they retired from the scene a couple of years ago. But, we should not forget what Gael Greene in New York magazine called their "Dinner of the Century," marking Paul Bocuse's triumphant entry into town.*

"In all of American history," she wrote in 1971, "there was perhaps only one meal that could rival it for portent—that first Thanksgiving potluck of venison, eels, roast duck, leeks, watercress, wild plums, homemade wine."

What the native Americans hosting the English settlers served in 1621 and what Paul Bocuse served his New York hosts 350 years later sounds familiar. "The Bobbsey Twins" of Gaelic food criticism, Gault and Millau, dubbed it Nouvelle Cuisine," reported Gael, "The time was ripe. America was riding a sensuality explosion."

Gael was on the mark, but Henri Gault and Christian Millau, who had flown Paul in for this dinner, never managed to trap him into their nouvelle cuisine. The recipe for goulash that Paul sent me I see as his salute to the unmistakable good regional cuisine of Paul Kovi's Hungary. "Food you can recognize on your plate," as Paul calls such cuisine.

SERVES 4

3 1/2 tablespoons butter

7 ounces lean smoked bacon, diced

1 3/4 pounds rump steak, larded with fatback and cubed

7 ounces onions, peeled and chopped (see note)

Salt and freshly ground pepper to taste

2 tablespoons Hungarian paprika (see note)

Heat the butter in a large saucepan over medium heat, add the bacon, and brown lightly. Add the steak and onions, sprinkle with the salt, pepper, and paprika and stir together. Reduce the heat to low and cook uncovered for 10 to 15 minutes. Add the tomatoes with the bouquet garni and wine. Cover and continue to cook over low heat, stirring occasionally, for at least 75 minutes, or until the meat is tender. The meat should always be covered by the cooking liquid, so add water when necessary; do not bring to a boil.

Remove the pan from the heat and stir in the cream. Cook over low heat until all is blended and the sauce starts to thicken. Season to taste.

2 medium-sized ripe tomatoes peeled, salted, and cubed

1 bouquet garni: 1 sprig each of parsley and thyme, and a bay leaf, tied together

1 cup dry white wine

1 cup heavy cream or crème fraîche

❁ *In Paul Kovi's cookbook,* Transylvanian Cuisine, *his recipe entitled Ragout from Marrosszek, (Marosszeki Heranytokany, as Transylvanian readers will instantly recognize), included a pinch of caraway seeds and $1/2$ teaspoon of fresh-chopped marjoram. At the end of the cooking, $1/2$ pound of sliced mushrooms and, instead of heavy cream, sour cream was added and blended with 1 tablespoon flour to really thicken the sauce.*

❁ *If a recipe asks for 7 ounces of a vegetable, buy just over half a pound in the store and then you'll know that peeled and chopped it'll make about about 7 ounces. If you like onions, no harm in a little more or less, says Paul.*

❁ *Roumanian Transylvanian cuisine is fond of pepper and sweet paprika, whereas Hungarian Transylvanian cuisine prefers pepper and hot paprika. Paul Kovi described "the exciting and varied cuisine of this region, before its colorful tradition became swallowed up by the onslaught of gray uniformity we are experiencing throughout the world." Soon after writing this page, Paul Kovi, great American restaurateur and friend, passed away. The press Christmas dinner we liked to hold each year with Paul at the Four Seasons will not be the same without him.*

Steaks for the Chef's Day Off:
Rib Eye Steak Boned with Three Peppers

Côte de Boeuf Desossé aux Trois Poivres

**Jean Banchet with Paul Bocuse,
Orlando**

WHEN JEAN BANCHET OPENED HIS RESTAURANT *Le Français in Chicago, he began flying down for a couple of days with Paul Bocuse. "When Paul learned I had made it in a city like Chicago with my own resources, we've been great friends ever since. I stay at his house. We go to the market. I cook, simple things we don't get in restaurants. It's marvelous. 'Make me a soup, Jean,' Paul says. I look it up in the cookbook if I don't recall how it goes." I don't think he had to look this one up in the cookbook.*

SERVES 2

1 tablespoon clarified butter

2 rib eye steaks, 12 ounces each, boned

Salt to taste

1 tablespoon cracked black peppercorns

1/2 cup cognac

1/2 cup dry white wine

1 cup heavy cream or *crème fraîche*

1 cup veal glaze (see page 283)

1 tablespoon green peppercorns

1 tablespoon pink peppercorns

1 tablespoon unsalted butter

Heat the clarified butter in a heavy skillet over medium heat.

Season the steaks on each side with salt and cracked black peppercorns. Place in the skillet and cook until medium rare.

Remove the steaks from the pan and set aside. Pour off any fat. Add the cognac and white wine, bring to a boil, and reduce by one-third. Add the cream and bring to a gentle boil. Add the veal glaze, bring to a boil, and reduce by one-third. Reduce the heat to low. Add the green and pink peppercorns and whip in the butter.

Arrange a steak on each plate and pour the sauce around the steak.

Serve with french fries or potato purée and a well-seasoned salad of watercress or lettuce and arugula.

✳ *Freshly crushed peppercorns and the quality of the meat, says Hervé Riou, are important. Crush the peppercorns under the base of a cast-iron skillet.*

✳ *Dry white wine: Since Jean is from over the hill from Beaujolais and Mâcon, enjoy a white Mâcon or even, if you can find it, a white Beaujolais for the cooking and a glass before your guests sit down. A red wine—a Morgon or Fleurie from Beaujolais or a young Saint Emilion—would go well with the steak. This is relaxed cooking, so have a wine to relax with, too.*

✳ *Cognac in Paul's house: There is always a bottle of French cognac at hand alongside the wines.*

Working in Bordeaux in one of the old wine firms on the quayside called the Quai des Chartrons, I was privileged to take some of our English-speaking visitors on tours of the great châteaux, stopping in for lunch at the family's flagship vineyard, Château Pontet Canet.

During my four years there, roast lamb with green peas and potatoes boiled *à l'anglaise* was served every time. The wines varied—a champagne as a welcome, then a white Graves and the Medoc reds leading up to a fine old vintage, '47 or '61, depending on the importance of the guest. But always, it was the lamb that had grazed on the salt meadows running down to the Gironde estuary and the sea, *agneau pré-salé,* considered some of the finest lamb in France. Excellent lamb is reared in Ouessant in Brittany, on the land around Mont St. Michel in Normandy, from Auvergne to the Alps and the herb-scented foothills of Provence. But the château owners of Bordeaux knew that the flavor of Pauillac lamb together with their fine wines made the perfect marriage.

In Haro, in the Rioja wine district of Spain, I tasted my first baby lamb roasted on an earthenware pan in a bread oven and served with a bottle of the owner's red wine. Arriving in America on Long Island, I found the local butcher had legs of baby lamb until a supermarket swallowed up the small butcher. In 1989, aboard the SS *France*, I sailed with thirty-three chefs of France, who applauded the lamb that Lea Linster cooked for us (see page 135). When Pan Am flew from Nice, Roger Vergé gave me a navarin of lamb in small bowls that filled the cabin with the scent of Provençal cooking when the flight attendant raised the cover (see page 138).

When Paul Bocuse and Jean Troisgros first came to America in the late sixties and seventies, they were defending the French cuisine of their restaurants against the new wave, *nouvelle cuisine*. Give us cuisine that you can recognize on the plate, declared Paul. When you visit France, said Jean, you come to eat the cuisine of France, just as I go to America to enjoy the cooking of America.

Nouvelle cuisine is the past, with its sponsors, Gault and Millau, long retired from the scene. Paul told me he saw Henri Gault on television last year, regretting their magazine's error in encouraging chefs to create new dishes every day, in the name of *nouvelle cuisine*. Other diversions will be encountered, like the globalization of produce with its lack of respect for the seasons and the natural ripeness of what is shipped. One has to be hopeful that France will always have the producers and the markets for what the chefs need in their kitchens, hopeful that there will be sons and daughters ready to carry on the great traditions of French cuisine that gave us an unbroken chain of marvelous chefs, with such leaders as Carême, Escoffier, Point, Brazier, Bocuse, and Troisgros. This is the land of soups, fish, shellfish, beef, lamb, veal, pork, chicken, game, foie gras, truffles, cheeses, bread, butter, cream, desserts, fine wines, and champagne.

We raise our glass to France.

Roast Lamb with Potatoes

Gigot d'Agneau aux Pommes de Terre

**Margaridou,
Auvergne**

THIS WAS ONE OF THE DISHES *country people carried over to the baker who cooked it in his oven after he had finished making the morning's bread, as we would do in Paris on Christmas Day with our turkey that was too big for the oven.*

Margaridou liked to cook a fair-sized leg, or gigot, weighing about three pounds. This meant there was always cold lamb for the next day.

SERVES 4

3 tablespoons butter

1 sprig thyme

1 bay leaf

4 large white potatoes, peeled
    and thinly sliced

Salt and freshly ground pepper
    to taste

1½ cups water

1 leg of lamb, about 3 pounds

3 garlic cloves

Preheat the oven to 350°F.

Spread a layer of butter inside an ovenproof earthenware or cast-iron casserole, adding the sprig of thyme and bay leaf.

Place the sliced potatoes out like a bed on the casserole. Season with salt and pepper, and add the water. Prick the leg of lamb and insert the three garlic cloves. Cover the leg in a fine layer of butter, season with salt, and lay it over the potatoes. Place in the oven. Cooking time can be calculated at 10 minutes per pound. Halfway through its cooking, when the roast starts to turn golden, remove and baste with its juice, and turn it over so that it roasts on all sides.

At the end of cooking time, let the roast rest in the oven with the door slightly ajar for a few minutes. Place the roast on a large warm dish and surrounded with vegetables of your choice, cooked while the gigot is in the oven.

✳ *In other parts of Margaridou's region, people served gigot with green beans instead of potatoes. A green salad to follow is excellent.*

✳ *Mint sauce adds to the flavor (see page 288).*

✳ *A secret of cooking in the days of Margaridou, says Hervé Riou, remembering his apprenticeship, was a wood or coal fire. When the oven was white hot, they put the gigot in the oven; it was seared on the outside and cooked with the wood or the coal or red hot embers. Today, not having a wood or coal fire, we first seared the gigot on all sides in a little oil over a high heat on top of the oven to brown it nicely. Then we put the ovenproof skillet in a preheated 350°F oven, at 10 minutes per pound. A handful of peeled potatoes and onions were added to the pan before putting it to roast in the oven.*

✳ *A young, fresh red wine would go well here. Or even better, look for a wine of the year like Beaujolais Nouveau or the youngest Chianti you can find.*

Roast Leg of Lamb

Gigot d'Agneau

The Mère Brazier,
Restaurant Mère Brazier,
Lyon

THE MÈRE BRAZIER PREFERRED TO COOK *a round leg of lamb. She considered that easier to carve, starting from the thin end lengthwise. She did not recommend pricking the meat with garlic, since some find the aroma too strong. For perfectly cooked lamb, Mère Brazier suggested that cooking should not start until the guests had arrived for apéritifs.*

SERVES 4

1 leg of lamb, about 2³/4 pounds
2 cloves garlic, halved
3 tablespoons olive oil
Salt and freshly ground pepper
    to taste

Preheat the oven to 425°F.

Rub the leg lightly all over with the garlic. Wrap the haunch of the leg with aluminium foil and brush the meat with the olive oil.

Place the leg on a rack in a roasting pan. Season with salt and pepper. Cook for 15 minutes per pound—about 45 minutes for a 2³/4-pound leg. Baste frequently.

Serve on piping hot plates, garnished with seasonal vegetables, french fries, and a watercress salad.

※ *Roast lamb where I come from calls for mint sauce (see page 288).*

※ *For her wine, Mère Brazier would suggest a Beaujolais, Côte-Rotie, or red Hermitage for this lamb.*

Lea's Lamb Baked in a Galette of Potatoes (Bocuse d'Or, 1989)

Agneau en Galette de Pommes de Terre

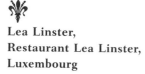

Lea Linster,
Restaurant Lea Linster,
Luxembourg

IN THE WINTER OF 1989, *while New York and Paris shivered, thirty-three chefs of France were aboard the MS Norway, transforming her back into the SS France of transatlantic history, for a week's gala cruise in the Caribbean.*

Each day luncheon and dinner were cooked by a different set of chefs, including Pierre and Michel Troisgros, André Daguin, Jean-Paul Lacombe, Jean-Pierre and Paul Haeberlin, Joel Robuchon, Patrick Lenôtre, and Lea Linster.

Paul Bocuse was the godfather of our cruise, standing on the quayside at Fort Lauderdale as the great liner cast off, and waiting for us with a barbecue on a desert island during our last day at sea, for the chefs "day off."

The super-star of the cruise turned out to be Lea Linster, a young chef from Luxembourg. The other chefs agreed that she cooked the best dish on the cruise—her lamb in a galette of potatoes that had won her the Gold Medal at the Bocuse d'Or Competition in Lyon earlier that year. Happy to be aboard, her joie de vivre also made her a winner.

Refreshed, sunburnt, and well-fed, thirty-three chefs flew back to France. Here is Lea's little lamb of a recipe, sent complete with kisses from the chef herself—as it says on the check, everything included, tout compris.

SERVES 4

Lamb stock

4 tablespoons peanut oil

1 loin of lamb, about 2¹/₂ pounds, boned and trimmed of fat

1 pound bones and pieces of lamb

1 onion, diced

continued

To make the lamb stock, one day in advance, heat 3 tablespoons of the peanut oil in a skillet over medium heat and sauté the loin, lamb bones, and other pieces of lamb. Take care not to burn the oil. Remove the skillet from the heat, remove the meat and bones, and place them in a stockpot. Carefully drain off excess fat.

Sauté the onions, carrots, and garlic in the remaining peanut oil in the same skillet. Remove the vegetables and

2/3 cup minced carrots

1 head garlic, halved

1 bouquet garni: 1 sprig each
    of thyme, rosemary, and
    parsley, and a bay leaf,
    tied together

1 tablespoon tomato paste

Salt and freshly ground pepper
    to taste

1 sprig rosemary

2 tablespoons butter plus
    2 tablespoons cold butter,
    cut into pieces

5 large potatoes, about 1/2
    pound each

2 tablespoons peanut oil

1/2 pound broad beans,
    such as fava beans, shelled

1 quart salted water, Evian,
    Volvic, or American spring
    water, not city tap water

Beurre blanc sauce

1 cup chicken stock
    (see page 282)

1 sprig thyme

2 tablespoons heavy cream
    or *crème fraîche*

3 1/2 tablespoons butter

Salt and freshly ground pepper
    to taste

drain off any excess fat. Place the vegetables in the stockpot with the bones.

Over medium heat, deglaze the skillet with 1 quart water. Pour this into the stockpot. Cover the ingredients in the stockpot with water. Add the bouquet garni, tomato paste, salt, and pepper. Cook over medium heat for 2 hours, checking regularly that the water remains at the same level add more water, if needed.

Pour out the lamb stock through a fine-mesh sieve into a saucepan and refrigerate. The fat will solidify on the surface and can be removed easily.

The next day, gently simmer the lamb stock over medium-low heat for 2 or 3 hours more and pour through a fine-mesh sieve. Add the rosemary, butter, salt, and pepper. Pour through a fine-mesh sieve again. Set aside.

Preheat the oven to 425°F.

Peel and cut the potatoes on a vegetable slicer or by hand in long, fine julienne strips. Squeeze the water out of the potatoes and mold them into a thin layer like a thin pancake, or *galette*. Heat the oil in a skillet over medium heat and cook the potatoes on one side only.

Wrap the potatoes, golden side out, around the lamb. Place the lamb in a roasting pan and roast for 20 minutes under the broiler.

Meanwhile, prepare the garnish. Put the salted water in a large saucepan and over medium heat, bring to a boil. Add the broad beans and cook for 5 minutes. Remove from the heat and set aside to cool. Remove their skins and return the beans to the cooking liquid until ready to serve. The beans should look very green.

To make the *beurre blanc* sauce, put the chicken stock and thyme in a small saucepan, and over medium heat, cook until it reduces slightly. Add the heavy cream and stir in the butter. Add salt and pepper.

Place the lamb on a warm, deep serving platter. Reheat the beans and place them with the lamb. Serve the sauce on the side.

❋ *For two other garnishes, any classic vegetables will go with this dish.*

❋ Beurre blanc *should be prepared just before serving, or it will separate if left to stand more than 30 minutes.*

❋ *Lea, aboard the SS France, cooked her raw loin of lamb inside the* galette *for 20 minutes. Everyone in the ship's restaurant that day stood up and cheered her.*

Navarin of Spring Lamb with Baby Vegetables

Navarin d'Agneau Printanier

Roger Vergé,
Restaurant Le Moulin de Mougins,
Côte d'Azur

FOR ANOTHER MAIN ENTRÉE DISH FOR PAN AM, *I asked Roger for something full of the aromas and colors of his south of France. Again, here he is in his kitchen at Mougins, teaching us his recipe step by step.*

SERVES 6

2¹/₂ to 3 pounds lean shoulder or leg (*gigot*) of lamb

1 tablespoon olive oil

1 tablespoon butter

4 medium-sized carrots, washed and sliced

2 medium-sized onions, sliced

1 head garlic, chopped

4 ripe medium tomatoes

2 tablespoons all-purpose flour

1 bay leaf

¹/₂ cup chicken stock (see page 282) or water

Salt and freshly ground pepper to taste

Vegetable garnish

2 bunches baby carrots, washed and sliced

¹/₂ pound baby turnips, scraped and sliced

¹/₂ lb small white onions, peeled

Pinch sugar and salt

"A navarin, like all stews of meats and vegetables that simmered over a fire in the old days," Roger explained, "is so good when it comes to the moment of serving. It is still simmering when you carry it out to the table and you lift the lid off the casserole, and you have the marvellous smell of the fresh thyme. One wants to eat it, *on a envie d'en manger!*

"Start by cutting away any fat and deboning the lamb and chopping the meat into 2¹/₄ x 2¹/₄-inch pieces. For the in-flight meals we had small round individual china cocottes with lids, and we cut the meat into smaller pieces. Cook the meat in a little oil and butter in a big cast-iron casserole with a lid, stirring all the time with a wooden spoon until it is seared but not brown. Add the carrots, onions and some garlic. Don't forget the ripe tomatoes. Remove the seeds and just cut them in quarters and drop them in. Add the flour, stirring well, and then the bay leaf. Pour in some white stock or even a little water. Real chicken stock is even better."

I have heard Roger admit he has used a chicken bouillon cube with some water. Why not, if no true chicken stock is at hand?

"You leave it to cook in the casserole, making sure the heat is not too high. The secret of a good stew is leaving it to simmer gently, gently. Watch the meat and when it is really cooked as if melting, *bien fondant*, remove and drain the sauce from the meat piece by piece. Reduce the sauce left in the casserole a little. Put the meat into a clean casserole, adding the sauce, and finally, the vegetable garnish…

"The vegetables for the garnish are cooked apart. Cook the carrots in a medium saucepan of salted water, boil for 4 minutes and drain. Cook the turnips the same way for 5 minutes and drain. Cook the onions in a saucepan in a little boiling water with a pinch of salt and sugar, until all the water evaporates. Add these vegetables to the stew.

"The potatoes should be cooked right at the end. Blanch them in boiling salted water for a couple of minutes, drain and without letting them cool add to the navarin sauce so they finish cooking in the stew and take on the taste of the navarin. That's how I like potatoes best.

"After the ratte potatoes, add the green peas which are still bright green and crunchy from a little cooking in another saucepan, and the green beans also green and crunchy, and a big bunch of thyme, close the lid of the casserole and slowly bring it to boil and then leave it to gently simmer. Add some knobs of butter and you are ready to serve.

"Place the casserole in the middle of the table and in front of everyone, lift the lid and all the lamb, the vegetables, and the perfume from the bouquet of thyme will escape. It smells so good, it's *formidable!* Sprinkle a little parsley on each serving.

"The meal is all there. You can start with a little salad or a cocktail of shrimps. After the navarin you can serve a good farmhouse cheese and an apple tart. You have there a marvelous meal."

1/2 pound ratte (see note) or other small potatoes, peeled

5 tablespoons shelled baby peas

1/2 pound small green beans, stringed

1 large bunch of fresh thyme

1 1/2 teapoons butter, in knobs

1 bunch parsley

❊ The gigot, or leg, of lamb, is frequently listed on menus in French restaurants in America. It's one of the most popular cuts of lamb in France.

❊ Fresh vegetables, fresh herbs, fresh milk, fresh butter, fresh cream, fresh everything. Unless the chefs said "dried," these chefs only use fresh produce. So fresh there is dew still on the salads picked that same morning in Paul Bocuse's garden. Fish that arrived the night before in the port and shipped overnight. So I have not indicated "fresh" for each ingredient. Though looking at vegetables, fruits, and herbs in some stores and supermarkets today still, you might be better advised to use frozen produce sometimes. How old is the milk? How fresh are the eggs? Paul always says that good frozen vegetables are better than poor-quality fresh vegetables.

❊ Ratte potatoes are small, yellow-skinned potatoes to be found in good farmers' markets and gourmet stores.

❊ For farmhouse cheeses, see page 247, and for Apple Tart, see page 261.

Mechoui of Lamb with Coucous

Mechoui de Coucous d'Agneau

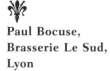

**Paul Bocuse,
Brasserie Le Sud,
Lyon**

ONE SUMMER IN PARIS IN THE FIFTIES, *when I was working as assistant to fashion designer Jacques Esterel, our little boutique off the Avenue Champs-Elysées was home to budding film stars with photographers from Paris-Match magazine next door. I worked long hours, six days a week, and seldom a vacation. One day Jacques walked out to catch a plane for a week on the Côte d'Azur. He walked back three minutes later to ask me to join him.*

Friends had lent him a farmhouse on their property at Mougins on the hill outside Cannes, where today Roger Vergé has his restaurant. The Cannes Film Festival was on. Hosting a party for a film company for whom Jacques had designed the costumes, we roasted on a barbecue a whole sheep, called a mechoui, on the hillside. The film itself was not great. The cinema emptied as word went around, "Esterel's cooking a mechoui."

In his Brasserie Le Sud in Lyon with its sunny menus and tablecloths, Paul Bocuse offers a mechoui as the Tuesday plat du jour, accompanied ideally by a carafe of Côtes de Provence rosé. Then you should drive straight on, south down the road to the Mediterranean.

SERVES 4

3/4 cup chickpeas, soaked
    overnight

1 8-quart couscous pan
    (*couscoussière*) (see note)

2 small shoulders of lamb,
    boned and cut in pieces

3 garlic cloves, chopped

1 cinnamon stick

1/2 teaspoon each saffron, ground
    turmeric, and ground ginger

1 teaspoon freshly ground
    pepper

7 1/2 tablespoons butter

1 large bunch fresh parsley,
    finely chopped

continued

Drain the water from the chickpeas and place them in the couscous pan with the shoulders of lamb, the garlic, cinnamon, saffron, turmeric, ginger, pepper, 4 tablespoons butter, three-quarters of the chopped parsley, three-quarters of the coriander, and the tomatoes. Fill the pan with 3 cups water, or enough to cover.

Bring to a boil over medium heat. Reduce the heat to low and cook, covered, for 90 minutes, or until the chickpeas are tender.

Remove the lamb from the pan and set aside in a little broth to keep warm. Add the carrots, turnips, broad beans, raisins, salt, and pepper to the pan. Increase the heat to medium and cook for 15 minutes. Add the zucchini and cook for another 10 minutes.

1 large bunch fresh coriander,
  finely chopped

1 pound ripe tomatoes, peeled
  and crushed

3 cups water

1 pound carrots, cut into 1-inch
  sticks

1 pound turnips, large ones
  halved or quartered

1/2 pound fresh broad beans,
  such as fava beans, shelled

1/2 pound raisins

Coarse salt and freshly ground
  pepper to taste

1 pound zucchini, halved or
  quartered

1 pound couscous (see page 298)

One small jar *harissa* (see note)

Meanwhile, steam the couscous for about 20 minutes—if you are using a *couscoussière*, let the couscous cook in the top portion above the liquid. Turn the couscous out into a bowl to release the moisture, add the remaining butter, and cover.

Check the seasonings of the broth, then add the rest of the herbs.

Serve the broth and the vegetables in a soup tureen and place the lamb in a large warm bowl. Pass the *harissa* in a serving bowl.

※ *A couscous pan, or* couscoussière, *is a stainless steel set of pans fitting one into the other. The meat and vegetables cook in the lower part and the couscous in the top part, which has holes in its base and lid for the steam to escape. This pan is available from Bridge and Zabar's in New York, from Sur La Table, and from other outlets (see page 298). Or it can be replaced by a large lidded kettle fitted with a colander lined with a cheesecloth.*

※ *Harissa is a purée of red chili peppers, garlic, and herbs. Paul recommends buying it in a jar in Oriental stores like Kalustyan (see page 298).*

※ *Tomatoes, in good, old country dishes like this one, are chopped or cut up and added to the cooking. For finer cooking, or haute cuisine, the seeds may be removed.*

※ *If using precooked chickpeas, drain them first.*

※ *This is a simple couscous. Others use artichokes, leeks, onions, and the North African* merguez, *a very hot sausage of beef and mutton—this can be obtained from D'Artagnan (see page 298).*

※ *For a full-scale* mechoui, *use a whole lamb or mutton. Dig a pit in your garden and lay a big fire. Over this you can roast a whole lamb on a spit over really hot embers, as we did on that hillside in the South of France. At an authentic mechoui in North Africa, the alternative to sheep and lamb is gazelle or camel.*

Of all the meat raised in America, veal has perhaps undergone the most dramatic changes in quality.

"When I first arrived in the sixties," recalls André Soltner, "the veal was really a catastrophe. It was red and didn't look like veal. I would not put veal on our first menus when we opened Lutèce, I was so disappointed with what I saw.

"Since the seventies, there's a fantastic change in the veal, with the quality of veal called *plume de veau*. I took Alain Chapel down to the market then, and he told me he was not able to get nice veal like that in France. When I first showed Paul Bocuse all those loins of veal at the Fourteenth Street Market—200 loins of veal, one as white as the other—he was speechless.

"Our meat in America, for example, beef, cooks a little differently as it's more greasy, there's more fat in it. You have to cook it a little more."

Veal Kidneys Sautéed in Madeira

Rognons de Veau Sauté au Madère

**Georges and Paul Bocuse,
Restaurant du Pont,
Collonges-au-Mont-d'Or, Lyon**

"Paulo! Attention! Don't let the kidneys boil or stew!" Georges Bocuse warned his son Paul. It was in the kitchen of the family hotel-restaurant on the banks of the river Saone that Paul Bocuse, aged seven, received his first cooking lesson. His real apprenticeship of nine years took him on through three of the greatest kitchens in France. Today's great chefs of France learned on the job. There was neither time nor means to afford going to culinary school such as exists today for aspiring chefs.

SERVES 4

2 veal kidneys

Salt and freshly ground pepper
    to taste

4 tablespoons (1/2 stick) butter

1/4 cup madeira wine

1/2 cup thickened veal or chicken
    stock (see page 282)

Slit the kidneys in half lengthwise, remove the membranes, slice each half again diagonally in half, and cut into bite-sized pieces. Season with salt and pepper.

Heat 2 tablespoons butter in a skillet over high heat and when it starts to sizzle, add the kidneys and sauté rapidly for 4 or 5 minutes, or until brown. Never allow the kidneys to boil or stew. Remove the kidneys, drain, and keep warm.

Add the madeira to the skillet and cook over high heat to reduce by half. Add the veal or chicken stock, bring to a boil, and cook for 2 minutes to reduce by half. Stir in the remaining butter to thicken the sauce.

Put the kidneys back into the sauce, stir, and serve very hot in 4 warm bowls.

※ *Mère Brazier in her restaurant in Lyon, where the young Bocuse began his apprenticeship, would dip the sliced kidneys in flour before they were sautéed, which helped to thicken the sauce. Sometimes she replaced the madeira with a dry white or red wine or added to the sauce some chopped mushrooms that had been presautéed in butter.*

※ *For the wine, Paul and his father in the family inn would recommend their Beaujolais, which they themselves went up each year to the vineyards to buy at harvest time. Mère Brazier liked to serve a red Rhône or a chilled rosé.*

Veal Sweetbreads in White Wine

Grillons de Ris de Veau Jean Troisgros

**Jean Troisgros,
Restaurant Troisgros, Roanne
and Georges Troisgros,
New York**

On the menu at Fernand Point's *where Jean Troisgros apprenticed, there was a breaded escalopes of veal sweetbreads, Ris de Veau Maréchale, named after le maréchale de l'hopital, a "splendid creature though born of poor folk," known locally in the seventeenth century for her love of fine dining and gargantuan feasts.*

Here is another father-and-son recipe. Georges sat in his home in New York and wrote this old favorite of his father. They used to cook it together when Jean came to New York and stayed with him.

SERVES 4

1 1/2 pounds veal sweetbreads

4 teaspoons butter

2 pounds spinach, well-rinsed

Salt and freshly ground pepper
    to taste

3 shallots, chopped

1 tablespoon red wine vinegar

3 3/4 cups dry white wine

1/2 cup veal stock (see page 282)

1 1/2 pounds white mushrooms

Soak the sweetbreads in cold water for one hour. Blanch them for 5 minutes and then drain so that the nerves and skin can be removed easily. Break them up by hand into small knobs. Heat 1 teaspoon butter in a skillet over medium heat and sauté them for 10 minutes, so that they remain crunchy and yet still soft.

Meanwhile, put 1 teaspoon butter, the spinach, salt, and pepper in a saucepan and cook over medium heat. Set aside in a warm place. Heat 1 teaspoon butter in a saucepan over medium heat and sauté the shallots until lightly brown. Deglaze the pan with the red wine vinegar and white wine, cook until it reduces by half, and add the veal stock. Set aside in a warm place. Heat the remaining butter in a skillet over medium heat and sauté the mushrooms. Set aside.

When the sweetbreads are cooked, immediately serve with a vegetable garnish, such as new potatoes and the vegetables. A green side salad goes well with this.

Rump of Veal in Casserole

Quasi de Veau

**Raymond Oliver, Paris,
and Grandmère Bocuse,
Collonges-au-Mont-d'Or, Lyon**

This is the family dish Raymond and Paul grew up on. Paul served it at the luncheon for American food writers in 1997 when he launched his cookbook, Paul Bocuse's French Cooking *at André Soltner's Lutèce restaurant. Paul flew in with Roger Jaloux from his kitchen in Collonges and in André's tiny kitchen, three Meilleurs Ouvriers de France chefs cooked a marvelously simple quasi de veau.*

He served this dish as a salute to his old friend Raymond Oliver, and as a salute to grandmère Bocuse. Finally, it was a salute to the French cuisine that runs through his cookbook.

Paul Bocuse's French Cooking *cookbook I rank along with the works by Ali-Bab, Pelleprat, and Oliver. It is the most complete work published in the past twenty years on French cooking by one of the great chefs. It's out of print today, so buy a secondhand copy when you see one.*

Today, in this age when the kitchen belongs to the chef, when the chef is patron, *every chef has his cookbook of his cuisine, what he cooks in his kitchen. Paul Bocuse, André Soltner, Jean and Pierre Troisgros, Roger Vergé, and the others, it is the duty of each to write his own personal record of the chef, the man, and his work (see Bibliography, page 302).*

For the recipe of Quasi de Veau, *see Introduction on page xiv.*

To Cook a Ham and Pease Pudding

Cuire un Jambon

**Adapted from Auguste Escoffier,
Savoy Hotel, London**

ONE OF THE BIG EVENTS OF THE YEAR *in a French village was the day the pig was slaughtered. Killing Monsieur meant every part of him was used: charcuterie, patés, sausages, saucissons, boudins, ribs, loins, ears, tail, offal, even the feet (Trotters, see page 155). Nothing was wasted. Pride of place, a ritual, went to the hanging of the legs of ham, freshly cured and cooked, from a stout beam in the kitchen.*

Until I came to America, there always seemed to be a farmer in my life—from the mountains of Wales and Scotland to the hills of Auvergne and Provence, from Saint Emilion to the Basque country in the Pyrenees which produces the inimitable jambon de Bayonne—*taking down a ham, cutting off some slices, hanging it back aloft. I lived and taught English for two years in the* lycée *at Biarritz, down the road from Bayonne where the smoked ham is king.*

Here is an adaptation of the great Auguste Escoffier's recipe for a good boiled ham. In his days as chef de cuisine at the Savoy Hotel in London, the piece of boiled ham, or whole roast of beef, were wheeled out on a silver chariot to your table in the dining room and ceremoniously carved for you. We have omitted the silver chariot.

SERVES: DEPENDING ON THE SIZE OF THE RAW HAM YOU BUY AND ON HOW MANY PEOPLE WALK THROUGH THE DOOR, WHEN THEY HEAR YOU HAVE COOKED A HAM

1 Virginia ham, salted,
for boiling

Soak ham in cold water for at least 6 hours—some recommend 12 hours—to draw out the salt. Make sure the ham is well-covered with the water. Do not refrigerate.

Scrape and cover again with fresh cold water. Bring to a boil, reduce heat and simmer until tender and the bones can be slipped out of the meat. The time for cooking varies according to the quality and weight of the ham, but allow approximately 18 to 20 minutes to the pound.

If the ham is to be eaten cold, it should be left to cool in the cooking liquid. Do not let it stand all night in its cooking liquid.

When ready to serve, drain and strip off the skin and place on a serving platter ready to carve.

Sliced boiled ham can be served hot or cold with boiled potatoes and spinach or fresh green peas.

❋   *In England, slices of freshly cooked ham would be added to cold turkey and served the day after Christmas. Or we served the ham, hot or cold, with a purée of fresh peas. Or with pease pudding made from dried peas—what Mrs. Beeton, who wrote English cookbooks a century before Elizabeth David, called the "indispensable" pease pudding, as follows.*

Pease Pudding à la Madame Beeton

1 pound large sweet peas,
freshly gathered

2 tablespoons (1/4 stick)
unsalted butter

Cook the peas in a saucepan over high heat. Drain, reserving the cooking liquid, and pass the peas through a fine-mesh sieve. Return the purée to a skillet. Stir in the butter and add a little cooking liquid so that it returns to a purée consistency. Paul Bocuse likes to add some heavy cream or *crème fraîche*, stirring it into the purée.

❋ *Freshly gathered peas: Paul always says a package of frozen peas is better than some poor-looking peas.*

❋ *Ham is excellent for omelets (see page 34) and sandwiches.*

❋ *A slice of boiled ham can be an alternative to the bacon used in the Eggs on a Dish Gare de Lyon (page 38).*

Petit Salé of Pork with Lentils

Petit Salé aux Lentilles

**Paul Bocuse,
Brasserie L'Est,
Lyon**

"WHERE I COME FROM, *every time we made a soup,*" said Paul, "*we dropped in a piece of salted ham,* petit salé. *In the Perigord and Gascony, they add pieces of* confit *of goose to the soup and call it a* garbure *(see page 20)."*

SERVES 6

2 pounds salted loin of pork

1¼ pounds salted pork brisket

1 small salted pork knuckle

1 pound, 12 ounces green
  Puy lentils

2 cloves garlic, unpeeled

1 onion, spiked with 1 whole
  clove

2 carrots, peeled and sliced

1 bouquet garni: 1 sprig each
  of thyme and parsley, a bay
  leaf, and a small stick of
  celery, tied together

½ teaspoon peppercorns

1 cooking sausage, about
  1 pound, Lyonnais or
  2 mild Italian sausages

1 tablespoon lard

5 ounces back streaky bacon
  in one piece, rind removed
  and cut in small pieces

Salt to taste

Soak the loin, brisket, and pork knuckle for 30 minutes in a large pot of cold water. Remove the meat and wash under cold water.

Place all the pork in a large stock pot and refill with cold water to cover. Bring to a boil over medium heat and cook, bubbling, for 1 hour.

Wash the lentils thoroughly in cold water. Place them in a skillet filled with cold water and cook over high heat, at the boil, 10 minutes. Drain the lentils and add them to the pork. Add the garlic, onion, carrots, bouquet garni, and peppercorns, and cook over high heat for 1½ hours. Forty minutes before the end of the cooking, add the sausage. Melt the lard in a saucepan over medium heat and cook the streaky bacon until brown, then mix in with the lentils.

When ready to serve, remove the garlic, onion, and bouquet garni. Adjust seasonings to taste.

Remove the pork and sausage from the pot, cut them into pieces, and lay them in a bed of lentils in a warm, shallow serving dish.

※ Lard is pork fat melted down for cooking fat, used for larding and barding. Country folk in France also talk about a slice of lard, as we would say a slice of bacon, meaning a fatty, streaky slice cut from a belly of the pig. Daniel Boulud's breakfast every morning as a child was an egg and slice of lard (see page 153).

Braised Spiced Pork Belly

Lard Braisé aux Racines et Lentilles

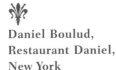

Daniel Boulud,
Restaurant Daniel,
New York

"WHEN I WAS A CHILD, *my parents always kept two or three pigs on the farm that we slaughtered each year for hams and sausages and lard. Every morning, before walking to school, my breakfast was an egg and slice of lard," says Daniel Boulud.*

"My lard-and-lentils dish, a little transformed today from those days, comes of my nostalgia for that childhood."

SERVES 6 TO 8

Spices

1 teaspoon coriander seeds
1/2 teaspoon fennel seeds
2 teaspoons black peppercorns
1/4 teaspoon whole cloves
2 pieces star anise
One 3-inch long cinnamon stick
1 cup coarse salt
1/4 cup sugar
1 teaspoon finely chopped garlic
6 sprigs parsley
2 bay leaves
6 sprigs sage
6 sprigs thyme

One 4-pound slab fresh,
    very lean pork belly
1 large carrot, peeled and diced
1 large onion, peeled and diced
1 green celery leaf, diced
2 gallons chicken stock
    (see page 282)

One to 2 days ahead, preheat the oven to 400°F.

Toast the coriander seeds, fennel seeds, peppercorns, cloves, star anise, and cinnamon stick on a baking sheet for about 5 minutes. Remove from the oven, and using a mortar and pestle or a food processor, crush toasted spices and herbs, adding the salt, sugar, garlic, and herbs.

Score the skin of the pork belly with a sharp knife in a cross-hatch pattern, and rub well with the herb-and-spice mixture. Set into a large container, cover, and refrigerate for 1 or 2 days.

On the day of cooking, preheat the oven to 350°F.

Scrape the surface of the pork belly lightly to remove the excess herb-and-spice mixture and discard. Put the pork in a large braiser with the carrot, onion, and celery. Add the chicken stock to cover the pork belly and bring to a boil over high heat. Cover with a lid and place the pan in the oven.

Cook for 2 1/2 to 3 hours, or until the pork is tender. Remove the pork carefully from the braising liquid and place it in a shallow roasting pan. Roast approximately 1 hour, basting occasionally with cooking juices, until the pork is nicely glazed. When ready to serve, accompany this dish with braised potatoes or lentils. Either of these may be cooked using one part cooking liquid reserved from the pork and one part water.

* *For a braiser, use a deep ovenproof casserole or marmite with a lid that can cook in the oven and on top. Le Creuset makes a wide range of sizes of these pots (see page 297).*

* *Daniel means the green celery leaf, diced, not a celery stalk. He calls it a branch of celery.*

Pig's Trotters

Friands des Pieds de Porc

André Soltner,
Lutèce Restaurant,
New York

"I AM ALWAYS BEING ASKED AS A CHEF, *what is my favorite dish," tells André. "That doesn't exist,*
because yesterday I felt like eating a trout. And in eight days I shall feel like eating a lobster, and eight
days later I shall feel like a slice of ham. Or some pig's trotters." Like some of his recipes, this one
requires some preparation a day in advance.

SERVES 8

2 pig's feet
1 pork knuckle
1 medium-sized onion
1 celery stalk, washed
1 small leek, washed
1 carrot, peeled and washed
10 sprigs parsley
2 sprigs thyme
1 bay leaf
2 garlic cloves, chopped
1 teaspoon salt
Pinch freshly ground pepper
2 cups dry white wine

Noodle dough

1 pound (3¹/₈ cups) all-purpose
    flour, sifted
Pinch finely crushed salt
3 large eggs
6 egg yolks
1 teaspoon white wine vinegar

continued

One day ahead, put the feet and knuckle in a pot and cover barely with cold water. Bring the water to a boil and skim the foam off the surface. Add the onion, celery, leek, carrot, parsley, thyme, bay leaf, garlic, salt, pepper, and wine.

Cover the pot, leaving the lid slightly ajar. Reduce the heat to low and cook for 1 hour. Remove the vegetables, reserving them to slice and serve with a vinaigrette. Cook the meat for 2 to 3 hours more, or until the meat is tender.

Remove the meat from the liquid and set aside to cool. When it is cool enough to handle, remove the meat from the bones and cut into ¹/₄-inch cubes.

To make the noodle dough, one day ahead, combine the flour, salt, eggs, egg yolks, vinegar in a mixing bowl and mix thoroughly by hand—or with an electric mixer—until the dough is smooth and elastic. To prevent the dough drying out, wrap it in cheesecloth and set aside for 1 hour, until it becomes firm.

Meanwhile, blanch the sweetbreads in boiling water for 4 minutes, then chill under cold, running water. Peel them carefully, removing all tough membranes. Cut into ¹/₄-inch cubes.

Sweetbreads

1/2 pair of sweetbreads

5 tablespoons butter

1/2 cup mushrooms, sliced

1 teaspoon Dijon-style mustard

Flour for dredging

4 tablespoons white wine vinegar

1/2 cup veal stock (see page 282)
    or water

Salt and freshly ground pepper
    to taste

Melt 2 tablespoons butter in a casserole, add the sweetbreads and mushrooms, and cook gently for about 5 minutes. Add the pork and cook for 5 more minutes. Add the mustard, salt and pepper to taste.

On a floured board or other flat surface, roll out the noodle dough in a very thin sheet about 12 inches x 8 inches wide. Heat water to boil and poach this sheet for 4 minutes. Remove from the water with a spatula and place the noodle sheet on a sheet of plastic wrap 2 inches wider all around than the dough. Spread the meat over the noodle sheet and roll into a cylinder. Use the film to hold everything together as you roll, taking care not to roll the plastic film into the meat. When the cylinder has been rolled out, wrap the film around the outside and tie firmly at each end with twine. Refrigerate the cylinder overnight.

When ready to serve, cut the sausage into 1/2-inch-thick slices and dredge them in flour. Heat 1 tablespoon butter in a skillet over medium heat and sauté the slices for 3 minutes each side, or until nicely browned. Arrange the slices of meat on warm plates.

Drain the fat from the skillet, add the remaining vinegar and *fond de veau* or water and cook over high heat to reduce by half. Whisk in the remaining 2 tablespoons of butter, and cook over high heat for 2 minutes.

Pour this sauce around the slices of meat and serve hot.

VARIATIONS WITH PORK

The recipes in the book can be cooked with other main ingredients than those listed by the chef. The chefs use the same recipe with other fish, other meat, other vegetables, other fruit than those given here. It can depend on what is available at the market, what looks freshest, what is in season.

Pork can be roasted like beef or lamb, a shoulder or *carré* of pork, or some loin chops as a change from lamb chops. André Soltner gives us his recipe for pig's trotters (see page 155). There are age-old country recipes for pig's tails (cook like pig's trotters, says Escoffier), ears, heads, kidneys, tongues, and the rest of the pig. *Boudin noir*, or black pudding as it is called in the North of England, is the most delicious of sausages, but it requires a pint of pig's blood that is not available in this country. The village *charcuterie* store in France makes it once a week, often on Wednesdays. Buy some and take it to the home of a friend who will cook it for you, just as I ask Jeannie's daughter Liz in London to cook me fresh kippers. Order *boudin*—or fresh kippers—when next you see them on a menu. Paul's cookbooks recommend you buy *boudin* already prepared at a delicatessen, but today there are few stores over here that sell the real, genuine *boudin*.

The master of *charcuterie* in Lyon for years was the legendary René Besson, known as "Bobosse," from the village of Clochemerle, Vaux-en-Beaujolais. One day, Paul asked Bobosse to take Jeannie and me to his village. Bobosse drove the narrow country roads at high speed, telling stories with his charcutier's head turned round to us. "I'm so madly in love with my Beaujolais," he cried to us. "I know all the little roads to my Vaux! Whenever I return from a trip, I don't go straight home. I take the car and drive into the Beaujolais." He points. "That's my best friend's house with the pond. I brought him ducks from my pond, but when I got home the ducks had flown back home, too!" One more bend, we arrived in one piece.

Over the years, I have been going at dawn with Paul to the market in Lyon. After he had visited the Mère Richard and the other produce stalls, we would walk over to the café to find Bobosse and the chefs, Paul's colleagues, for a *machon* of a dozen oysters, some Bobosse *charcuterie*, like sausage and patés. Over some chilled Beaujolais, they would talk.

"The *machon* is the best time of day," says Paul, "when you can hear all the stories which end up being the truth in a matter of years."

Sauerkraut with Meats and Sausages

Choucroute Garni à l'Alsacienne

André Soltner,
Lutèce Restaurant,
New York

THIS IS A DISH, choucroute, *known the world over, and we have the chef who knows it better than anyone this side of the Atlantic.*

"In Alsace, as a child, I grew up with choucroute *cooked by my mother, but perhaps only a couple of times a year," says André Soltner. "People imagine we eat it all the time, but when I worked Chez Hansi, an Alsatian restaurant in Paris, we cooked a* choucroute *with champagne, that was for the tourists.*

"Choucroute Garni was never on my menu at Lutèce, but customers who knew me well liked to order it in advance for their whole table. I say it myself, our choucroute *was as good as the best* choucroute *you will eat in Alsace."*

André suggests you can also start with sauerkraut already prepared (see note).

SERVES 8 TO 10

For 5 lbs sauerkraut

2 white cabbages, about
    5 pounds each

1 cup coarse salt

4 teaspoons juniper berries

2½ tablespoons cooking lard

1 large onion, peeled and
    finely sliced

2 cups dry white wine, like an
    Alsace Pinot Blanc

1 cup water

1½ pounds smoked bacon,
    in one piece

Salt and freshly ground pepper
    to taste

Preheat the oven to 325°F.

Three weeks ahead, prepare the sauerkraut for the choucroute, if you do not use a commercial sauerkraut—see note. Remove any green or spoiled leaves and core the heads. Wash, drain, and shred the leaves. Arrange the cabbage shreds in layers, in a stoneware or enamel pot—not metal—sprinkling some coarse salt and juniper berries over each layer. Press the cabbage down, cover with a cheesecloth, and place a small lid on top with a clean, heavy stone or weight (not metal) on top of that. Let marinate. After 3 or 4 days, remove the weight, lid, and cloth and spoon off any foam formed on top of the cabbage. Add some cold water to just cover the cabbage. Replace the cloth, lid, and weight and refrigerate. After 3 weeks, the sauerkraut will be ready for the *choucroute*.

On the serving day, preheat the oven to 325°F.

Remove the *choucroute* from the refrigerator or from the package and wash in cold water. Drain and give a second wash. Drain and, taking the choucroute in handfuls, squeezing out the remaining water. Set aside. In a large stockpot, ideally with a heavy bottom, heat 2 tablespoons lard over medium heat, and cook the onion until it softens, but does not brown. Add the wine, 1 cup water, and the smoked bacon. Cover and cook over medium heat for 20 minutes.

Season the *choucroute* with pepper and salt, and add it to the pot, covering it with the bacon. Bury the bouquet garni in the *choucroute*. Place a circular sheet of parchment paper over the *choucroute*. Cover the pot with a lid and place it in the oven for 1 hour. Then add the pork loin to the pot and return to the oven to cook for another 30 minutes.

Boil the potatoes in salted water and set aside, keeping them hot.

Cook the bratwursts in a pan of unsalted boiling water for 10 minutes, then reduce the heat, add the frankfurters and cook for 10 minutes more, without boiling.

Heat the remaining 1/2 tablespoon lard in a sauté pan over medium heat, and sauté the blutwursts until browned. Season the *choucroute* to taste and prepare for serving. Slice the bacon and pork loin. Slice the bratwursts and blutwursts diagonally in thirds. Pile the *choucroute* in the center of a large, warm serving dish, and place the meat and potatoes around and on top of the *choucroute*.

❀ *Good commercial sauerkraut, André says, is to be found in stores, but avoid canned sauerkraut.*

❀ *Since he suggests Alsace Pinot Blanc in the cooking, that would be the ideal wine to serve. Among my memories of* choucroute *dinners past in small Alsace bistros, I remember the fresh, young Pinot Blanc, the house wine in chilled stoneware pitchers, and the* choucroute à l'alsacienne, *served by young ladies in their Alsace national costumes and headdresses, and that it was a heady dish.*

1 bouquet garni: 1 teaspoon caraway seeds, 1 bay leaf, 10 juniper berries, 2 garlic cloves, unpeeled and cracked, wrapped in a cheesecloth and tied with kitchen string

1 1/2 pounds smoked pork loin, precooked

16 to 20 small potatoes, peeled, preferably new potatoes

4 smoked bratwursts

8 to 10 frankfurter sausages

4 blood sausages, or blutwurst

Chapter Five

Chicken

**POACHED CHICKEN
STUDDED WITH
BLACK TRUFFLES**

THE MÈRE BRAZIER,
LYON

**CHICKEN SAUTÉED
WITH WHOLE GARLIC**

JEAN DUCLOUX,
TOURNUS

**STEAMED CHICKEN,
ALEXANDRE DUMAINE**

BERNARD LOISEAU,
SAULIEU

**BRESSE CHICKEN
IN A SOUP TUREEN**

CHRISTIAN BOUVAREL,
COLLONGES-AU-MONT-
D'OR, LYON

**CHICKEN BRAISED
IN CREAM WITH
WHITE LIVERS AND
VONNAS PANCAKES**

GEORGES BLANC,
VONNAS

**CAPON WITH
WINE**

MARGARIDOU,
AUVERGNE

**CHICKEN
POACHED IN
NEW BEAUJOLAIS**

PAUL BOCUSE,
COLLONGES-AU-MONT-
D'OR, LYON

**ROASTING CHICKEN
COOKED IN
SEA SALT**

PAUL BOCUSE,
COLLONGES-AU-MONT-
D'OR, LYON

**CHICKEN ROASTED
ON A ROTISSERIE
OR SPIT OVER A
WOOD FIRE**

PAUL BOCUSE,
COLLONGES-AU-MONT-
D'OR, LYON

**CHICKEN IN
CREAM COOKED
IN A WOK**

PAUL BOCUSE,
BRASILIA

**CHICKEN ROASTED
PROVENÇAL-STYLE**

ARIANE DAGUIN,
NEWARK, NEW JERSEY

**THE FRENCH
CHICKEN HOT DOG**

ARIANE DAGUIN,
NEWARK, NEW JERSEY
AND JÉRÔME BOCUSE,
ORLANDO

**TAJINE OF CHICKEN
WITH CONFIT OF
LEMONS AND
BLACK OLIVES**

PAUL BOCUSE,
LYON

The Bresse Chickens

"THE BRESSE REGION IS A GASTRONOMIC PARADISE where they prepare a cuisine slowly simmering in the pot," wrote Gaston Derys of the Academie Rabelais in Lyon sixty years ago.

Like no other chickens in the world, Bresse chickens wear an appellation label as strictly defined as that of the fine wines of France. At thirty-five days old they are set free to roam the pasture where they can scratch around for worms, snails, slugs, insects, and the like to augment their daily feed of cereal flour, maize, and dairy products. For the next nine weeks they have space, at least ten square meters a bird. Then into an indoor cage for eight to fifteen days for their flesh to whiten so that, at sixteen weeks, they can be slaughtered, ready for the table.

"A good Bresse chicken and capon," says Paul Bocuse, "should weigh between two-and-three-quarters and six pounds, sometimes more. They can be distinguished by their size, their whiteness, the fine grain of their skins, and their large necks and feet with long spurs.

"The Bresse capons, young roosters that have been castrated, can be seen in the markets here around Christmastime. We like to roast them on the spit, but if you do not have a spit, in the oven."

A dozen of the chefs gathered in this book were born and reared in or around the Bresse country, home of the most succulent spring chickens, roasting chickens, hens, cockerels, and capons of France. Fernand Point and the Mère Brazier were born in the Bresse. Paul Bocuse, Alain Chapel, Jean-Paul Lacombe, Roger Jaloux, Pierre Orsi, Georges Blanc, Georges Perrier, and Daniel Boulud come from just down the road, in and around Lyon.

Paul Bocuse's parents, when their teenage son was threatened with deportation to Germany during World War II, until he was old enough to join the French army, hid him on a chicken farm in the Bresse region where he learned everything about raising and preparing these quality-controlled (*appelation controlée*) birds.

Chickens ran wild in the backyards of every home in Bresse, becoming the "Sunday roast" more often than any other meat, so that today, on the menus of these chefs, chicken can be found cooked in more ways than any other product. Thus, to the importance of butter and cream in their cooking, add chicken.

So many are the ways to cook the noble chicken that Escoffier gave 180 recipes for chicken in his classic cookbook, *Ma Cuisine*. Ali-Bab gave 75 chicken recipes in his *Gastronomie Pratique*; Raymond Oliver's *La Cuisine* and *Paul Bocuse's French Cooking* each offer more than 30 chicken recipes.

LYON

Just south of the Bresse region where the world's finest chickens are raised, stands France's third city, Lyon. Two major rivers of France, the Saone and the Rhone, meet there and flow on south to the Mediterranean.

The cuisine of Lyon has been renowned since the sixteenth century when Rabelais lived there and published his *Pantagruel* and *Gargantua,* listing regional fare still served to this day—"soups *lionnoise,* roast capons with their cooking juices, hens, trout, turbot, raised meat pies."

This century saw Lyon ranked gastronomic capital of the world by the first president of the Academy of Gastronomes, the legendary Curnonsky, "whose entire entire life was devoted to eating and to thinking, talking and writing about eating," wrote Richard Olney, the American foodwriter, living in Provence.

Curnonsky rated the Mère Brazier the "greatest cook in the world." First in the history of the Michelin awards, she ran two 3-star restaurants, one in Lyon and one in the suburbs. Her granddaughter, Jacotte Brazier, today manages the one in Lyon with the same menus, the same warm welcome.

Poached Chicken Studded with Black Truffles

Volaille Demi-Deuil

The Mère Brazier,
Restaurant Mère Brazier,
Lyon

EUGENIE BRAZIER, KNOWN AS THE MÈRE BRAZIER, *was a favorite among company directors in Lyon, a world center of the silk trade. She offered two menus that only varied depending on the season and the market. They came from far and wide to taste her Bresse chicken poached and studded with truffles* à la Mère Brazier.

Like a family tree, recipes have many roots. They are handed down and adapted a little here, a little there over the years. Many of them have truly country roots. The Mère Brazier learned this next one while working in the kitchen of another from Lyon's tradition of women cooks, the Mère Filioux who had brought the recipe from her home in the Bresse country.

Remembering the days of his apprenticeship in the Mère Brazier's kitchen, Paul Bocuse always has on his menu this poularde en demi-deuil Mère Brazier. "We cooked fifty of these 'hens in mourning' every Sunday, so that with those juices we finished up with marvelous stocks, even if we had never been to cooking school to learn the name for them."

In 1995 Lyon hosted the world's leaders for the annual G7 conference. The region's great chefs— Paul Bocuse and company—cooked a series of presidential dinners, sharing the media front pages with the heads of state. One of the dishes served was the poached chicken studded with truffles.

SERVES 4

1 black truffle

1 teaspoon cognac

Sea salt and freshly ground pepper to taste

1 chicken, about 3^1/2 pounds

3 quarts water

2 to 3 medium-sized carrots, chopped

1 bouquet garni: sprigs parsley, sprig thyme, sprig rosemary, and 1 bay leaf, tied together

Clean and peel the fresh truffle and marinate in the cognac. Season with salt and pepper. Slice into slivers about ^{1}/4 inch thick. Slip the truffle slices under the breast skin and under the thigh skin. Truss the bird with kitchen string under each thigh.

Fill a large Dutch oven or stock pot with the 3 quarts water, bring to a boil over high heat, and add the carrots and bouquet garni. Plunge the chicken in the water, reduce the heat to medium, cover, and poach for about 45 minutes, or until tender.

Let the chicken sit in its poaching liquid for 30 minutes before serving. Remove the chicken, cut into serving pieces and distribute among 4 soup bowls. Ladle some poaching liquid over each portion and serve, passing the cornichons and mustard in a separate dish.

Dijon-style mustard and cornichons

❋ *The quality of chicken was the secret of this easy recipe, the Mère Brazier would say, and it should ideally come from the Bresse or from the Dombes region that lie across the river Saone from Beaujolais country. In America, look for an organic free-range chicken. (See page 297.)*

Though impractical for the home cook, the Mère Filioux once confided to Elizabeth David, the distinguished English food writer visiting her in the fifties, "You need to cook a minimum of twenty birds at the same time, every one a Bresse chicken, so that their different aromas and savors are blended at the same time in this broth."

❋ *Paul Bocuse recommends poaching the chicken "without great haste."*

❋ *Fresh truffles are best, but they are expensive. The new truffle "harvest" arrives in January when the chefs buy at the starting price. Otherwise, it is less expensive, and easier in America, to rely on canned truffles. (See page 297.)*

❋ *There is no substitute for truffles, but fresh chanterelle might be considered. Remove sand from stems, wash, drain, and stew in a tightly closed pan over high heat for several minutes, shaking so they do not stick, and they will release their water. Cut into thin slices and follow as for truffles. But try it with truffles at least once.*

❋ *Sea salt is now available in many stores. (See page 297.)*

❋ *The Beaujolais of the year or a young Saint Emilion would be fine for the wine. In summer months, the Beaujolais might be slightly chilled.*

Chicken Sautéed with Whole Garlic

Poulet Sauté aux Gousses d'Ail en Chemise

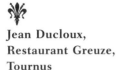

**Jean Ducloux,
Restaurant Greuze,
Tournus**

"NOUVELLE CUISINE! *No time for it," exclaimed Jean Ducloux, seventy-seven years old. "Served up by young chefs who've barely learned traditional French cooking. You think sometimes you're in Japan."*

So this is what he serves his good friend Paul Bocuse when he comes for dinner and they sit round the table and talk of old times.

SERVES 4

One 3-pound chicken
Salt and freshly ground pepper
    to taste
4 tablespoons butter
6 garlic cloves, unpeeled
1/2 cup dry white wine,
    Mâcon-style
2 tablespoons water
Small bunch parsley,
    chopped

Preheat the oven to 475°F.

Cut the chicken in 8 pieces—2 legs, 2 wings, 4 pieces of breast—and season with salt and pepper.

Heat the butter in a large cast-iron skillet over medium heat and add the chicken and garlic. Partially cover the skillet with aluminum foil or a lid and cook slowly for 40 minutes in a 475°F oven.

Remove from the oven and place chicken pieces on a warm serving dish. Deglaze the skillet with the white wine and two tablespoons of water. Pour the juices and garlic over the chicken and garnish with chopped parsley.

Steamed Chicken, Alexandre Dumaine

Poularde á la Vapeur Alexandre Dumaine

**Bernard Loiseau,
Restaurant Côte d'Or,
Saulieu**

FOLLOWING IN THE STEPS OF A GREAT RESTAURATEUR *is an enormous challenge. Jacotte Brazier inherited the cuisine established by her grandmother, the Mère Brazier. Patrick Henriroux, a few years ago, took over Fernand Point's legendary Pyramide and has already two Michelin stars. The other great stop for food lovers on the Paris-Mediterranean road was La Côte d'Or at Saulieu, home of the distinguished chef Alexandre Dumaine until his death in 1974. The following year, the young chef Bernard Loiseau, who had apprenticed under Jean Troisgros in Roanne, came to work in the Côte d'Or kitchens and bought the restaurant in 1982.*

Totally restructuring the kitchens and restaurant, Loiseau won his 3 Michelin stars in 1991 and today is constantly in the papers and on television and radio in France. He is known for promoting his cooking with water, cuisine à l'eau, and this recipe he gave me from Alexandre Dumaine's days is perfectly at home on the Côte d'Or menu in 1999.

SERVES 4

1 large chicken, at least 3 to 4 pounds

1 ounce canned truffles, cut in thin slices

Marinade

3 1/2 tablespoons cognac

4 tablespoons Madeira wine

6 tablespoons truffle juice (see note)

Stuffing

2 1/2 ounces carrots, cut in julienne strips

continued

One day ahead, prepare the chicken and the marinade. Truss the chicken and place it in a deep ovenproof dish. Cut the truffles in thin slices and slide a slice under the skin of each side of the breast and each thigh of the chicken.

To make the marinade, combine the marinade ingredients in a saucepan. First, pour in and *flambé* the cognac and Madeira. Add 6 tablespoons of truffle juice. Set aside in the refrigerator to chill. When cold, spoon it over the chicken and refrigerate the chicken for 24 hours. Every 6 hours or so, turn the chicken around in the dish so that it is completely marinated.

On the day of cooking, to make the stuffing, steam the julienne of carrots for 8 minutes in a covered double boiler. Remove and set aside to cool in a stainless steel bowl. Repeat

2¹/2 ounces leeks, cut in
    julienne strips
2 ounces turnips, cut in julienne
    strips
1¹/2 ounces foie gras, diced
1 young chicken liver,
    finely chopped
Coarse salt or sea salt and freshly
    ground pepper to taste
3 tablespoons truffle juice

Oxtail bouillon

1¹/2 quarts chicken stock
    (see page 282)
1 oxtail (see note)

Rice

20 tablespoons (2¹/2 sticks) butter
1 cup basmati rice (see note)
3 tablespoons truffle juice
¹/4 ounce truffles, chopped

this operation 7 minutes for the julienne of leeks, and 3 minutes for the julienne of turnips. Add the diced foie gras and sautéed chopped chicken liver to the bowl of vegetables. Season the stuffing with salt, pepper, and 3 tablespoons of truffle juice. Ladle in some marinade from the chicken and fill the chicken with the stuffing. Season the chicken with salt and pepper.

To prepare the oxtail bouillon, put 1¹/2 quarts chicken stock and 1 oxtail into a saucepan and cook for 30 minutes.

When ready to cook the chicken, pour the oxtail bouillon and the chicken stock into a large, deep casserole or poaching pan. Cook it over a low heat and gradually let the liquid come to a boil. Place a metal roasting rack inside the pot on which rests the ovenproof dish holding the marinated chicken. Cover the stockpot with a tight lid and cook over medium heat for 1¹/2 hours.

Thirty minutes before the chicken has finished cooking, heat the butter in a skillet, add the rice, and cook for 1 minute so that the outer skins—envelopes, André Soltner calls them—holding the rice grain are broken. Pour in 1³/4 cups of chicken liquid from the stockpot and bring to a boil, cover tightly and return to the oven for 20 minutes. Once the rice is cooked, add the truffle juice and chopped truffles. Season and set aside.

When ready to serve, ladle the hot basmati rice onto a warm serving dish.

Using a ladle, scoop some cooking liquid from the stockpot and pour it onto each of the 4 warm soup plates. Add some rice and stuffing from the chicken. Place a piece of chicken on each plate and cover with some more bouillon. Lightly sprinkle some *fleur de sel,* or sea salt, on the pieces of chicken.

✻ *Bernard Loiseau, like his colleague Paul Bocuse and others, enjoys the ceremony of carrying the rice and the stockpot containing the chicken into the dining room. He opens the lid at the table, lifts out the chicken on to a carving board, and cuts it up. Or you carve in the kitchen and serve on a platter.*

✻ *The additional truffle juice: Cook some truffles for 1 hour in a little water, Bernard explains, with a pinch of coarse salt added.*

✻ *Oxtail: Take whatever oxtail the butcher can find for you.*

✻ *He likes to add a little marinade into the bouillon to give it more body.*

✻ *A double boiler, or* bain marie, *is a useful piece of kitchen equipment if you like to steam. Use a steamer basket that sits over a saucepan of water, or ideally, a saucepan that comes with its steamer insert.*

✻ Fleur de sel, *the finest of salts, comes from salt marshes of Gerandes in Brittany and Noirmoutier, south of the mouth of the River Loire. Hervé Riou, who worked as a youngster on the marshes at Noirmoutier, recalls, "At dawn they let in a little of the sea over the marshes that have become a kind of salt bed, so that during the day the evaporation by the sun produces a light shimmering coat of salt crystals on the surface of the water. At sunset we carefully skimmed the surface with butterfly nets for the salt crystals,* fleur de sel. *Underneath lay the ordinary, everyday salt.*

   "A slice of country bread with 3 or 4 crystals of fleur de sel, *on some* demi-sel *butter," sighs Hervé Riou, "that is heaven. You die." Recently* fleur de sel *became available in some gourmet stores and health-food stores here. (See page 297.)*

Bresse Chicken in a Soup Tureen

Volaille de Bresse en Soupière

**Christian Bouvarel,
Restaurant Paul Bocuse,
Collonges-au-Mont-d'Or, Lyon**

WHEN THESE CHEFS DISCOVER A TALENTED YOUNGSTER, *they send him as apprentice to the finest, toughest cooking schools they know—the kitchens of their colleagues. Fernand Point sent his young turks, Paul Bocuse and the Troisgros brothers, for their baptism of fire at the Lucas-Carton Restaurant in Paris. So Paul sent fourteen-year-old Christian Bouvarel, after two years in the Bocuse kitchen at Collonges, on to the Restaurant Oustau de Baumanière in Provence, to the Haeberlins at the Auberge de l'Ill in Alsace, to Maurice Bernachon's house of chocolates in Lyon, to Gaston Lenôtre's patisserie in Paris and finally in 1974 back to the Bocuse kitchen at Collonges.*

Winning his Meilleur Ouvrier de France in 1993, Bouvarel has risen to be one of Paul's three chefs de cuisine.

SERVES 4

2 artichoke bottoms, quartered

2 cups sliced carrots

2 cups trimmed and sliced
   green beans

2 cups peeled and sliced turnips

2 cups sliced leeks

1 cup crushed peas

2 cups sliced fresh mushrooms

1 cup sliced celery

One 3-pound chicken, trussed

2 ounces fresh foie gras, diced

1 cup chicken stock
   (see page 282)

Sea salt and freshly ground
   pepper to taste

1 pound Flaky Pastry dough
   shaped in a circle
   (see page 286)

1 egg yolk

Supreme sauce (for recipe,
   see page 285)

Preheat oven to 375°F. Bring a large saucepan of water to a boil and briefly blanch all the vegetables. Set aside vegetables and reserve the cooking liquid.

Place the chicken in a large ovenproof soup tureen, adding the vegetables and their cooking liquid, the foie gras, the chicken stock, and salt and pepper. Place the flaky pastry dough over the tureen like a lid, pressing down and brushing the edges with the egg yolk.

Put the tureen in the oven for 1 hour, 15 minutes.

Meanwhile, prepare the Supreme sauce, following the instructions on page 285.

When the chicken is cooked, remove the chicken from the oven, place on a warm platter, and serve with a rice pilaf and with the Supreme sauce on the side.

* *Supreme sauce should be white and creamy. If too thick, dilute with more cooking liquid from the pot.*

Chicken Braised in Cream with White Livers and Vonnas Pancakes

Poulet de Bresse au Foie Blond et Crêpes de Vonnas

Georges Blanc,
Restaurant Georges Blanc,
Vonnas

FOUR GENERATIONS AGO IN THE 1870s, *the Blanc family were farmers in the Beaujolais region. They crossed the river Saone to open an inn in the fairground of the village of Vonnas. The cooking at the Mère Blanc's was what Georges Blanc today calls "woman's cooking," cuisine de femme, relying on the best produce from the countryside around, the Bresse and the Dombes. From this period came a long line of women cooks each with her restaurant, from the Mère Blanc to the Mère Filioux and the Mère Brazier in Lyon.*

Georges continues this family tradition of fine cuisine renowned for the quality of produce. He has built a Relais & Château class hotel with a heliport, convention center, and gift stores and he has written a number of cookbooks, the most recent The Natural Cuisines of Georges Blanc. *He gives us the recipe for the dish he served at the President of France's dinner cooked by the great chefs of the region for the G7 Heads of State on their official visit to Lyon in 1995.*

SERVES 4

1 whole fresh foie gras, cold, raw

One 3-pound free-range, organic chicken

Salt and freshly ground pepper to taste

4 tablespoons (1/2 stick) butter

1 onion

1/2 pound small white mushrooms, quartered

2 heads garlic, unpeeled

1 bouquet garni: 1 sprig each of tarragon, thyme, and parsley, and a bay leaf, tied together

continued

One hour ahead, press the raw foie gras through a wire strainer, or *tamis*, over a bowl so that veins and other impurities stay behind and the bowl contains a purée of foie gras. Cover and refrigerate.

To prepare the chicken, cut off the legs, thighs, wings, and wing tips. Season with salt and pepper. Put the chicken breast and pieces and 1 tablespoon butter in a large saucepan and cook over high heat.

Add the onion, mushrooms, the unpeeled garlic, and the bouquet garni. Cook until they turn a uniform color, then add 1 cup of white wine and reduce by half. Pour the cream over the chicken, covering it completely, and cook for 30 minutes.

1 cup dry white wine,
     Macon-style
2 cups heavy cream
1 ounce truffle juice
1 tablespoon white wine vinegar
3 cloves garlic, peeled

Vonnas pancakes

1 pound white potatoes
2 cups whole milk
5 tablespoons all-purpose flour
3 large eggs
4 egg whites
3 tablespoons extra-heavy cream
     or *crème fraîche*
2 tablespoons clarified butter

Meanwhile, start preparing the Vonnas pancakes. Peel the potatoes and cook in salted water, drain, and while adding the milk, whisk into a purée. Set aside to cool. Stir in 3 tablespoons flour, the eggs, egg whites, and the remaining cream until the potatoes take on the consistency of pastry cream, or *crème patisserie*. Add some of the remaining flour, if necessary.

Heat 2 tablespoons clarified butter in a flat, nonstick skillet as if for an omelet. When the pan is very hot, make the four pancakes, by pouring in 1 tablespoon of the pancake mixture for each pancake. The mixture shapes itself into a round. Turn them over with a spatula, and they are cooked. Remove from the skillet with a spatula and place on wax paper.

Remove the pieces of chicken from the pan and set aside to keep warm.

Pour the sauce through a fine-mesh sieve and add the purée of fresh foie gras, stirring constantly, to make the liaison. Add the truffle juice and vinegar and simmer for 5 minutes. Season to taste and set aside.

When ready to serve, place the chicken on the serving dish surrounded by the peeled garlic heads. Serve with the sauce in a sauceboat and the Vonnas pancakes.

※ *Georges Blanc also adds a garnish of blond chicken livers, cooked* à point, *giving further richness and depth—and a thousand and one more calories—to this dish.*

※ *The chef prefers white potatoes. The taste and the look of the dish counts.*

※ *Pancakes: Whatever batter you have left over, make some more pancakes. They will be delicious with a second serving of George's chicken in cream. "Worth the journey," says the Michelin guidebook of its three-star restaurants.*

※ *A word from Joel Somerstein, chef de cuisine of Waters Edge Restaurant in Queens in New York who, after the Culinary Institute of America, worked eight months' apprenticeship in the Georges Blanc kitchen. "Twice a day* at Blanc's we cooked batches of chicken braised in cream with white livers and Vonnas pancakes. The Bresse chicken was the finest, but this dish truly depends on the quality of the cream. Whereas cream in America is at 40 percent fat, farmhouse cream and the cream in restaurants like Blanc is nearer 60 percent. This dish is about cream."

❋ Fresh foie gras is the raw fattened liver of a duck or goose. "One of the greatest of all culinary products," says André Soltner, who as a child growing up in an Alsace village, was taught how to force-feed every day his family's couple of geese with corn, ready for the Christmas dinner. Many families sold the foie gras, or fattened liver, to hotels, but André's mother served the foie gras, as a terrine, followed by the roasted goose.

    Georges Blanc, like his mother, too, starts this recipe with a whole fresh foie gras. This greatest of luxuries, priced at around $50, or more depending on the weight and the price of foie gras, is once again being packaged in plastic in France—from Périgord, Alsace, and the Landes—and shipped from France. Buy it only from the very best store where you know they respect shipping dates and cold storage, as they do at Citerella's and Balducci's in New York. This is far from paté of foie gras in a tin. Paul Bocuse advises: Reject livers that do not have a clear pink color or that are marbled with black veins. Some livers look fine, but when cooked, turn grey. Others, when heated, soften and turn to liquid. Finally, it is best to choose your foie gras with someone with experience. Another reason for you to go to Lyon and here, Georges Blanc's in Vonnas.

    Simpler, cheaper, of course, there is available the tin of purée of foie gras, but it is miles from the quality of the fresh foie gras. Remember.

❋ Fresh American duck foie gras is available from D'Artagnan. (See page 298.)

❋ The wine with foie gras that Jean-Pierre Haeberlin savours is a glass of Chateau d'Yquem; for some, the splendid richness of fresh foie gras calls for opening an equally splendid bottle of champagne. For the list of a dozen champagne houses available in this country, see page 264.

Capon with Wine

Coq au Vin

**Margaridou,
Auvergne**

THIS DISH GOES BACK TO THE SIXTEENTH CENTURY *when, in the old hosteleries of France, cooks would prepare it rapidly in front of the guests, over a great wood fire. For our recipe, we went into the hills of Auvergne, where the roads and the rivers still followed the lie of the land, where the inns and dining were more modest, where* coq au vin *was a feast. A meal fit for a king, in your home, when Margaridou was cooking.*

SERVES 4

One 4-pound capon, grain-fed
    if possible
1/2 cup *eau-de-vie* liqueur or
    cognac
1/4 pound lean pork fat, (lardons)
    cut into strips
3 1/2 tablespoons butter
1 bouquet garni: 1 sprig thyme
    and 1 bay leaf, tied together
1/4 pound whole white mush-
    rooms, washed and peeled
Flour for dredging
3 1/2 bottles Beaujolais
Salt and freshly ground pepper
    to taste
4 large slices of bread, buttered
    and browned like croutons
2 tablespoons butter
2 tablespoons all-purpose flour

Cut the capon into 4 to 6 pieces. Put them in a frying basket, pour the liqueur over them, and *flambé,* or singe them, without letting them burn.

Put the pork fat into a large casserole or Dutch oven and cook over high heat. Add a knob of butter, the bouquet garni, and the whole mushrooms. When the mushrooms begin to turn golden, dredge the pieces of the capon and sauté them until golden.

Add the wine to cover, season to taste, and bring the liquid to a boil. Reduce the heat to medium to low heat, and cook, covered, for 1 hour. The capon should be cooked, but not falling off the bones.

When ready to serve, arrange the buttered crouton slices on an ovenproof serving platter. Place a piece of the capon on each crouton slice.

Put the juice through a fine-mesh sieve and return to the Dutch oven. Add a knob of butter and the flour, and stirring, cook over medium heat until it thickens into a fine sauce.

If this last stage has been a little slow, cover the serving platter with a buttered sheet of aluminum paper and place it in a preheated 435°F oven for 2 minutes. Serve immediately.

※ *Margaridou liked to use a young capon, advising in her cookbook, "An older bird will have more flavor but it will require more cooking time." She cooked her* coq au vin *in a large pot hanging over the wood fire in the family kitchen-living room fireplace. Because it is rare to find a fireplace in which to cook today, our* coq au vin *is cooked on top of the oven. She cut up her chicken "in as many pieces as you have guests."*

※ *If a capon is not available, use a roasting chicken.*

※ *Flambé originally meant singed. In an age before supermarkets, chickens came from the backyard of one's home. When we needed a bird for dinner, it was drawn, plucked, and singed over a flame to remove the small stubs of quills still in the skin. Margaridou's* coq au vin *was special, so she first poured some of her eau-de-vie liqueur over the bird to give its cooking an even richer taste. To flambé in a restaurant is a ceremony that calls for the flambé trolley, complete with bottles of cognac and respectful silence as the dish is set aflame, or* flambéed.

※ *To singe is to lightly pass over the skin with a flame, without burning—that is without leaving burn marks. When birds were plucked, I remember from my childhood days, the farmer singed the body of the chicken to eliminate the little stubs left by the feathers removed from the skin. A bird* flambéed, *or singed, is imparted that little taste of fire.*

※ *For the wine, Margaridou felt her* coq au vin *deserved the best local red, a bottle of Chanturgue. The Mére Brazier cooked her* coq au vin *in red Burgundy and served the same wine or a Chateauneuf-du-Pape.*

Paul Bocuse tells how in the French countryside, it is still possible to find a grain-fed rooster or cockerel, and the blood of the cockerel from when it is killed. Add 1/2 cup of wine and 1 tablespoon of vinegar before the blood coagulates; it will be excellent to use in the cooking liquid for the sauce. The day before cooking his coq au vin, *he marinates the bird in Beaujolais from the Fleurie region and adds 1 carrot, 1 onion, 1 bouquet garni, thyme, garlic, and peppercorns, setting it aside for 24 hours in the refrigerator.*

NEW BEAUJOLAIS
BEAUJOLAIS NOUVEAU

On the third Wednesday of November at midnight, the new vintage of Beaujolais, barely a month in bottle, officially leaves the cellars. Trucks drive up to Paris, planes fly out of Lyon and Paris to all corners of the world. Banners in the bars, bistrots, and restaurants announce that "The New Beaujolais has arrived."

A well-made Beaujolais Nouveau reaches its peak end of December, early January. Contrary to what you may have been told, it can still be excellent to serve for the next six months, while waiting for that vintage's more matured Beaujolais to arrive after Easter and settle down, ready for drinking.

In six months it may lose its natural sparkle and effervescence that it had in its first months in the vat. You will never taste that fabulous champagne-like wine in full fermentation, bubbling away in the cellars, since it has had to be subdued enough to be bottled or the corks would fly out as soon as it travels. Bottled, it is still a lovely young wine and and true young wines are rare today.

In the old times in Lyon, the bistrots competed for the best Beaujolais Nouveau. Cafés would go through a barrel of wine a day, over 300 barrels a year. They understood the refreshing excitement about a young wine.

When Beaujolais Nouveau arrives in America and the price is right—well under $10, and usually a dollar cheaper per bottle when it arrives by ship in December—buy some bottles or even a case for your cellar.

Chicken Poached in New Beaujolais

Poulet au Beaujolais Nouveau

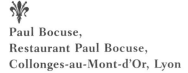

Paul Bocuse,
Restaurant Paul Bocuse,
Collonges-au-Mont-d'Or, Lyon

PAUL BOCUSE HAS HIS OWN VINEYARD *in Beaujolais and his longtime friend Georges Duboeuf bottles it for him with the Paul Bocuse label designed by Alain Vavro. So we know where Paul is at midnight on the third Wednesday of November.*

From mid-November to spring, poach the chicken in the Beaujolais Nouveau; from May until mid-November, poach it in any Beaujolais at hand.

SERVES 4

3 tablespoons olive oil

1 whole chicken, fleshy and
    tender, about 3 1/2 pounds

1 garlic clove, crushed

1 1/2 crushed shallots

1/2 bottle Beaujolais Nouveau

1 1/2 tablespoons butter

1 sprig parsley, chopped

Salt and freshly ground pepper
    to taste

Heat the olive oil in a deep skillet over medium heat and sauté the chicken lightly. Add the garlic and shallots. Pour the 1/2 bottle of Beaujolais Nouveau over the chicken. Bring to a boil, reduce the heat to low, and poach, covered, for at least 1 hour, or until tender. The slower the cooking, the better the taste. After cooking, remove the bird to an ovenproof serving plate and keep warm.

Make a reduction (enough to fill a coffeecup) of the juice in the skillet. Blend in the butter, ideally with an electric hand blender. Pour the sauce over the chicken and sprinkle with some chopped parsley, salt, and pepper.

※ *Use the same Beaujolais for cooking and drinking.*

SERVING AND DRINKING BEAUJOLAIS

There are two major styles of Beaujolais, with, of course, all the differences of character of each winemaker, of which there are hundreds in Beaujolais.

Beaujolais, born and bred in Beaujolais by the Beaujolais winemaker himself, tends to be the wine that quenches thirst, the wine to quaff without a moment's reflection. Other wine regions of the world have tried to imitate Beaujolais Nouveau, but they cannot attain that lightness that the soil, the weather, and the winemaker gives it.

The born and bred Burgundy winemaker buys the wine in Beaujolais and brings it back to his cellars in Burgundy to make it in the same style as his other Burgundies, naturally a more full-bodied Beaujolais.

What is the right temperature to drink this wine?

Beaujolais is one of the rare red wines, since it is young and fresh, to appreciate slight chilling. A quarter of an hour in a bucket of water and ice or in the cooler. Not too cold.

"I always serve my Beaujolais cool, *frais*," says Paul, "but there are some restaurants I know who still serve Beaujolais at 70°F! Take three bottles of the same Beaujolais and try this blind tasting on some friends who are connoisseurs—they must be friends or you may lose them. So as not to do any publicity for anyone," says Paul with a smile, "take three bottles of Paul Bocuse Beaujolais, my wine. One bottle you chill to 55°F, another to 57°F, and the third to 70°F. You say to your friends, 'Here are three different wines, tell me which is the best. You'll see, it is always the freshest and coolest wine that wins."

My favorite Beaujolais winegrower, the late Comte Henri de Rambuteau, who lived quite simply in his family château in the heart of Beaujolais, told me, "We drink Beaujolais as new as possible. The best wine is the wine in the vat, so I never bottle any of the Beaujolais we drink in my home. We keep going back to the cellars. I like it as young and as cool as possible. You wouldn't do it with a Beaujolais Growth or Bordeaux château wine, but with our wine from the south of Beaujolais, it's not shocking to put ice in the wine. I put ice in my glass of Beaujolais."

Roasting Chicken Cooked in Sea Salt

Poulet de Bresse au Sel de Mer

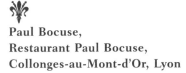

Paul Bocuse,
Restaurant Paul Bocuse,
Collonges-au-Mont-d'Or, Lyon

"An ancient recipe I brought back from China," Paul told me. "The fishermen who lived along the beaches would build a heap of salt on the sand and inside they placed their meat, gigot or chicken, and cooked it, adding a few potatoes."

SERVES 4

1 Bresse or free-range roasting
    chicken, about 3 1/2 pounds
Freshly ground pepper to taste
2 pounds, sea salt

Preheat the oven to 450°F.

Prepare the chicken as if for roasting. Pepper the chicken lightly.

Take a large braising pan, preferably of cast-iron, line it with foil—enough extra foil to enclose the whole chicken—and cover the bottom with a thick layer of sea salt.

Place the chicken in the center of the salt, breast down. Cover the chicken completely with the remaining salt in a thick crust, pressing down the foil all round to enclose and seal in the bird.

Place the pan in a preheated 450°F degree oven and cook for 1 hour, 15 minutes.

Remove from the oven and place the chicken, still in the foil, on a serving platter. Tear off the foil and carry the chicken out to your guests. In front of them, break open the block of sea salt. If all's well, the chicken cooked this way will look a beautiful golden color and should be just perfectly cooked, *à point*. "The iodine in the sea salt," says Paul, "will bring out a marvelous flavor and its flesh should be most succulent."

Chicken Roasted on a Rotisserie or on a Spit over a Wood Fire

Volaille de Bresse à la Broche au feu de Bois or à la Rôtisserie

Paul Bocuse,
Restaurant Paul Bocuse,
Collonges-au-Mont-d'Or and
Brasserie Le Nord, Lyon

ON BEING HONORED BY THE CHAINE DES RÔTISSEURS *in New York's harbor aboard MS* Royal Viking *in 1989, Paul thanked his hosts, "I was one of the forerunners of roasting on a spit. The first spit I had in my restaurant dated from 1765. I recall that in 1950 the best manufacturer of roasting spits was Monsieur Giraudon, and it was he who had the idea for the Chaine des Rôtisseurs. From my first day as restaurateur, I've never stopped roasting chickens, ducks, pigs, rabbits, and other game on the spit over a fire. For me, the best dish in the world is a real Bresse chicken cooked on the spit."*

I have been visiting Paul for more than twenty years now, and each time I look at the menu, I know I will order the chicken roasted on the spit. He has a grand fireplace center stage at the back of the restaurant, with an even larger one in his banquet hall. He can be seen basting the bird or piece of meat himself, as the spit turns, or stoking the fire.

SERVES 4

1 roasting chicken, about 3 1/2 pounds

Salt and freshly ground pepper to taste

3 1/2 teaspoons unsalted butter, melted

Carefully clean and rinse the chicken in cool running water and pat dry with paper towels. Season it inside and out with salt and freshly ground pepper, and truss with kitchen string so the wings are tight against the breast.

Put the chicken on the spit or rotisserie and brush with melted butter. From time to time during the 45 minutes of cooking for a bird this size, baste the chicken with the juice that falls into the drip pan. To appreciate the qualities of cooking on a spit over wood fire or on a rotisserie, the chicken should be served and eaten as soon as it has finished cooking—that is, when the juices run clear.

Serve the concentrated juice from the drip pan in a sauceboat.

❀ *Clean and rinse the chicken: Maybe I am particularly sensitive, but I am surprised these days to find, from different stores, that the chickens have not been fully cleaned. Vestiges of blood and small pieces often remain and I have to insist on scraping until the inside cavity of the chicken carcass is really clean.*

❀ *We do not know today how long a chicken has been on the shelf or how long in storage. In the country we knew.*

❀ *If you have a large party: Friends the other day were preparing a dinner for over thirty guests and supreme of breast of chicken was on the menu. I suggested they have the breasts shipped overnight from D'Artagnan (see page 298); this way they are assured the parts arrive ready for cooking. D'Artagnan's chickens are organic, roam freely in naturally lighted areas, and are raised by Amish and Mennonite farmers in Pennsylvania.*

SOME TIPS FOR ROASTING ON THE SPIT OVER A WOOD FIRE

❀ Fleshy birds make the best roasting chickens, with some fat to prevent them drying out while on the spit or rotisserie.

❀ Roasts can be cooked in the oven or on a spit which, though seldom used nowadays, is far superior to the oven, because the open air causes the moisture to evaporate and the meat browns delicately.

❀ For more flavor use certain woods, like grape vine, which transfer their aroma to the roast.

❀ When the browning has taken place, the intensity of the heat is reduced by adding less wood to the fire or by moving the meat away from the heat or by using some protective measure such as a screen.

❀ Use a drip pan to gather the fat and cooking juices—use the juices for frequent basting.

❀ "A true chicken," says Paul, "should be flambéed—put it on a plate and a little cognac or armagnac over it and set it alight."

❀ Once roasted, the chicken should be removed from the fire, presented to your guests, carved at the table and served.

❀ "Try to find a farm-raised chicken if you can't have a Bresse chicken," advises Paul. "It should be a chicken well-covered in flesh, between 4 pounds and 4½ pounds. A true chicken, not one that's been standing up without sleep in a shed."

Chicken in Cream Cooked in a Wok

Poulet à la crème Cuit dans un Wok

Paul Bocuse,
Presidential Palace, Brasilia

"THE PREPARATIONS HAD BEGUN THREE MONTHS EARLIER, *for fear that something indispensable would be left undone for lack of time. They brought in live chickens from Ciénega de Oro, famous all along the coast not only for their size and flavor, but because in colonial times they had scratched for food in alluvial deposits and little nuggets of pure gold were found in their gizzards...the women wore evening gowns and precious jewels...at each place was a menu printed in French, with golden vignettes.*" *Gabriel Garcia Marquez in* Love in the Time of Cholera *could have been describing the day Paul Bocuse was invited by the President of Brazil to Brasilia, to cook a dinner for fifteen in the new presidential palace. Paul arrived to find all the fine china, glassware, silverware and a splendid new kitchen for him. They had forgotten one, indispensable thing. The kitchen equipment.*

"*So I cooked for fifteen with only one pan,*" *recalled Paul.* "*Look at the Chinese, they manage to do all their cuisine in one pan. You can start with the soup, then a* poulet à la crème, *followed by crêpes. You can cook a whole meal in a Chinese-style pan. Their pan, the wok, is thinner than ours. A steel pan with slightly high edges, not teflon but real steel like our grandfathers had in the kitchen, will do fine.*"

We have adapted the Mère Brazier's poulet à la crème *for cooking with a wok.*

SERVES 4

One 3 1/2-pound chicken, preferably free-range or organic
1 teaspoon butter
1 medium-sized onion, chopped
2 cups heavy cream or *crème fraîche*
2 egg yolks
Juice of 1 lemon

Cut the chicken in four pieces.

Melt the butter in the wok, add the chopped onion and pieces of chicken, and cook slowly over medium heat, stirring constantly.

When the chicken is nearly cooked, stir in the heavy cream over the pieces of chicken and allow to bubble for 10 minutes, constantly tossing the chicken in the wok. Remove the pieces of chicken and keep them hot in the serving dish.

Stir the egg yolks and lemon juice into the sauce in the pan and beat until it thickens. Pour through a fine sieve onto the chicken pieces and serve.

Chicken Roasted Provençal-Style

Poulet Provençal

**Ariane Daguin,
D'Artagnan,
Newark, New Jersey**

ARIANE DAGUIN, BORN IN THE GASCONY REGION OF SOUTHWEST FRANCE, *grew up in a family of restaurateurs who ran the Michelin two-star restaurant Hotel de France in Auch. By the age of eleven, she was boning ducks, melting duck's fat, and force-feeding geese.*

To escape from a family life that revolved around foie gras, foie gras, and still more foie fras, she ran away to America. There, ironically, she founded, with a Texan, George Faisan, a highly successful fine food company they called D'Artagnan. It supplies American-bred foie gras, chicken, duck, buffalo, and other game to all the best restaurants of America. Most of the fresh foie gras came from France, shipped by great Périgord fortresses like the Rougié family and from Alsace and the Landes regions.

Ariane and George's organic, free-range chickens are rated the best this side of the Atlantic, but Ariane admits the day she tasted Bresse chicken in France left an indelible memory of flavor. Living in America, while you are waiting for the Bresse chicken from Bresse to one day be available at the local meat store, her own chickens are an alternative.

Ariane, our girl from Gascony, cooks this dish on the grill.

SERVES 4

1 medium eggplant

Coarse salt

2 zucchini

1 red bell pepper

2 bunches scallions

One 3$\frac{1}{2}$-pound organic,
    free-range chicken

Olive oil

1 garlic clove, peeled

1 teaspoon each dried thyme,
    rosemary, and lavender

Freshly ground pepper

continued

One day ahead or the same day, slice the eggplant into $\frac{1}{2}$-inch-thick slices, place on paper towels, and sprinkle with coarse salt to extract the water. After 10 minutes, pat dry. Turn the slices over and repeat. Set aside.

Slice the zucchini and bell pepper into 1-inch-thick slices. Wash the scallions and cut off the ends and tops.

Cut the chicken into 8 parts and rub them with olive oil and garlic. Sprinkle with thyme, rosemary, lavender, pepper, and salt.

Vinaigrette

1 teaspoon balsamic vinegar
3 tablespoons olive oil
Pinch chopped herbs
1 garlic clove, crushed

Except for sprinkling with the salt, which cannot be done the day before, you can prepare this recipe to this point the night before, placing the vegetables in a covered container in the refrigerator.

To make the vinaigrette, mix the vinegar, olive oil, herbs and garlic in a roasting pan or bowl. Toss each vegetable into the bowl and mix. Add salt to taste, if chicken is prepared the day before. Add the chicken and toss in the same marinade.

Place chicken parts skin side down on a hot grill of a barbecue to start, taking care not to burn skin. Turn heat to medium and grill parts till cooked and let rest 10-15 minutes before serving.

Grill the vegetables under medium hot grill until soft.

Serve immediately on warm plates with the vegetables in the center of the plate and with some chicken on top.

ROASTING ON THE SPIT:
THE FIRE — LE FEU

"The fire for me is the magic of our cooking," declares Paul Bocuse. "Too many cooks today don't know how to make a fire! Modern ovens only require them to turn a button. The cook who doesn't see the flame is not in the same profession. It's important that part of our cuisine is still made on a fire."

Jean Troisgros had the same respect for the fire. His son, Georges, began his apprenticeship by rising every day at dawn to cut the wood, lay the fire, and light the family's wood- and coal-burning ovens in the kitchen at Roanne. Like his cousin Claude, he continued his apprenticeship in the Paul Bocuse kitchen, lighting the fire there, too.

The French Chicken Hot Dog

Le Chien Chaud au Poulet

Ariane Daguin,
D'Artagnan,
Newark, New Jersey,
with Jérôme Bocuse,
Chefs de France Restaurant,
Disney World, Orlando

"I HAVE NEVER WORKED WITH PAUL BOCUSE," *said Ariane, "but with his son, Jérôme, manager at the Chefs de France Restaurant in Walt Disney World, we created the French chicken hot dog."*

SERVES 4

4 French brioches or a French baguette, quartered

4 small onions, stewed into a compote

12 black Nice olives, pitted and sliced

4 sundried tomatoes

1 sprig basil leaves, finely chopped

1 garlic clove, crushed

Juice of 1 lemon

4 D'Artagnan chicken sausages

4 teaspoons Dijon mustard

"After warming the brioches lightly in the oven, split open and add a little touch of the Mediterranean on each—onions, a couple of olives, 1 sundried tomato, basil, a pinch of crushed garlic, a drop of lemon juice. Finally, Jérôme adds the hot chicken sausage with some real Dijon mustard.

"He put a notice outside the restaurant The French Chicken Hot Dog! *Le Chien Chaud.* They sell a ton of it every week." Selling like hot dogs.

❊ *D'Artagnan chicken sausages, "100-percent natural without nitrites, preservatives or artificial casings," are available (see page 298). If quality is less of a concern, supermarkets also carry packaged chicken sausages in the frankfurter department.*

Tajine of Chicken with a Confit of Lemons and Black Olives

Tajine à la Volaille de Bresse aux Citrons
Confits et Olives Noires

Paul Bocuse,
Brasserie Le Sud,
Lyon

FOR HIS SEVENTIETH BIRTHDAY, Paul Bocuse flew a party of fifty friends for a weekend of celebrations in Marrakesh, Morocco. They stayed at the palatial Mamounia Hotel, managed by an old friend, Robert Bergé, formerly manager of the Parker-Meridien and Peninsula hotels in New York.

On his return, Paul added this touch of North African cuisine to the menu of his brasserie in Lyon, Le Sud, alongside other Mediterranean fare like osso bucco, paella, gazpacho, and tiramisu. For this sunshine cuisine, he added to his wine list two Moroccan wines, rosés, to join the Chiantis, Riojas, Beaujolais, Rhônes, and some Côtes de Provence by the winemakers of St. Tropez.

This recipe is prepared in a tajine, the earthenware Moroccan dish with a lid (see note). This way to the cuisine de soleil!

SERVES 4

Chicken

1/4 cup fresh ginger

1 medium-sized white onion

3 garlic cloves, crushed

3 stalks celery, chopped

1 teaspoon coriander seeds

2 ripe tomatoes

4 1/2 pounds Bresse or
    free-range chicken

3 1/2 tablespoons olive oil

1/4 teaspoon saffron threads
    or saffron powder

1 teaspoon ground cumin

1 small green bell pepper

Preheat the oven to 350°F.

Peel the ginger and the onion and chop fine. Peel and crush the garlic cloves. Chop the celery. Crush the coriander grains. Blanch the tomatoes and dice them. Cut the chicken into 8 pieces. Heat the skillet over medium heat.

Add the olive oil and the pieces of chicken. Cook until golden on both sides. Add the onion. Cook for 5 minutes. Add the garlic, ginger, celery, saffron, coriander, cumin, green bell pepper, tomatoes, black olives, salt, and pepper. Stir well and pour in the white wine. Bring to boil.

When ready to start cooking, place everything except lemons in the tajine, cover, and cook in the oven for

45 minutes. At the end of cooking, add the lemons and cover again. Let rest 10 minutes, with your oven door slightly ajar, before serving.

Serve straight from the tajine.

❖ *If you do not have a tajine, a clay roasting pot or a Le Creuset pot with a lid will do well.*

❖ *Candied lemon: Because preserving lemon is complicated and requires preparation at least 1 day ahead, Paul recommends jars of candied lemon already prepared. These can be found in gourmet stores. To prepare an authentic lemon confit, read Paula Wolfert's* Couscous and other Good Food from Morocco.

❖ *The tajine of chicken can be accompanied by couscous, the wheat semolina that is traditional in North Africa.*

❖ *To crush coriander seeds more easily, place them in a kitchen towel and crush with a pastry roller.*

❖ *For another North African dish, see Mechoui of Lamb (page 141).*

3/4 cup pitted black olives, ideally Nice or Greek Kalamata olives

Salt and freshly ground pepper to taste

1 cup dry white wine, Macon-style

1 medium-sized jar of *confit* of lemons, preserved lemons (see note)

Chapter Six

Game

Rabbit, Duck, Pigeon, Squab, Turkey, Venison

**RABBIT STEW
WITH NOODLES**

ANDRÉ SOLTNER,
NEW YORK

**RABBIT WITH
BASIL SAUCE AND
FRESH NOODLES
WITH PORT AND
SMALL VEGETABLES**

ROGER VERGÉ,
MOUGINS, CÔTE D'AZUR

**SALMIS OF SQUAB
WITH CONFIT
OF CABBAGE
IN ITS TARTLET**

GEORGES PERRIER,
PHILADELPHIA

**FOIE GRAS, THE
FATTENED LIVER
OF A DUCK,
JUST AS IT IS**

ADAPTED FROM ALI-BAB

**FATTENED FRESH
LIVER OF DUCK
OR GOOSE**

CLAUDE TROISGROS,
RIO DE JANEIRO

**SQUAB ROASTED
IN GARLIC WITH
MERLOT WINE
SAUCE**

ARIANE DAGUIN,
NEWARK, NEW JERSEY

**VENISON ROSSINI
MEDALLIONS IN
SAUTERNES**

ARIANE DAGUIN,
NEWARK, NEW JERSEY

**NOISETTE
OF VENISON
WITH GRAND
VENEUR SAUCE**

JEAN BANCHET,
CHICAGO

**TURKEY IN
THE POT**

PAUL BOCUSE,
HYDE PARK, NEW YORK

"*Hunting,* la chasse, *is that privileged time for meeting your friends* in nature's surroundings," said Paul Bocuse, "then together around a good table. As the old saying goes, 'The table is, one might say, the lady of the house, *l'entremetteuse.*"

Rabbit Stew with Noodles

Civet de Lapin

André Soltner,
Lutèce Restaurant,
New York

SOLTNER RECALLS THE SIXTIES *when the restaurateur André Surmain invited him to New York.*

"I put rabbit on the menu—the only place to buy it was in Italian markets on Ninth Avenue—but customers never ordered it. When I suggested my rabbit stew they would tell me they liked rabbits as pets, but they would never eat rabbit. In the eighties, when people became concerned over calories and fat, they learned rabbit was low-fat and I began selling rabbit. Some evenings, I would have ten or fifteen orders of rabbit. Some days I made it my lunchtime plat de jour *and sold out."*

SERVES 4

Marinade

1 bottle red wine, such as Bordeaux, Burgundy, Rhône, or Beaujolais

1 medium-sized onion, peeled and chopped

2 shallots, peeled and halved

3 garlic cloves, peeled, green germs removed

1 carrot, trimmed, peeled, washed, and chopped

1 bay leaf

1 sprig thyme

Salt and cracked pepper

Cooking the rabbit

1 rabbit (fryer), about 3 pounds, cut in 12 pieces with bone in

1/4 pound smoked bacon in one piece, not strip bacon

3 tablespoons butter

Twelve to 24 hours ahead, put the 12 pieces of rabbit in a terrine or bowl and cover with the marinade ingredients. Set the bowl aside in a cool place or in the refrigerator. Gently mix the ingredients from time to time.

On the day of cooking, cut the bacon in small pieces, about 3/4-inch x 1/4-inch x 1/4-inch. Put them in a saucepan and cover them with cold water. Bring to a boil and cook for 4 minutes and then drain.

Heat 1/2 tablespoon butter in a heavy-bottomed saucepan over medium heat, add the bacon, and sauté for about 3 minutes. Add the chopped pearl onions and cook about 8 minutes, or until golden brown. Add the mushrooms and sauté quickly over high heat. Remove the bacon, onions, and mushrooms from the pan with a slotted spoon and set them aside. Leave the fat in the pot and add the lard.

Remove the pieces of rabbit from the marinade and drain them, reserving the marinade with its vegetables and herbs. Wipe the rabbit dry, and add to the fat in the pot.

Sauté over medium heat for about 10 minutes, or until browned. Season with salt and pepper. Sprinkle the rabbit in the pot with flour and stir it around, sautéeing for another 1 or 2 minutes, or until the flour is slightly browned.

Pour the marinade into the pan with its vegetables and herbs and bring to a boil. Cover with a lid, reduce the heat to low, and simmer for about 35 minutes, or until tender. Check the meat from time to time, adding water—about 1/2 cup at a time—to keep the meat moist.

Remove the pieces of rabbit with a slotted spoon and set aside in a shallow bowl. Spoon the onions, mushrooms, and bacon over the meat. Taste the sauce in the pot and add salt and pepper. Strain the sauce through a fine-mesh sieve and pour over the rabbit.

Cook the noodles in a saucepan of salted water and then sauté in the remaining butter for 2 minutes. Serve with the rabbit.

❋ *Boneless loins of rabbit, as well as whole rabbits, are available from D'Artagnan (see page 298).*

16 pearl onions, peeled

1/4 pound mushrooms, washed and sliced

1 tablespoon lard

1 tablespoon all-purpose flour

1 pound fresh or dried noodles

Salt and freshly ground pepper to taste

Rabbit with Basil Sauce and Fresh Noodles with Port and Small Vegetables

Cul de Lapereau à la crème Basilic avec
Nouilles Fraîches au Porto et aux Petites Legumes

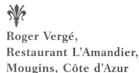

**Roger Vergé,
Restaurant L'Amandier,
Mougins, Côte d'Azur**

FLYING IN TO NICE AIRPORT, *along the Côte d'Azur coastline, a number of small hills stand out below like molehills. The villages of Mougins above Cannes, like Ramatuelle and Gassin above St. Tropez, were built on top of hills to be safe from marauding pirates arriving from the sea. Roger Vergé has his second smaller restaurant, L'Amandier, in the village of Mougins where in the summer months he holds his cooking school. Morning "hands on" classes are taught recipes like the one that follows, then they sit down in the restaurant to eat what has been prepared.*

SERVES 2 TO 3

Hindquarters of domestic rabbit, (about 2 ½ lbs.), comprising the saddle and two hind legs

1½ tablespoons butter

Salt and freshly ground pepper to taste

1 small sprig thyme

2 tablespoons warm water

1 tablespoon chopped shallot

3 tablespoons dry white wine (from the bottle you plan to drink with the meal)

5 tablespoons heavy cream

1 egg yolk

Vegetables

3 tablespoons little sticks carrots

Preheat the oven to a low heat.

To prepare a whole rabbit, cut it in two just behind the ribs. Make one clean cut to avoid crushing and splintering the vertebrae. Reserve the front half. Cut halfway through between each vertebrae with the point of a knife. Remove the kidneys and the fatty parts. Season all over with salt and pepper.

Spread the butter over the bottom of an enamelled cast-iron casserole just large enough to hold the rabbit. Put in the rabbit and the thyme. Cover the pan and cook over a very low heat for 20 minutes. Check carefully occasionally to see that the rabbit does not start to brown. Before the butter starts to burn, add 2 tablespoons warm water and reduce the heat lower still. Keep the pan well-covered. The rabbit is perfectly cooked when a fork inserted in the thickest part of the leg produces beads of colorless liquid; if the juices are still rosy, cook for a few minutes longer. When the rabbit is cooked, wrap it in foil and keep warm.

Increase the heat to medium, add the chopped shallot and dry white wine, and deglaze and reduce until about 2 to 3 tablespoons liquid remain. Add half the cream, and bring to a boil again for about 2 minutes. No more. Remove from the heat.

Whisk together the remaining cream and egg yolk in a bowl. Pour the contents of the bowl into the the pot that is off the heat and then return to the heat, whisking all the time. Bring almost to a boil and strain through a fine-mesh sieve into a small saucepan. Season with salt and pepper. Cover and set aside in the warmth of the low-heated oven with the door open.

To prepare the vegetables, cook them in salted water until crisp-tender—2 minutes for the zucchini, 5 minutes for the carrots, 15 minutes for the asparagus tips. Drain and set aside.

To make the noodles, bring 2$\frac{1}{2}$ quarts salted water to a boil in a large casserole. Add the olive oil and the noodles, stirring them to prevent sticking. Fresh pasta should boil for 2 minutes; follow package directions for dried pasta. Taste from time to time to make sure the pasta stays firm.

Meanwhile, bring the port to a boil in an 8-inch casserole, reducing it until only 1 tablespoon remains. Add the carrots and zucchini and continue cooking until the liquid evaporates.

Remove from the heat, add the diced tomatoes and butter, mixing the vegetables together until the butter is melted.

Drain the pasta immediately when it is cooked in a colander and using two forks, mix with the vegetables and butter.

2 tablespoons little sticks zucchini

12 asparagus tips

Noodles

2$\frac{1}{2}$ quarts salted water

1 tablespoon olive oil

10 ounces dried noodles or 14 ounces fresh noodles

6 tablespoons white port or red port, if preferred

2 tablespoons diced tomatoes

4 tablespoons butter

1 teaspoon fresh-chopped basil

1 teaspoon fresh-chopped parsley

Juice of $\frac{1}{2}$ lemon, optional

2 tablespoons blanched and slivered almonds

Salt and freshly ground pepper to taste

Just before serving the rabbit, add the chopped basil and parsley to the cream sauce, and if you like a sharper flavor, add the lemon juice. Check the seasonings.

Place a piece of rabbit on each warm plate and cover lightly with the sauce. Next to the rabbit, place some pasta, sprinkle the pasta with almonds, and decorate with asparagus tips.

* *Saddles of rabbit with the bone in, as well as whole rabbits, are available from D'Artagnan (see page 298).*

Some tips from Roger:

* *When adding to or substituting for any of the vegetables, use the same quantity of each vegetable. Always keep the color scheme in mind. You can use broccoli, spinach leaves, mushrooms, peppers, and peas. If fresh vegetables are not available, you can use frozen, but the the flavor will not be as good.*

* *If you do not have the time, simple buttered noodles (tagliatelle) also go very well with the rabbit.*

* *For wines that go well with this dish, try a white Côtes de Provence, Hermitage white, white Macon, or a Pouilly-Fuissé.*

A tip from me:

* *Check when Roger has his next cooking classes. (See page 308.)*

Salmis of Squab with a Confit of Cabbage in Its Tartlet

Salmis de Pigeon au Choux Confits et sa Barquette

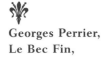

**Georges Perrier,
Le Bec Fin,
Philadelphia**

BORN IN LYON, *Georges Perrier learned his passion for cooking from an Alsatian mother and a Lyonnais father. Apprenticed first at La Baumanière under chef Raymond Thuillier, he then went to La Pyramide under Madame Point, who had succeeded her husband. Georges came to America in 1967 and opened his own restaurant, Le Bec Fin, in downtown Philadelphia in 1970 with many of the dishes from those days on the menu. When food writer Craig Claiborne wrote in the* New York Times *that he had just tasted the most extraordinary* quenelles *down in Philadelphia, "They were the* quenelles *like we made them at La Pyramide," said Georges. The recipe Georges chose for me with his favorite bird, the pigeon, is a little complicated but, in Georges' words, worth the effort.*

SERVES 4

Salmis of squab legs

4 squabs

2 tablespoons coarse salt

2 sprigs thyme, chopped

2 cloves garlic

6 black peppercorns

3/4 cup rendered duck fat
(see page 298)

Tartlets

1 shallot, chopped

1 tablespoon butter

1/2 pound wild mushrooms,
peeled and chopped

1 tablespoon vermouth

continued

Twelve hours ahead, to make the salmis of squab legs, remove the legs only from the squab carcasses and sprinkle with the salt. Cover and refrigerate for 12 hours. Rinse off salt, pat dry, and put in a heavy pot with 2 sprigs thyme, 2 cloves garlic, peppercorns and 3/4 cup rendered duck fat. Set aside in the refrigerator. Reserve the remaining squab for later.

Preheat oven to 250°F.

Cut a piece of parchment paper to fit over opening of the pot and cover the squab legs. Bake in the oven for 2 hours. Remove legs from fat when cool enough to handle and remove all meat and skin from bones. Rough cut meat and skin and set aside.

To prepare the tartlet fillings, start by cooking 1 chopped shallot in butter in a small tightly covered skillet until the

1/2 cup heavy cream or
    crème fraîche

2 sprigs fresh thyme, chopped

Four 2-inch tartlet shells or pans

Puff pastry to cover tartlets
    (see note)

1 large egg, beaten

Sauce

2 shallots, chopped

1 tablespoon butter

1/2 pound wild mushrooms,
    peeled and chopped

1 cup red wine

1/4 teaspoon sugar

1 1/2 cup squab stock (reserved
    from the cooking)

1 tablespoon foie gras (or
    mousse of foie gras)

5 chicken livers

Cabbage

1 young green cabbage

1/4 cup bacon, diced and
    blanched

3/4 cup rendered duck fat
    (see page 298)

Olive oil

Salt and freshly ground pepper
    to taste

shallot is translucent. Add 1/2 pound chopped wild mushrooms and cook until all the liquid from the mushrooms has evaporated. Deglaze the pan with the vermouth, and then add heavy cream and reduce by half. Add the chopped leg meat and chopped thyme. When cool, divide the filling between tartlet shells, add puff pastry to cover the shells and brush with an egg wash. Set aside in the refrigerator until ready to bake.

To prepare the squab, first remove the squab from the refrigerator, season with salt and pepper, and sear in hot oil in a skillet until browned on all sides and cooked medium rare. It will finish cooking later. Take from the pot and allow to cool.

Remove the meat from the carcasses. Set aside. Pour the cooking liquid through a fine-mesh sieve and set aside in a separate pan.

To prepare the sauce, take a saucepan with a lid that closes tightly and sweat 2 chopped shallots in 1 tablespoon butter. Add the remaining chopped mushrooms and cook 2 or 3 minutes on medium heat. Add the chopped up bones of the squab, red wine, and sugar to the pan and bring it to a boil. While boiling, hold a lit match over the pan to ignite the alcohol in the fumes. When all the alcohol has burned off, add the squab cooking juice. Reduce the heat to medium and cook slowly for 20 minutes. Finish the sauce by blending 1 cup of the squab stock with the foie gras and chicken livers, bringing it to a boil. Add salt and pepper to taste, and pour it through a fine-mesh sieve.

Preheat the oven to 400°F.

To make the confit of cabbage, cut the cabbage into quarters and remove the core. Separate the leaves and cut out the thick ribs in the center of the leaves. Blanch the leaves in boiling salted water, remove, and dip quickly into ice water to keep the green color. In a large pot, combine blanched leaves, blanched diced bacon, and 3/4 cup rendered duck fat and cook over medium heat for 30 minutes. Pour off excess duck fat and keep cabbage warm.

Assemble the tartlets and bake in the oven for 15 minutes, or until the tops are cooked and lightly brown. Bake the breasts during the last 5 minutes at the same temperature to finish cooking. Reheat the sauce and cabbage.

Place a spoonful of cabbage on each plate and 2 breasts on the cabbage at four o'clock and eight o'clock positions. Put the tartlets at twelve o'clock and sauce the plate in front of each breast.

❋ *Georges uses 1 tablespoon of foie gras or mousse of foie gras. Read on. What happens when it is a whole, fattened foie gras? See page 198.*

❋ *Whole or boneless squab, also breasts of squab, are obtainable from D'Artagnan (see page 298).*

❋ *A couple of these recipes the chefs have given us, because they are in stages, cook the fish or, here, the meat, only "medium rare." Follow the instructions, or at the later stage it will be too dried out when cooked further.*

❋ *If you like your meat served medium, or* seignant *in French: Medium means* à point. *Well-done, for Hervé, means "massacred, destroyed."*

❋ *Tartlet shells or pans are obtainable in a good kitchen equipment store or catalog (see page 297).*

Foie Gras, the Fattened Liver of a Duck, Just as It Is

Foie Gras du Canard au Naturel

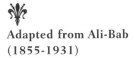

Adapted from Ali-Bab
(1855-1931)

HENRI BABINSKY, WRITING UNDER THE PSEUDONYM OF ALI-BAB, *was a civil engineer travelling round the world, prospecting for gold and diamonds, and collecting recipes and cooking for his colleagues as he went. His monumental cookbook,* Practical Gastonomy, *was published in 1907, revised in 1928— a few years before Michelin gave its first three stars to Fernand Point and the Mère Brazier. Foie gras was a deep, sensual pleasure for them and for Ali-Bab.*

French cuisine rises to real heights when it comes to foie gras. Whether the foie gras comes from producers in the Périgord, Alsace, or Gascony regions, or from families with their own ducks and geese in the courtyard behind the house, France is home of the foie gras.

Comtesse Irline de Rambuteau, wife of my old Beaujolais friend Henri, puts on her long country dress, her boots, and a headscarf and, twice a day, goes out to their farm to force feed her geese. Walking into Paul's kitchen, after a morning with him at the market, his chef Roger Jaloux has, laid out on the kitchen table, a load of baskets filled with fresh foie gras, just arrived from foie gras producer Jean Rougié in Perigord. My Saint Emilion winegrower Alain Querre, after a day at the foie gras fair in Gascony, stands in his kitchen canning the fresh foie gras for the New Year.

When I asked Paul for a recipe for foie gras, he replied, "Take the simplest." This one from Ali-Bab is almost identical to the foie gras au naturel *recipe by the Mère Brazier.*

SERVES 1

1 whole foie gras,
    a fattened duck liver
Salt
Extra-virgin olive oil
1 tin-lined copper sauté pan

Take one beautiful duck liver, ideally just when winter is getting really cold. Lightly salt the liver. Over medium heat, heat a sauté pan that has been rubbed with some drops of olive oil. Place the liver in the pan.

Place the pan over high heat, shaking the pan constantly so that the liver does not stick to it. After 12 to 15 minutes, the liver should be a fine golden color and ready, *à point.* Serve it immediately on a warm plate.

❋ Ali-Bab liked to add a little lemon juice. The best livers came from the mallard duck, he declared. "Prepared this way," he wrote, "foie gras of duck is a dish worthy of the gods. With its appetizing, flavored, rosy form, it charms one's senses and seduces even the most delicate of stomachs."

❋ Imported French fresh foie gras is now available from D'Artagnan (see page 298), and in certain fine gourmet stores. For Rougié's fresh and canned foie gras, see page 300.

❋ For wine, the Mère Brazier liked to serve it with a glass of Alsace Riesling. Jean-Pierre, Paul, and Marc Haeberlin in Alsace treat themselves to a glass of the great Sauternes, Château Yquem, each Christmas when they serve foie gras that Paul and Marc have prepared. For Ali-Bab, "Serve the best wine you have in the house, from right in the back of the cellar." Gerard and Elyane Boyer, in the heart of Champagne at Les Crayères in Reims, would guide you to one of 192 champagnes on their wine list, possibly a vintage brut from your favorite champagne house.

Fattened Fresh Liver of Duck or Goose

Foie Gras Exotica

Claude Troisgros,
Restaurant Claude Troisgros,
Rio de Janeiro

CHEFS ARE A MOVEABLE FEAST *in themselves. The fortunate ones begin by being apprenticed out in restaurants across France, Europe, the world. If they had labels on their baggage like liner passengers of yore, what a display! In France, if there is a family restaurant to tend, they return home.*

Claude Troisgros was one out of the nest who got away. When I would fly down to Rio and stay with him, watching him walk happily through the market each morning to buy what he needed for eight tables at his first restaurant, Roanne, he was already dreaming. Roanne and Rio de Janeiro. New York and Miami Beach.

Foie gras with jicama, caperberries, kumquats, star anise, nira, and honey. Claude takes one of the glories of France, foie gras, and this is what he brings back from the market to go with it. He serves it as an appetizer, or to follow his Lobsters Oh Marcoco! *(page 103). France alive and well in the New World. A good reason to make the trip to Rio, go and see the markets there, and dine* chez *Claude. In the meantime, enjoy the reading and imagine Claude is cooking this for you.*

SERVES 4

Sauce

2 teaspoons honey
1 teaspoon balsamic vinegar
2 teaspoons grated ginger
2 teaspoons demi-glace
  (see page 283)
3¹/2 tablespoons butter
Juice of ¹/2 lime

Fruit

4 caperberries
4 kumquats, preserved, *confit*
1 star fruit, preserved, *confit*

Put the honey and vinegar in a saucepan and cook until it becomes a light caramel. Add the ginger and demi-glace and cook over medium heat to reduce by half. Strain the sauce through a fine-mesh sieve. Before serving, stir in the butter and lime juice. Reheat the sauce, but do not boil.

To prepare the fruit, put caperberries, kumquats, and star fruit in a large saucepan with the sugar, water, and the cinnamon, clove, and star anise. Cook gently over low heat until the fruit is tender.

Slice the jicama into slivers measuring 0.12 inch (3mm). Cook them in boiling water with some salt and the vinegar until tender.

When ready to serve, cut the foie gras into 4 slices. Season and sauté in a very hot skillet. Drain on a paper towel.

Arrange the jicama slices in the center of each plate. Cover with the sauce. Place a slice of foie gras on top. Drain caperberries, kumquats, star fruit, cashew nuts, and garnish the foie gras with the fruit, nira, and pink and white peppercorns.

1/2 cup water
1/2 cup sugar
1 cinammon stick
1 whole clove
1 star anise
1 large jicama
Salt to taste
1 teaspoon balsamic vinegar
One 1 1/4-pound foie gras,
1 tablespoon butter
4 cashew nuts
Nira or chives
4 pink peppercorns, crushed
4 white peppercorns, crushed

❋ *Imported fresh French foie gras, since December 1998, is available in some of the best gourmet stores, such as Citerella in New York. It's also available from D'Artagnan. (See page 298.)*

❋ *Cutting jicama into such small slivers shows how finely Claude works. He means you to use the indispensible mandoline that chefs use to slice ingredients from paper thin to 1/2 inch. Many home cooks now have one. (See page 299.)*

❋ *Star anise is the eight-pointed pod from a shrub that grows in the Far East. It has an anise flavor. If you cannot find the caperberries or some other ingredients, remember this recipe comes from Claude's restaurant in Rio.*

❋ *Claude called me yesterday from the Blue Door restaurant in Miami where he is consultant chef. The same management and Claude are opening a restaurant in the restored St. Moritz Hotel in New York for November 1999, and a restaurant and hotel in London in 2000. Watch these chefs.*

Squab Roasted in Garlic with Merlot Wine Sauce

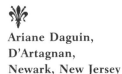

Ariane Daguin,
D'Artagnan,
Newark, New Jersey

Squabs, pigeoneaux, are raised peacefully on farms in America. From the same family, the wood pigeon, or palombe, is wild and considered fair game to the French on its autumnal migration across southwest France. Through harvest time the Bordeaux winegrower can be seen out shooting whatever flies over his vineyard. In the Pyrenées mountains along the Franco-Spanish frontier, my Basque friends took me to see the pigeons being lured up the valley to the mountain top where they had stretched nets between trees to trap and shoot the birds. Then down to the local inn where the owner's wife had prepared us the succulent pigeon pie, salmis de palombes. *I was researching a program for the French radio on one of my ancestors, the Duke of Wellington, who passed that way, over La Rhune mountain, to celebrate with champagne one of the bloodiest of his victories at Toulouse—three years before Waterloo in 1815. Did they offer Wellington squab or pigeon pie on the victory menu in Toulouse?*

SERVES 6

18 garlic cloves, peeled

6 squabs, about 1 pound each

4 cups rendered duck fat, heated

2 cups Merlot wine

1/2 cup heavy cream or
  crème fraîche

Salt and freshly ground pepper
  to taste

Blanch the garlic cloves in boiling water for 10 minutes. Drain.

Preheat the oven to 450°F degrees.

Rinse the squabs and dry them inside and out with paper towels. Stuff two garlic cloves inside each squab and season with salt and pepper inside and outside. Place the birds in a roasting pan just large enough to hold them in one layer. Rub the duck fat all over them. Roast the squabs in the oven for 20 minutes, basting 3 or 4 times during the cooking. Remove from the oven and keep the squabs warm.

Skim off the fat from the roasting pan with a spoon. Deglaze the pan with the wine, scraping the bottom to get up every brown piece of meat. Pour the liquid into a small saucepan, add the remaining garlic, cook over medium heat, and reduce by half. Add the cream and reduce over high heat, without stirring, for 2 to 3 minutes, or until the sauce starts to thicken and is well blended. Spoon the sauce over the squabs and serve immediately. A rice pilaf makes a good side dish.

❋ *Squab, or* pigonneau, *is a red-meat bird like duck, not to be confounded with cornish hen, or* poussin, *a white-meat bird like chicken. It is a possible alternative here. Both are obtainable from D'Artagnan. (See page 298.)*

❋ *For rendered duck fat, see D'Artagnan listing on page 298.*

❋ *Another way to remove the fat before deglazing: Pour the contents into a defatting pitcher, if you have one, and pour the liquid beneath the fat back into the pan. Or carefully pour the fat off into a bowl and deglaze what is left.*

❋ *Provide finger bowls, because squabs with their small bones are best eaten with the fingers.*

Venison Rossini Medallions in Sauternes

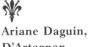

Ariane Daguin,
D'Artagnan,
Newark, New Jersey

"I HAVE ADAPTED AN ESCOFFIER RECIPE," *says Ariane.* "*Instead of a* filet mignon *of beef, I have a* filet mignon *of deer, or* chevreuil, *and a little garniture with some foie gras in the sauce to make a liaison and a slice of hot liver in the deer. Make sure the sauce is strong,* bien relevé, *with deer stock. In winter we add some dried cranberries, some green and black pepper, and make a liaison of the sauce with some mousse of foie gras.*"

Bob the farmer, Jeannie's neighbor in the Appalachians, sometimes gives us venison shot during the hunting season. Wild venison has a big, strong taste. A taste of the soil, goût de terroir, *as my winemakers would say.* "*No comparison with game reared on farms,*" *says André Soltner.*

SERVES 6

One 3-pound venison loin or strip or boneless leg filet

Salt and freshly ground pepper to taste

1 tablespoon olive oil

4 tablespoons D'Artagnan demi-glace or 2 tablespoons venison demi-glace and 2 duck or veal demi-glace or 4 tablespoons of either one

1 small D'Artagnan terrine of foie gras or 6 slices terrine de foie gras, about 2 1/2 to 3 ounces each (see note)

1/2 cup Bordeaux Sauternes wine

1 tablespoon duck fat

Garnish

3 apples, peeled and diced

2 medium turnips, chopped

Cut the venison loin into 6 equal medallions, 1/4 inch thick. Season with salt and pepper on both sides. Heat the oil in a skillet over medium-high heat. Sauté the medallions for 2 to 3 minutes on each side until medium rare. Remove from the heat and keep warm.

To make the sauce, heat the demi-glace in a saucepan over medium heat. When reduced by half, whisk in 4 tablespoons of foie gras, the 1/2 cup wine, salt, and pepper.

To make the garnish, heat 1 tablespoon duckfat in a large skillet over medium heat and sauté the fruits and vegetables until golden brown. Season to taste.

When ready to serve, place a medallion in the center of each warmed plate. Cut the terrine of foie gras in 6 slices of 2 1/2 to 3 ounces each, and place on top of each medallion. Place 1 slice of truffle on top of the foie gras, if desired. Spoon the sauce over the medallion. Serve the vegetables on the side.

* *Boneless strip loin and leg of venison, mousse and terrine of foie gras, duck fat, demi-glace, and venison stock are available from D'Artagnan (see page 298).*

* *The wine Ariane uses in the cooking and recommends for the table is the exquisitely sweet wine, Sauternes from Gascony's neighbor, Bordeaux.*

1/4 pound green grapes

1 big shallot, chopped

2 pounds wild mushrooms, cleaned and chopped

1 clove garlic, chopped

1/4 cup fresh parsley, chopped

1 truffle, sliced (optional)

Noisette of Venison with Grand Veneur Sauce

Jean Banchet,
Restaurant Le Francais,
Chicago

"This morning we set out about sunrise after taking breakfast of our venison and fish," wrote *Captains Merriweather Lewis and William Clark in their journal, June 13, 1805, on their expedition launched by President Jefferson to open trade across the unexplored territory bounded by the Pacific Ocean.*

America was once a land rich in game like venison and fish. By the turn of this century much of that had been hunted down. Much of the land where the deer and the buffalo roamed has been taken over by man. Too many rivers have been polluted. In France, the last of the salmon in the Loire has gone, there is virtually no more fishing in the Saone, the Seine, and the Rhône. Though today in America, there are still the hunters and fishermen, what is hunted cannot be sold. The venison and freshwater fish in our stores has to come from farms.

Jean and Paul are hunters. This is a true hunter's recipe.

SERVES 4

2 pounds Scottish venison,
  on the bone, marinated
  2 days (see note)

Marinade

2 tablespoons olive oil

2 cups dry red wine,
  Bordeaux-, Beaujolais-,
  or Burgundy-style

1 medium-sized onion, diced

1 stalk celery, diced

1 carrot, diced

1 bay leaf

1 sprig fresh thyme

6 juniper berries

Two days ahead, to make the marinade, put the venison loin in a large bowl or casserole. Put the oil and red wine in a bowl and whisk together. Stir in the remaining marinade ingredients and pour over the loin to cover completely; the air cannot touch the meat. Set aside in a cool place for 2 days, turning the venison frequently in the marinade.

One day ahead, to make the sauce, heat the oil in a large, heavy saucepan over medium heat and brown the bones, trimmings, and vegetables. Transfer to a bowl. Pour the vinegar and red wine into another saucepan and bring to a boil, reduce the heat to medium and reduce the volume by three-quarters. Add the bay leaf, juniper berries, thyme, crushed pepper, chicken stock, and veal demi-glace. Return the bones, trimmings, and vegetables to the saucepan, bring slowly to a boil, then reduce to a simmer for 2 hours. Strain the sauce into another heavy saucepan, cool, cover, and refrigerate.

On the serving day, heat the sauce in the saucepan, bringing to a boil, reduce and cook slowly for about 45 minutes, to reduce to 2 cups. Reduce the heat heat. Just before serving, remove from the heat and whisk in 2 teaspoons red currant jelly and 1 tablespoon butter.

Cut the loin into 8 equal medallions. Heat the remaining 2 tablespoons butter in a heavy skillet until hot but not smoking. For medium rare, sauté the medallions about 3 minutes on each side.

Fill each mushroom cap with $1/2$ teaspoon red currant jelly and place 2 caps on each plate. Place a medallion of venison on top of each mushroom, and surround with some roasted chestnuts. Cover with sauce. Serve hot.

❋ *The born hunter, Jean goes out into the woods for his dinner. Here he asks for wild venison, preferably Scottish. We cannot buy wild venison so we have to ask a hunter to invite us to dinner, or buy D'Artagnan farm-raised venison (see page 298).*

❋ *Jean likes to serve this dish with a celery root puree and red cabbage.*

❋ *When Jean says leave the marinade in a cool place, he means cool. Wine should be at room temperature, people used to say, but today rooms are centrally heated. So cool to cold, but not in a refrigerator.*

1 tablespoon black peppercorns, crushed

Sauce

2 tablespoons vegetable oil

2 pounds venison bones and trimmings

1 medium onion, diced

1 stalk celery, diced

1 carrot, diced

$1/2$ cup red wine vinegar

2 cups dry red wine

1 bay leaf

6 juniper berries

1 sprig thyme

1 teaspoon black peppercorns, crushed

1 cup clear chicken stock (see page 282)

2 cups veal demi-glace (see page 283)

6 teaspoons red currant jelly

3 tablespoons clarified butter (see page 295)

8 medium button (white) mushroom caps, roasted

24 freshly roasted chestnuts, shelled and chopped

Salt and freshly ground pepper to taste

Turkey in the Pot

Dindon au Pot

Paul Bocuse,
At The Culinary Institute of America,
Hyde Park, New York

ONE COLD, SNOWY DECEMBER MORNING IN 1993, *I arrived at the Culinary Institute of America, invited by Paul Bocuse to be, as usual, his translator. I found him on the lawn outside the president's office digging a deep hole. Students in white uniforms and toques stood round him watching. Paul stopped and lifted from the hole a large brown paper bag. Applause. He handed the bag to Roger Vergé at his side and they walked off, the students following, to the CIA's new Danny Kaye Theatre.*

"Every December," Paul explained onstage to the students, drawing a turkey from the brown paper bag, "my great-great-grandfather would take his horse and cart to Cremieu, a little village known for the quality of its small black turkeys. Back home, after cleaning the turkeys and stuffing them with chopped truffles and sausages and wrapping them in sulphurized paper, placing them in a jute sack, he buried them six inches deep in the garden, as we did two days ago. The earth helps preserve the bird, while the flavor of the truffles and sausages permeates the meat."

A moment of reflection. This recipe comes from the old days when the countryfolk kept food in a cold larder or even, as here, in winter, under the cold earth outside. This is a recipe that is fun to read, but if you want to try it, Hervé recommends, use your refrigerator instead of going underground (see note).

SERVES 8

6 ounces shallots, minced

2 tablespoons walnut oil

10¹/2 ounces sausage meat

10¹/2 ounces chestnuts, peeled
and blanched

7 ounces fresh truffles, minced

One 6-pound turkey

Roll of parchment paper

1 newspaper

1 large brown bag, size of turkey

3 pounds veal knuckle

Cook the shallots in the walnut oil in a skillet with the lid tightly closed, and cool. Mix them with the sausage meat, chestnuts and truffles. Stuff the turkey.

Wrap the turkey in parchment paper, and then in newspaper, and place in a large brown paper bag. Secure tightly.

Put the turkey in a hole in the ground, cover the hole, and leave in the ground for about 12 hours to tenderize and develop the truffle flavor throughout the turkey.

Take the turkey out after the elapsed time, and gently poach it for a half-hour per pound, cooking the bird with the knuckle of veal, oxtail, and the usual *pot-au-feu* vegetables, and salt and pepper.

Serve in the cooking pot.

❉ *Paul and the young chefs had fun that day with this recipe from the old times before everyone had a refrigerator and the earth was clean from pesticides. "Make sure," Paul told them, tongue in cheek, "you mark the spot with a stick where the turkey is buried. Losing the turkey is the sign of a careless chef."*

❉ *Instead of digging a hole in your garden, marinate the turkey in the refrigerator. First, advises Hervé, place it on a dish and wrap it up tightly in ample aluminum foil to make it airtight. This way no odors from the refrigerator can reach your "turkey in the fridge" while it marinates for 12 hours with its stuffing of sausage meat, chestnuts, and truffles. Then cook the turkey, as Paul and Roger did, and you will have a great-tasting bird. You can use this recipe for Christmas—or any other time—with a goose or a capon.*

❉ *Paul asks for fresh truffles because they are in season and arrive in time for Christmas. At other times of the year, use tinned truffles that are packed and measured in ounces. Remember, in France a pair of kitchen scales is an important part of the chef's equipment. If you go to their cookbooks, their measures are in grams and kilos, as they are throughout Europe. Imported produce from Europe now carries both metric and American measures.*

❉ *Turkey for us at Christmas, even during the war, came with a stuffing of sage and onions and chestnuts. (See page 286.)*

1¹/2 pounds oxtail

3 pounds pot-au-feu vegetables:

    1/2 pound carrots, sliced

    1/2 pound onions, sliced

    1/2 pound turnips, sliced

    1/2 pound parsnips, sliced

    1/2 pound leeks, well washed and sliced

2 celery hearts, sliced

Salt and freshly ground pepper to taste

Vegetables

The chefs buy much of their produce—meat, fish, fruit, cheeses—early in the morning at local markets. Or they have it shipped in overnight from markets around the country, from Brittany, Normandy, the Mediterranean, or even flown in from overseas.

Freshest of all is what they grow in their own kitchen gardens. Paul Bocuse has two kitchen gardens, one a few minutes away on the hill overlooking his restaurant, the other alongside the river.

"Vegetables play an important role in my kitchen," he says. "We grow the best string beans, the best potatoes. We use neither insecticides nor chemicals on the garden, so they're the most natural vegetables possible from good well-exposed soils."

The kitchen garden reminds him of the seasons. "People seem to forget the world is round and that vegetables and flowers come up in the springtime. I like seasonal vegetables."

Young Spring Salad
from My Kitchen Garden

Paul Bocuse,
Restaurant Paul Bocuse,
Collonges-au-Mont-d'Or, Lyon

AFTER HIS DAWN VISIT TO THE MARKET IN LYON *and a bistrot breakfast or* machon, *Paul likes to drive his truck filled with local produce back to the restaurant, unload, and drive up to his kitchen garden on the hill of Collonges. Walking with his gardener, Marcel Besson, known as "Bobosse," Paul looks around his garden.*

"Each morning, before the sun rises, my gardeners gather the vegetables and fruit with all the freshness of the night on them, so that at midday we are able to serve vegetables and fruit picked only hours earlier."

SERVES 4

5 young carrots

3 stalks celery or celeriac

1 bunch radishes, about 6 pieces

1 head romaine, cos, or small
    butter lettuce

1 bunch watercress

1 handful lamb's lettuce,
    or corn salad (see note)

3 Belgian endives

1 small bunch arugula

Herbs such as parsley, chives,
    tarragon, and chervil

1 tablespoon red wine vinegar

3 tablespoons olive oil

Salt and freshly ground pepper
    to taste

Cut carrots and celery in julienne strips. Remove leaves from radishes. Coarsely chop the lettuce, watercress, lamb's lettuce, endive, and arugula, and place all the vegetables in a salad bowl.

Mix together parsley, chives, tarragon, and chervil. Add vinegar, olive oil, salt, and pepper. Taste and adjust seasonings. Pour over the greens in the salad bowl and toss the salad well.

❋ *Lamb's lettuce—mâche or corn salad—with its small dark green leaves, is everywhere today in America, even little stores. We would pick it wild in the fields, like dandelion leaves, but store salads today are cultivated. Also excellent when mixed with potatoes or beetroot.*

❊ Paul varies his salad dressing, using lemon juice, Dijon mustard, or walnut oil or blending walnut oil and peanut oil or olive oil.

❊ The Mère Brazier made her vinaigrette with $1/4$ cup each of finely chopped onions (tightly wrung in a kitchen towel), chopped parsley, chopped chervil, capers, salt, freshly ground pepper, a good wine vinegar, and 9 ounces of olive oil. For veal or lamb or other cold meat she would mix some chopped hard-boiled eggs into the salad.

Salad of French (String) Beans with Hazelnuts

Salade de Haricots Verts à la crème et aux Noisettes

Roger Vergé,
Restaurant Le Moulin de Mougins,
Côte d'Azur

ONE DAY IN THE LATE SIXTIES, *the two food writers Henri Gault and Christian Millau, renowned as the champions of* nouvelle cuisine, *came for dinner at Paul Bocuse's restaurant at Collonges. Returning to Paris, they wrote in their magazine* Gault-Millau, *"Paul brought out these string beans that were smelling fresh from the garden's soil. Simply extraordinary! There,* nouvelle cuisine *exists! We've just tasted it."*

"I remember explaining to them," Paul says, "that Fernand Point already was cooking young, fresh green beans and string beans like that, quickly in and out of the water, so that they were still crunchy in the mouth, thirty years ago." Jean and Pierre Troisgros, alumni of the Fernand Point kitchen, too, cooked their vegetables this way (see their Salmon Escalopes with Sorrel Sauce, page 50). Roger Vergé, who has written a cookbook solely on vegetables and plans another on potatoes, cooks his green beans this way, too.

SERVES 2

1 pound French (string) beans, (*haricots verts*, see note)

6 quarts water

2 tablespoons coarse salt

3/4 ounce hazelnuts, shelled

4 tablespoons *crème fraîche* or heavy cream, well-chilled

1 teaspoon strong Dijon-style mustard

Juice of 1/2 lemon

2 tablespoons chopped chervil

4 pale lettuce leaves

Salt and freshly ground pepper to taste

Place a large salad bowl in the refrigerator to chill. Trim and wash the beans in a colander.

Bring 6 quarts salted water to a boil in a large saucepan and drop in the beans and cook, uncovered.

After 4 to 5 minutes, sample a bean for doneness. Prepare a bowl of cold water and ice cubes. When the beans are still slightly crisp, drain them quickly and plunge them into the cold water. This stops their cooking and keeps the beautiful green color. Drain quickly and carefully, dry on a cloth, if necessary, and set aside in a cool place or in the refrigerator.

Cut the hazelnuts into thin slices with a sharp knife and toast lightly in a small cast-iron skillet over a high heat, stirring constantly. The nuts should not brown, but remain pale. Alternatively, toast the nuts in the oven or under a broiler. Set nuts aside on a plate to cool.

Thirty minutes before serving, remove the bowl and the cream from the refrigerator. Combine the cream, mustard, lemon juice, salt, and pepper in the bowl and whisk ingredients together. Add the chopped chervil and French beans, and toss together with a wooden spoon. Taste the dressing, adding salt, as needed.

Arrange 2 lettuce leaves in "open-hand" shape on each plate and spoon two mounds of dressed French beans on the lettuce, and garnish with roasted hazelnuts.

❋ *Haricots verts: Roger calls them French beans, also known as green or string beans.*

Some tips from Roger Vergé:

❋ *It is important to choose fresh French beans. To test for freshness, break one in half. If it breaks cleanly and crisply, it is fresh. If it bends and stretches, it is not. Ideally, look for the smallest beans, about the size of a prong of a large fork, with some white flowers still attached. If you can't get the finest, choose beans fresh enough to snap in half. Watch carefully as they cook.*

❋ *Do not cook the beans more than 2 hours ahead of serving or they will wilt.*

❋ *Cream: Roger actually asks for double cream,* crème double, *a very heavy cream to be found in France. "So heavy," says Hervé, "you give a few turns of the whisk and you have butter." He adds that it is, "très, très bon."*

Warm Salad of Ratte Potatoes with Fresh Truffles

Salade Tiede de Pommes Rattes aux Truffes de Richeranches

**Jean-Paul Lacombe,
Restaurant Leon de Lyon,
Lyon**

TEN YEARS AGO, JEAN-PAUL, ONE OF LYON'S MOST ELEGANT BACHELOR CHEFS, *married Fabienne, Georges Duboeuf's daughter. Fabienne left the family wine business to become Madame Lacombe and manage the front of house of the Lacombe family restaurant Leon de Lyon in the heart of Lyon.*

Vinegar was called vinaigre d'Orleans, *since the Middle Ages when the town of Orleans on the Loire river was the center for making vinegar and the Dukes of Burgundy barred the Beaujolais winegrowers from using the direct route from Beaujolais to Paris, so the wine had to travel by horse and cart over the hills and up the canals to the capital. Any Beaujolais that spoilt travelling over the hills was left in Orleans to be turned into vinegar.*

These chefs make their own vinegar, and Jean-Paul and Fabienne know exactly who to visit for the best wine for the "mother" of their vinegar. Ratte potatoes, small and round, can be found in some greenmarkets in America. Well worth the search, they are particularly attuned to truffles.

SERVES 4

1 pound ratte potatoes (see note on page 140)

10 ounces watercress or winter salad

2/3 cup truffle juice (see note and Bernard Loiseau's tip on page 169)

1 1/2 tablespoons aged red wine vinegar, (*vinaigre vieux*)

6 tablespoons virgin olive oil

2 1/2 ounces fresh truffles

Salt and freshly ground pepper to taste

Wash the potatoes, without peeling, and cook them in salted water for 15 to 20 minutes. Test for doneness with a sharp knife. Sort and wash the cress and set aside in a cool place.

Combine the truffle juice, vinegar, and the olive oil in a small bowl. Season and set aside.

Wash and brush the fresh truffle. Drain and dry with a paper towel and cut into small, thick sticks.

Peel the potatoes and cut them into slices and set aside in a mixing bowl, adding the truffles and vinaigrette. Cover the bowl with clear plastic and set it near a warm oven for 10 minutes so the contents can be infused with the aromas.

Serve in four small individual dishes. Spread some potatoes inside a tart ring if available, or in the shape of a tart, with some truffles on top. Remove the tart ring and add some cress leaves, seasoned, in a circle around. Set the dish on a plate and serve.

❋ *Aged red wine vinegar, vinaigre vieux, is just what it says it is, aged in oak barrels that give it a bouquet (like the bouquet of an old wine) and an acidity that has freshness to it.*

Some tips from Jean-Paul:

❋ *Individual dishes with covers are best for containing the aromas.*

❋ *We always prefer fresh truffles (mid-December to late March). The rest of the year, use top-quality tinned or bottled truffles and the juice they are in can be used for the vinaigrette. Or see Bernard Loiseau's tip on making truffle juice on page 169.*

❋ *Covering and slightly warming the salad means the truffle will add its marvellous aroma to the potatoes. I like to cut the truffle in batons so that I can really crunch the raw truffle.*

❋ *Our truffles come from the village of Richeranches near the Pope's palace in Chateauneuf-du-Pape. The locals say it is the best soil, terroir, for truffles.*

❋ *The Duboeuf Pouilly Fuissé aged in the barrel or Gerard Chave's white Hermitage or a red Châteauneuf-du-Pape are ideal for this dish.*

❋ *When mixing your vinaigrette, says Hervé, "The blender gives you a lighter, more homogeneous vinaigrette. Whisking by hand can mean a heavier vinaigrette." Jean Troisgros used a little wire whisk. Paul Bocuse prefers the whisk, too, and likes his vinaigrette "thickened and light."*

❋ *When are the potatoes cooked? Take a sharp knife and see if it will go in deeply and easily—that's better than trying to give you precise cooking times. It can also depend on the freshness of the vegetable or on your oven.*

❋ *Set near a warm oven for 10 minutes. You will need to preheat the oven to a low temperature, and set the dish on the open oven lid or on a tray nearby.*

Asparagus Tips in a Vinaigrette of Potatoes

Les Pointes d'Asperges à la Vinaigrette de Pommes de Terre

Bernard Loiseau,
Restaurant La Côte d'Or,
Saulieu

WHEN ASPARAGUS IS IN SEASON, *young and delicious, it appears many times on the Loiseau menu. He serves this vinaigrette of potatoes, sometimes a truffled vinaigrette, with filets of sole. He also serves a vinaigrette with roasted rock lobsters with what he calls dwarf leeks and eggs, and with escalopes of hot foie gras. Imagine.*

SERVES 4

1 pound Bintje potatoes, peeled

1 cup whole milk

3 tablespoons butter, melted

1 tablespoon shallots, chopped

6 tablespoons olive oil

Coarse salt and freshly ground pepper to taste

Drops lemon juice

28 young, white asparagus

Drops walnut oil

1 tablespoon chives, chopped

Cook the potatoes in water for 15 to 20 minutes, or until tender. Drain and dry in the oven for 2 minutes on 250°F. Mash the potatoes into a purée, adding the milk and the melted butter. Then add the shallots and olive oil. Season with coarse salt and freshly ground pepper and some drops of lemon juice. Keep warm in a bain-marie and cover.

Using a chef's knife, carefully peel the white stalk of the asparagus and remove the small leaves around the tips. Cut the stalks to about 6 inches long, tie them in 4 bunches of 7 each with kitchen string. Place in a large saucepan of boiling salted water and cook for about 10 minutes. Fill a large bowl with water and ice cubes. Remove from the heat, plunge the asparagus into a large bowl of iced water for 15 seconds so that they keep their color. Remove and drain.

Remove the string from the asparagus and place 1 bunch on each plate. Next to the asparagus, place a tablespoon of potatoes. Drizzle walnut oil and chives over the asparagus and serve.

✳ Loiseau uses the young white asparagus that he can find easily when they come in season. Green asparagus, as young as possible, can be used. always dipping in iced water for several seconds after cooking to preserve their green color.

✳ Bintje potatoes are yellow-skinned and floury, best before they reach maturity. The the ratte potatoes (see page 140) are yellow-skinned and firmer. Large mealy Idaho or Russet Burbank potatoes could replace the Bintje.

✳ Roger Vergé advises that when boiling potatoes, start them off in cold water. Boiling water immediately tends to toughen potatoes. Once again, to test if cooked, use the point of a sharp knife.

Just a Simple Panful of Chanterelle Mushrooms

Une Poelée de Girolles Tout Simple

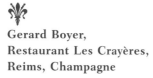

**Gerard Boyer,
Restaurant Les Crayères,
Reims, Champagne**

GERARD BOYER SERVED HIS APPRENTICESHIP AT LASSERRE IN PARIS *and in his father's restaurant in Reims. "You come and work here," Boyer Sr. told him, "but it's to be your decision, not mine. Quite simple. The day you feel you're not happy, there's a hole over there the builders did not close, the door." Gerard stayed, married Elyane and together went on, to turn the turn-of-the century Château Les Crayères into one of France's finest Relais and Châteaux hotel-restaurants. Gerard is a longtime travel companion of Paul Bocuse, and they call each other up on the 'chefs telephone'— every chef has one in his kitchen today—whenever they are offered a special event in New York or Rio that would be more fun to do together.*

Chanterelles are best in season in the fall, from the edge of the woods on the hillsides of Champagne. Gerard calls this a simple recipe, but notice the care he takes in cooking, like movements of a ballet, a pas de deux.

SERVES 4

2¹/₂ pounds of chanterelle mushrooms, of good size

3¹/₂ tablespoons butter

Salt and freshly ground pepper to taste

¹/₂ tablespoon chopped shallots

¹/₄ cup heavy cream or crème fraîche

2 tablespoons walnut oil

2 sprigs flat parsley, coarsely chopped

¹/₂ cup chopped chives

Thoroughly clean the chanterelles by washing them quickly under the tap. Drain and dry with a paper towel.

Sweat the chanterelles three times, each time on a medium-low heat in a covered nonstick pan. At the end of each sweating, strain off and reserve all the juice that comes from mushrooms. This way they will be reduced to about half their size.

In a skillet, melt a nugget of butter and when it looks a blond color, drop in half of these chanterelles, lightly salt and pepper them, add half the shallots and sauté everything.

Add $1/2$ cup chanterelle juice from the above reduction and bring to a boil. Add half the cream and bring to a boil again. Beat into a sauce with half the remaining butter, add half the walnut oil and after bringing to a boil again, add half the parsley and chives. Set aside.

Repeat the same operation with the other half of the chanterelle juice, cream, butter, walnut oil, parsley, and chives.

Mix the two preparations so that they are homogeneous. Season to taste. Serve in small warm bowls.

❀ *Cook the chanterelles in two operations, says Hervé, don't be tempted to make this into one operation. The chanterelles are delicate; they could break up if you try to turn them in the pan with too many at a time. Do it twice and then mix them well together and they will look good when served.*

Cabbage Gratin

Choux en Gratin

**Margaridou,
Auvergne**

"Contrary to popular belief," *wrote Margaridou in her journal, "cabbage is an extremely subtle vegetable. The colder the climate they grow in, the firmer the cabbage and the more tender they are cooked. Those grown in our village of Planèze, they're the best. Cooked, they melt in the mouth."*

SERVES 4

2 firm, green cabbage

3/4 cup heavy cream

2 cups grated cheese,
    such as Cantal, Gruyère,
    or Parmesan

2 tablespoons butter

Salt and freshly ground pepper
    to taste

Preheat the oven to 350°F. Butter a gratin dish.

Core and quarter the cabbages and blanch briefly in boiling salted water. Drain. Remove the white leaves and set them aside on a plate.

Place a layer of cabbage leaves on the bottom of the dish, then add a layer of heavy cream, then sprinkle a light layer of grated cheese, then another layer of cabbage leaves, heavy cream, cheese, finishing with a layer of cream. Put several pieces of butter on top. Season lightly with salt and pepper.

Bake for 45 minutes. Once golden brown, open the oven door, and let the cabbage rest a few minutes. Serve hot.

Some tips from Jean and Pierre Troisgros:

❋ *An excellent dish when fresh young vegetables are largely out of season.*

❋ *The grated cheese depends on your taste. Gruyère gives a more refined flavor; Parmesan has a stronger flavor. Margaridou in Auvergne, home of Cantal cheese, liked this old country-style cheese. (See Cheeses, page 247.)*

❋ *Adding small pieces of raw ham,* jambon cru, *with the cheese makes the gratin taste even better to us.*

❋ *The same dish can be made with young cauliflower.*

Gratin of Aubergines, Tomatoes, and Zucchini (Imam Bayildi)

Paul Bocuse,
Brasserie Le Sud,
Lyon

A DISH THAT ORIGINATED IN TURKEY, *where according to one legend, editor Sharon Bowers tells me, the Imam's young wife prepared this dish every night from the twelve barrels of olive oil that were her dowry. When the Imam demanded the dish on the thirteenth night, she shrugged. The oil was gone. Imam bayildi means "the priest fainted!" It is served with grilled steaks in Paul's brasserie Le Sud in Lyon, where the menu evokes the warmth of the Mediterranean—fisherman's soup (page 85), tajine of chicken (page 186), and couscous (page 141) with wines from Provence, Italy, Spain, and Morocco.*

SERVES 5 OR 6

4 medium-sized zucchini, unpeeled

2 small eggplant

5 medium-sized tomatoes

2 medium-sized onions

1 clove garlic

Salt and freshly ground pepper to taste

1 bouquet garni: sprig thyme and 1/4 bay leaf, tied together

3 1/2 ounces Gruyère cheese, grated (optional)

2 tablespoons butter or 3 tablespoons olive oil

Preheat the oven to 400°F. Butter or oil a large, ovenproof gratin dish.

Rinse the zucchini under cold water and dry them off. Cut them into 1/2-inch-thick slices, discarding the ends. Peel the eggplant and cut into 1/2-inch-thick slices. Dunk the tomatoes into a saucepan of boiling water for 30 to 45 seconds, remove, and peel. Cut them into slices. Peel the onions and chop finely. Peel the garlic clove and crush with a fork.

Lay the onions on the bottom, then place the zucchini, the tomatoes, and eggplant in layers. Season each layer with salt and pepper. Place the bouquet garlic and bouquet garni. The gratin should be one layer of each vegetable only; layer any leftovers similarly in another gratin dish. Sprinkle Gruyère and pieces of butter on top.

Bake for about 30 minutes, or until the top layer has begun to brown. Remove from the oven and serve.

❋ *This is an excellent dish to accompany grilled meats and roasts.*

Potato Gratin, Fernand Point

Gratin de Pommes de Terre, Fernand Point

Paul Bocuse,
Restaurant Paul Bocuse,
Collonges-au-Mont-d'Or, Lyon

THROUGH GOOD TIMES AND BAD, *the country people have depended on the potato. In homes, it went into soups and stews, served with meat, poultry, game, and fish. The chefs of France followed suit.*

One dish they esteem highly is the gratin of potatoes. Defending his or her gratin is a chef's point of honor. During World War II, the occupation authorities in Lyon summoned Fernand Point to trial for daring to add cream in time of war to his gratin dauphinois. *At his defense, the superbly Rabelaisian, majestic figure of Monsieur Point rose in court and was heard to declare, "Messieurs, no one has the right to betray the true* gratin dauphinois."

The recipe that follows is the "veritable gratin dauphinois" by Fernand Point, his one and only gratin of potatoes, as recorded by his favorite apprentice, Paul Bocuse.

SERVES 4

1 clove garlic, chopped finely

2 3/4 pounds potatoes, peeled and thinly sliced

2 large eggs

3/4 cup whole milk

2 to 3 tablespoons heavy cream or *crème fraîche*

Pinch freshly grated nutmeg

Salt and ground white pepper to taste

3 1/2 tablespoons butter

Preheat the oven to 350°F. Rub the sides of a large enamelled or cast-iron ovenproof dish with the garlic clove and butter liberally.

Lay thin layers of potatoes on the dish. In a separate bowl, combine the eggs, milk, cream, grated nutmeg, salt, and pepper in a mixing bowl and whisk. Spread a thick coating of this mixture over the potatoes in the dish, adding some knobs of butter.

Bake for about 45 minutes, or until the potatoes are slightly brown. Open the oven door ajar and let the dish set for a few minutes. Serve very hot.

❀ *Potatoes. So much depends on the quality of the ingredients. Jean and Pierre Troisgros recommend the French BF-15 potato but they are not yet being grown in the States. Choose firm rather than waxy potatoes. "Slice them thin," said Paul Bocuse. "Twelve one-hundredths of an inch thick," said the Brothers Troisgros. "Paper thin," said Richard Olney.*

❀ *Eggs: Point and the Mère Brazier used 2 eggs, Escoffier and Guerot used 1 egg, whereas Troisgros, Chapel, and Olney used no eggs.*

❀ *Cream, said everyone, except Escoffier and Bocuse who said "Non."*

❀ *Cheese, said everyone, but Point, who cried, "Never!" On that note, join in the fun and serve this or your own variation of the one and only potatoes au gratin.*

Dauphinois Potato Tart with St. Marcellin Cheese, Fernand Point

Tarte Dauphinoise de Pommes de Terre au St. Marcellin

Patrick Henriroux,
La Pyramide Restaurant,
Vienne, Rhône Valley

I have great respect for a young chef who sends me this recipe, one he created as a salute to his illustrious predecessor, Fernand Point. This was Point's favorite cheese, the one and only St. Marcellin, as ever supplied by the Mère Renée Richard from her cheese stall in the Lyon market.

SERVES 4

1¹/₄ pound potatoes, peeled

4 tablespoons butter

Salt and ground pepper to taste

7 ounces smoked ham, preferably belly

7 ounces large white onions, peeled and thinly sliced

4 tablespoons butter

Sprigs thyme, chopped

1 clove garlic

Dash olive oil (less than ¹/₈ teaspoon)

¹/₂ of a whole St. Marcellin cheese

Preheat the oven to 360°F. Butter the bottom of a 12-inch nonstick tart mold.

Set aside two potatoes and slice them as thin as potato chips. Salt and pepper the mold, and cover with the potatoes laid out in a circular pattern.

Cube the smoked ham and cut the remaining potatoes into ¹/₂-inch-thick slices and set aside.

Heat the 4 tablespoons butter in a sauté pan over medium heat and cook the ham for 3 minutes, remove, and drain them. Cook the onions in the sauté pan until soft, adding a little chopped thyme and chopped garlic. Heat the olive oil in a skillet over medium heat and cook the potato slices, then drain them.

Combine the ham, onions, and potatoes, seasoning lightly with salt. Layer this mixture on top of the potato slices in the mold. Cut the cheese into small pieces and spread over the tart.

Bake for 18 minutes. The cheese will melt and brown under the heat and spread over the tart. Remove from the oven and when cool enough to handle, unmold onto a serving dish. Serve with the juice of a roast and a salad of chicory.

✳ *St. Marcellin cheese is a small, round disc, about 3 inches in diameter and 3/4 inch thick. Madame Richard's is made from raw cow's milk; commercial St.Marcellin is made from pasteurized cow's milk (see Madame Richard and St. Marcellin, page 248).*

Onion Tart

Tarte à l'Oignon

André Soltner,
Lutèce Restaurant,
New York

WHEN JEANNIE AND I ANNOUNCED OUR ENGAGEMENT, *André Soltner graciously invited us to bring some colleagues for a glass of wine at Lutèce. Five of us sat in his little bar, and André brought out slices of onion tart he had just made and a bottle of the Trimbach Riesling. He sat with us, and told us about his onion tart that had been part of his childhood.*

"Today when someone asks for it in advance, I make a big one and send out slices to give to some of the tables. Other chefs send a glass of champagne to a friend, but I say why champagne? If someone wants champagne, he can buy it. But an onion tart he cannot buy."

SERVES 4

2 cups all-purpose flour, sifted

1 teaspoon salt

8 tablespoons (1 stick) butter

1/2 cup cold water

2 tablespoons lard

1 pound onions, peeled and chopped

1 large egg

1/2 cup heavy cream or *crème fraîche*

Pinch freshly grated nutmeg

Salt and freshly ground pepper to taste

Preheat the oven to 375°F.

Mix the flour and 1 teaspoon salt in a bowl. Rub in the butter with the fingertips, taking care not to work the dough too much. Make a well in the center of the mixture, pour in 1/2 cup cold water, and blend it into the mixture with the fingers until it is just moistened. Let the dough rest for at least 30 minutes.

Heat the lard in a skillet over medium heat, and cook the onions until they are slightly browned and tender. Remove the skillet from the heat.

In a small bowl, beat the egg and cream together and add to the onions. Add a pinch of nutmeg, salt, and pepper.

Roll the dough out, and line a 10-inch pie tin or tart pan with it. Fill with the onion mixture. Bake for 25 minutes, and serve very hot.

Georges Troisgros came out of the Lutèce kitchen to join us, and André found another bottle of his favorite Alsace Riesling to go with the onion tart.

The kindness of chefs.

Chapter *Eight*

Pastas

Catherine de Medici and her ladies from Florence brought with them to France their favorite pastas—vermicelli, tagliatelli, canelloni, spaghetti, ravioli, macaroni, and more. And some say it was Marco Polo who had introduced pasta to Italy from his travels to China. Noodles have long been popular in China and Vietnam. The revival of noodles in France in the last half of this century may have been influenced by the nation's involvement in Vietnam, when French civilians and soldiers were returning home.

"In the early seventies," Hervé Riou recalls, "fresh noodles, *nouilles fraîches,* were the rage on the menus of fashionable Parisian restaurants. We made our fresh noodles every day or two by hand, hanging them up in the kitchen to dry. Until then, fresh noodles was looked on as the classic accompaniment to a beef bourguignon in country inns and bistros. Gratins with their cheeses and cream were very French. I think of fresh noodles in Alsace and gratins from Lyon and around."

Fresh Noodles

Nouilles Fraîches

**André Soltner,
Lutèce Restaurant,
New York**

SERVES 4

1 pound (3 cups) all-purpose
flour, sifted

Pinch of finely crushed salt

3 large eggs

6 egg yolks

1 teaspoon vinegar

2 teaspoons peanut oil

5 tablespoons unsalted butter
or olive oil

Combine the flour, salt, eggs, egg yolks, and vinegar, in a mixing bowl and mix thoroughly by hand or with an electric mixer, until the dough is smooth and elastic. To prevent the dough drying out, wrap in a cheesecloth before setting aside for 1 hour.

Divide the noodle dough into pieces the size of a small egg. On a floured board, roll out each piece into a paper-thin sheet, and cut each sheet into strips 1/4 inch wide and 2 inches long.

Put the noodles into a saucepan of boiling lightly salted water, with a little oil added, and cook until tender but not soft, about 5 minutes. Drain thoroughly, but do not rinse. Add some knobs of butter or olive oil, to taste.

※ *As an alternative, the chefs suggest, there is excellent commercial pasta in good gourmet stores.*

※ *Some chefs, after cooking the noodles, cool them under running water, but others do not. If you are going to serve the noodles immediately, do not run them under water, says Hervé. If you are going to set them aside for 20 minutes or so, then run them briefly under water.*

※ *All the chefs agree, pasta is best when cooked at the last moment, just before serving.*

Small Noodle Dumplings

Spätzle

André Soltner,
Lutèce Restaurant,
New York

Dumplings are better known in America as spätzle. *In England, Jeannie and I grew up with plain old dumplings in steak and kidney pie or Irish stew. Dumplings, they told us as children, are from some far-flung outpost of the British Empire. "Dumpling. A short, chubby creature," says Jeannie's dictionary of the English language. "Origin unknown." André grew up with them, good hearty Alsace* spätzles, *with a tremor over the* ä.

SERVES 6

3 large eggs
Salt to taste
Pinch freshly grated nutmeg
5/8 cup cold water
2 cups all-purpose flour, sifted
1 tablespoon chopped parsley
1 tablespoon peanut oil
6 tablespoons (3/4 stick) butter

Put the eggs in a bowl. Beat the eggs to break them up, then add the salt, nutmeg, and cold water. With a wooden spatula vigorously stir this mixture into the flour and continue until small bubbles form and the mixture no longer sticks to the spoon. The paste should be soft. Stir in 1 tablespoon chopped parsley.

Bring a large pot of salted water to the boil. (Note the pot should be tall enough so that when a colander is placed over it, there is a few inches' clearance between the water and the colander bottom. The colander should have large holes.) Add 1 tablespoon peanut oil to the water and place the colander over the boiling water.

Put the paste in the colander and press down on the paste with a spatula to force it through the holes into the boiling water. Cook for about 2 minutes, or until the dumplings rise to the surface.

Remove the dumplings and put in ice water or hold them under cold running water until thoroughly chilled. Drain the dumplings in the colander, tossing them so that all the water drains off.

Melt the butter in a skillet over medium heat until it browns slighlty. Sauté the dumplings in the butter and add salt to taste. Serve very hot.

❋ *If you go to Alsace, the local bistrots serve a fresh, young, light white wine in a pitcher. Like the best rosés of Provence, it doesn't travel. But Jean Hugel's family make a Hugel Gentil which is delightfully near that little wine in the bistrot and should cost less than $10 per bottle in the store.*

Gratin of Macaroni

Macaroni au Gratin

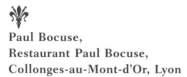

Paul Bocuse,
Restaurant Paul Bocuse,
Collonges-au-Mont-d'Or, Lyon

THE MÈRE BRAZIER AS A TEENAGER *was sent by her family to work on a farm. "Sometimes they gave us a gratin of macaroni. They cooked the macaroni in water, drained it, and seasoned it with a béchamel sauce and cream. It was good and years later my customers enjoyed it at my restaurant."*

Paul Bocuse has a macaroni gratin on the menu in his restaurant as garnish for Raymond Oliver's rumpside of veal, Quasi de Veau, Raymond Oliver *(see page 147). Paul served this dish on that day in the seventies at Lutèce when he presented his cookbook in America. To the disappointment of some, there was no sign of* nouvelle cuisine.

"Ridiculous fads for five or six purées on a plate, for the kiwi, for the taste for raw food borrowed from the Japanese, for peas chopped in four, all in the name of nouvelle cuisine!" *says Paul Bocuse. "A cuisine for those who had lost their appetite. But what we did do was positive. The chef came out of the kitchen where he had been a slave for decades, though it was Fernand Point who showed us the way in the thirties, the chef who became owner of his own restaurant."*

The Mère Brazier's gratin of macaroni and Paul's that follows are a legacy of the Romans who founded Lyon, and of the Italian influence in the days of the Rennaissance when this city was the silk-trade capital of Europe.

SERVES 6

Béchamel sauce

1 tablespoon butter
1/2 cup all-purpose flour
1 quart whole milk
Pinch salt and crushed pepper
Pinch freshly grated nutmeg

Macaroni

1 gallon water
Pinch coarse salt
10 ounces long macaroni

continued

To make the béchamel sauce, heat the butter in a casserole, blend in the flour, and add the milk, salt, pepper, and nutmeg. Cook over medium heat and stir constantly until it comes to a boil. Remove from the heat, cover, and let stand.

Preheat the oven to 400°F. Butter an ovenproof baking dish.

To prepare the macaroni, place 1 gallon water and a large pinch coarse salt in a large pot. Bring to a boil and add the macaroni. Cook for 15 to 20 minutes after the water boils again, making sure not to overcook the macaroni. It should remain al dente. Drain.

5¼ ounces Beaufort cheese

6 tablespoons light cream

Salt and freshly ground pepper
 to taste

2 tablespoons butter

3 tablespoons freshly grated
 Parmesan cheese

1 truffle (optional)

Cut the cheese into large slices. Add the cream and cheese to the béchamel. Blend in until the cheese is melted.

Layer the macaroni in the dish and cover with a layer of béchamel sauce. Alternate layers of macaroni and sauce, finishing with a layer of sauce. Spread the remaining slices of Beaufort over the dish. Dot with butter. Sprinkle with grated Parmesan or grated truffle. Salt and pepper to taste (optional).

Bake in the oven for 20 minutes. Remove and serve.

※ *Gruyère cheese can replace the Beaufort. Margaridou in the Auvergne made her gratin solely with the local Cantal cheese, since there was surely no Parmesan, Gruyère, or Beaufort available in her village store.*

※ *Any part of a truffle not used in the recipe can be kept fresh on some uncooked risotto in a glass jar. Truffles dry out, but it will give you some beautifully perfumed risotto for another day. "Though," advises Hervé, "I never leave them there more than five or so days."*

Le Cirque Spaghetti Primavera

Spaghetti Primavère, Le Cirque

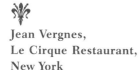

**Jean Vergnes,
Le Cirque Restaurant,
New York**

Paul Bocuse, Gerard and Elyane Boyer, all the Maccioni family, and I *were seated at a round table in the back of the new New York restaurant, Osteria del Circo, run by the three sons of Sirio Maccioni of Le Cirque 2000. In walked Jean Vergnes, in town, too, for the Pierre Franey memorial dinner. He joined us. Jean had been Sirio's first chef when he opened Le Cirque. "Remember, Sirio," he recalled, "the spaghetti appetizer I did for you? I have never sold so much in all my life. It was Le Cirque but I told you 'I'm old-school French,* vieux français, *I don't cook with olive oil. No oil. Only butter and cream.' So we used only butter and cream in that spaghetti and some garlic and tomatoes. It sold like hot cakes,* comme les petits pains! *It was* inimaginable! *A small plate, nine dollars. That was 1974."*

SERVES 4

1 bunch broccoli

2 small zucchini

4 asparagus spears, each about 5 inches long

1¹/2 cups green beans, trimmed, cut into 1-inch lengths

Salt and freshly ground pepper to taste

¹/2 cup fresh or frozen green peas

³/4 cup fresh or frozen pea pods, optional

1 tablespoon peanut, vegetable or corn oil

2 cups thinly diced mushrooms

1 teaspoon finely chopped fresh red or green hot chilies or about 1¹/2 teaspoon dried crushed red peppers

continued

Trim the broccoli and break it into bite-size flowerettes. Set aside.

Trim off and discard the ends of the zucchini. Do not peel the zucchini. Cut the zucchini into quarters. Cut each quarter into 1-inch or slightly longer lengths, for about 1¹/2 cups. Set aside.

Cut each asparagus spear into thirds. Set aside.

Cook each of the green vegetables separately in boiling salted water to cover for about 5 minutes, or until crisp-tender. Drain well, then run under cold water to chill, and drain again thoroughly. Combine the cooked vegetables in a mixing bowl. Then cook the peas and pea pods; about 1 minute if fresh, or 30 seconds if frozen. Drain, chill with cold water and drain again. Combine with the remaining vegetables.

1/4 cup finely chopped parsley

6 tablespoons olive oil

1 teaspoon finely chopped garlic

3 cups red, ripe tomatoes cut
    into 1-inch cubes

6 fresh basil leaves, chopped,
    about 1/4 cup, or about
    1 teaspoon dried basil

1 pound spaghetti or spaghettini

4 tablespoons (1/2 stick) butter

2 tablespoons fresh chicken broth
    (see page 282) or canned

4 ounces (1/2 cup) heavy cream
    or *crème fraîche*

5 ounces (2/3 cup) grated
    Parmesan cheese

1/2 cup toasted pine nuts

Heat the peanut oil in a skillet over medium heat and add the mushrooms. Add salt and pepper, shaking the skillet and stirring. Cook about 2 minutes. Add the mushrooms to the vegetables. Add the chopped chilies or crushed red peppers, and parsley.

Heat 3 tablesoons olive oil in a saucepan and add half the garlic, tomatoes, salt, and pepper. Cook over high heat about 4 minutes, stirring gently so as not to break up the tomatoes any more than necessary. Add the basil, stir and set aside.

Add the remaining 3 tablespoons olive oil to a large skillet, also the remaining garlic and the vegetable mixture. Cook over medium heat, stirring gently, just long enough to heat through.

Drop the spaghetti into boiling salted water. Cook until almost but not quite tender, al dente. When ready, the spaghetti must be slightly al dente. Drain well. Return the spaghetti to the kettle.

Select a pot large enough to hold the drained spaghetti and all the vegetables. To this, add the butter. When it melts, add the chicken broth, 1/2 cup cream, and cheese, stirring constantly. Cook gently on and off the heat until smooth. Add the spaghetti and toss quickly to blend. Reduce the heat to very low and add half the vegetables and pour in the liquid from the tomatoes, tossing and stirring.

Add the remaining vegetables and if the sauce seems too dry, add about 1/4 cup more cream. The sauce should not be soupy. Add the pine nuts and give the mixture one final tossing.

Serve equal portions of the spaghetti mixture in four to eight hot soup or spaghetti bowls. Spoon equal amounts of the tomatoes over each serving. Serve immediately.

✳ *Jean Vergnes was talking seriously when he suggested this recipe to Sirio, who was opening what many imagined would be a purely Italian restaurant. Jean was born in a village in the Isère-Dauphine region of the French Alps, home of the St. Marcellin cheese and* gratin dauphinois. *He was sauce chef,* saucier, *at the Hotel de Golf in Deauville at La Reine Pedauque in Paris and, in 1950, at the Waldorf-Astoria in New York. He went on to be executive chef at the Colony Restaurant and Maxwell's Plum and finally, at Le Cirque. "As a simple country boy whose hometown could not be located on a map, I was overwhelmed by the restaurant's success," Jean Vergnes wrote in his cookbook,* At Le Cirque Restaurant.

For more than twenty years Sirio had a series of splendid executive chefs at Le Cirque: Jean Vergnes, Daniel Boulud, and Alain Sailhac. Each cooked in the French-style for this great Italian restaurateur.

Gnocchi, Grandmother Troisgros

Les Gnocchi de la Mémé Forté

Claude Troisgros
from Grandmère Troisgros,
Roanne

ROANNE IS A SMALL COUNTRY MARKET TOWN *fifty miles northwest of Lyon on the N7 highway, not known for its cuisine until the Troisgros family—father, mother and two sons—came to town and took over the hotel opposite the railroad station, and gave it one of the finest restaurants in the world.*

I began knowing the great chefs there. Over lunch with the brothers Jean and Pierre one day, Pierre told me how much he looked forward to dinner at home as his Italian mother-in-law, who cooked him "the best gnocchi in the world."

Twenty years later, his son Claude in Rio de Janeiro sent me this recipe, adding, "My brother Michel, my sister Anne, and myself were all brought up on a regular diet prepared by our grandmother, Mémé Forté. One dish marked our childhood and is unforgettable. La Mémé would never reveal to us her recipe, so I have tried to reconstruct it from memory."

SERVES 4

Gnocchi

1 1/2 pounds potatoes

1/4 cup ricotta cheese

1 egg yolk

3/4 cup freshly grated
  Parmesan cheese

2 tablespoons all-purpose flour

Pinch nutmeg

Salt and freshly ground pepper
  to taste

Preheat oven 425°F.

To prepare the gnocchi, wrap the potatoes in aluminum foil and bake for 40 to 60 minutes. Peel them while hot and put the through a food mill to purée. Set aside to cool.

Put 2 cups of the potato purée in a bowl and add the remaining ingredients, making small, round balls in gnocchi shapes. Bring a saucepan of salted water to the boil and add the gnocchi, reduce the heat to medium, and cook for about 3 minutes. Remove and place the gnocchis in a deep, warm serving platter.

To make the tomato sauce, heat the butter in a skillet with a lid and cook the garlic and chopped onions over medium heat until light brown. Add the diced tomatoes, thyme, and bay leaf, and cook for about 15 minutes. Season to taste. Add the chopped parsley.

For the finishing touch, *le toque final,* cover the gnocchi with tomato sauce. Sprinkle Parmesan cheese over the dish as copiously as you like it.

Tomato sauce

2 teaspoons butter

1 garlic clove, finely chopped

1 teaspoon chopped onion

8 tomatoes, peeled, seeded, and diced

1 teaspoon chopped thyme

1 bay leaf

Salt and freshly ground pepper to taste

1 teaspoon chopped parsley

Extra freshly grated Parmesan cheese for serving

Big Ravioli with Lasagne and Mushrooms

Big Raviole

**Claude Troisgros,
Restaurant CT,
New York**

It takes more than courage to come to New York *and open a restaurant. I remember in the seventies the words of Jean Troisgros while we were driving to lunch with his best friend, Paul Bocuse, "If I was younger, I would open a restaurant in New York."*

Brother Pierre's son Claude did just that twenty years later. Flying in from Rio in 1994, he created at CT Restaurant a new flavor of French cuisine blended with what he had discovered in Brazil. He found himself showered with praise, bringing back memories of the days when Jean and Pierre were being discovered in Roanne.

Ruth Reichl, then restaurant critic of the New York Times, *wrote in her review about a dinner enjoying "the remarkable taste of the big ravioli filled with a mousseline of taro. Taro is an unctuous subtance with a luxurious texture that is the perfect vehicle for white truffle oil. The pillow of pasta is covered with a creamy mushroom sauce, and it is so irresistible that the woman is seduced."*

Gael Greene wrote in New York Magazine, *"I dare anyone to resist...the wild mushrooms in a taro-root mousseline with a tantalizing hint of cream and truffle oil, all wrapped in a filmy 'big raviole.'"*

Claude apprenticed in the Bocuse kitchen at Collonges. Paul found him his first post in Rio. "Claude's the one most like Jean," Paul said one day after dining at CT where he had written across the kitchen wall, "Bravo, les gars!" Well done, lads.

After two years of success, the rent rose out of hand and Claude decided to close CT and return to Rio. He sent me this recipe from those heady days in New York.

SERVES 4

To make the taro root mousseline, cook the taro root cubes in salted water for 40 minutes, drain, and purée in a blender. Bring the $1/2$ cup cream to a boil and mix in the taro root purée. Season. Add the white truffle oil, remove from the heat, and set aside.

To make the sauce, clean the white mushrooms and chop in blender until finely minced. Sauté the mushrooms with 1 tablespoon butter over medium heat for 10 minutes, stirring constantly.

Place in a cheesecloth and squeeze excess water into a bowl. Discard the mushrooms. Reduce mushroom water by 80 percent and add $1/2$ cup cream. Boil the mixture, whisking vigorously to emulsify (as for a cappuccino). Season with salt and pepper to taste.

To prepare the mushrooms, stem and clean them. Cook for 5 minutes in boiling salted water. Drain, heat the butter in a skillet, and sauté the mushrooms with the minced shallots.

When ready to assemble the dish, cook the lasagna al dente in boiling salted water. Heat the butter in a skillet over medium heat and cook the lotus roots. Use a sharp knife to determine doneness.

Place one lasagna noodle in each large soup plate and top with taro root mousseline and cover with another lasagna noodle. Place some mushrooms on top and cover with the sauce. Decorate with a strip of lotus root and a sprig of chives. Serve.

Taro root mousseline

$1/2$ pound taro root, peeled and cut into $1/2$-inch cubes

$1/2$ cup heavy cream or crème fraîche

1 tablespoon white truffle oil

Sauce

$1/2$ pound fresh white mushrooms

1 tablespoon butter

$1/2$ cup heavy cream or crème fraîche

Salt and freshly ground pepper to taste

Mushrooms

$1/4$ pound chanterelles

$1/4$ pound shiitake mushrooms

$1/4$ pound oyster mushrooms

2 tablespoons butter

2 shallots, minced

Ravioli

8 lasagna noodles, 4 inches x 4 inches wide

2 tablespoons butter

4 lotus roots, peeled and finely sliced

4 sprigs fresh chives, chopped

Chapter Nine

Cheeses *and* Bread

FOR A PAUSE
IN THE MEAL

**GRANITÉ OF
BEAUJOLAIS NOUVEAU**

PAUL BOCUSE,
COLLONGES-AU-MONT-
D'OR, LYON

CHEESES

**ST. MARCELLIN
CHEESE**

THE MÈRE RICHARD,
LYON

CHEESE SOUFFLÉ

PAUL BOCUSE,
LYON

CANTAL CHEESE

MARGARIDOU,
AUVERGNE

BREAD

**A SIMPLE
WHEAT BREAD**

ADAPTED FROM
LIONEL POILANE,
PARIS

For a Pause in the Meal

THERE COMES A MOMENT IN EVERY MEAL when a pause is welcome.
In Beaujolais country, the pause in a meal is serious. On St. Vincent's Day,
when the winegrowers celebrate their patron saint of winegrowers, my friend
Comte Henri de Rambuteau, mayor of his village La Brede, was always guest
of honor. "The ladies are invited to this banquet," said Henri. "The whole family
comes. We sit down about midday, a course is served about every hour, all day.
After dessert, about 5 P.M., there's a pause, *le trou de milieu*. In fact, they go off
to milk the cows and return to sit down again about 7 P.M., bringing with them
some more friends. Since they've also visited their own cellars, the ambience is
now getting very Beaujolais. Late into the night each one gets up to sing a song
or tell a story. I have my story to tell. You mustn't surprise them. They don't
appreciate a new story."

Granité of Beaujolais Nouveau

Granité au Beaujolais Nouveau

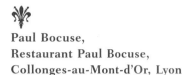

Paul Bocuse,
Restaurant Paul Bocuse,
Collonges-au-Mont-d'Or, Lyon

EVERY YEAR, GEORGES DUBOEUF INVITES ALL HIS WINEGROWERS, *some fifty or sixty of them, to celebrate the new harvest at a luncheon at Paul Bocuse's restaurant in Collonges. Imagine the stories told, the Beaujolais poured, and always, this next recipe for the moment of pause.*

When I was with Pan Am, I flew a dozen of them to New York for a Wine Summit at Windows On The World. The oldest of them, Johannes Papillon, at the pause in the dinner, looked out of the windows at New York by night, at his feet far below him, and exclaimed, "See! the stars are dancing!"

SERVES 6 TO 8

1 bottle Beaujolais Nouveau wine

1/2 bottle Evian mountain spring water

2 tablespoons sugar

1 cup crème de cassis

Pour the wine and water into a large, deep bowl, adding and stirring in the sugar and *crème de cassis*. Place in the freezer for one or two hours, stirring the liquid frequently with a wooden spoon to obtain a snow-like consistency.

When ready to serve, spoon out into goblets or individual bowls.

* *Preferably use a mountain spring water like Evian or Volvic to avoid the chlorine in tap water.*

* *Serve between the fish and meat course or after the meat course.*

* *Crème de cassis is as old as the hills, though commercially popular in France only since 1841. As mayor of Dijon in Burgundy, the late Canon Kir made it fashionable in the sixties by creating a drink named Kir—dry white wine with a spoonful of this sweet liqueur made from black currants. Crème de cassis is to be found in wine stores among the liqueurs. A syrup that is a nonalcholic version is to be found in gourmet stores, but this recipe and true kirs call for the liqueur, crème de cassis. (See page 301.)*

Cheeses

FRANCE HAS OVER 350 DIFFERENT CHEESES produced from cow's or goat's milk. Each region has several cheeses and each cheese has its season when it tastes best. Among the best known are Camembert, Boursin, Brillat-Savarin, Pont-l'Eveque, Livarot (from Normandie); Munster (from Alsace); Bleu de Bresse (Bresse); St. Marcellin (Dauphiné); Tomme, Beaufort, Reblochon, Vacherin (Savoie); Cantal, Bleu d'Auvergne, Fourme, Roquefort, St. Nectaire (Auvergne); St. Paulain (Anjou); and Brie, Explorateur, Fontainebleau (Ile-de-France).

Paul introduced me to Madame Renée Richard. Roger Vergé on the Côte d'Azur introduced me to the Ceneri family with their cheese store and cellars for ripening their cheeses, in the back streets of Cannes. Robert Ceneri and his son are kings in their Aladdin's cave of shelves and shelves of ripening farmhouse cheeses, and Madame Ceneri who runs the store, became like family for me when I was working on Pan Am's Nice to New York first-class menu. "What is your budget?" Robert asked me. For the next three years, twice a week, he drove his car to Nice airport with a half a dozen trays, laid out with five or six of the finest, ripe cheeses of France. Every day, our passengers, the crew, pilots, and captain flew to New York delighted. Word got out, and some passengers would ask for just a glass of wine and the cheeses—all for the same budget cost as the mediocre cheeses supplied on other routes. I was even able to upgrade economy class to a slice of Beaufort. The joys of cheeses from France.

St. Marcellin Cheese, le Fromage St. Marcellin
The Mère Renée Richard, Les Halles Market, Lyon

This is soft cow's milk cheese that Madame Renée brings to the market from her friends in farms up in the hills of the Isère region that runs alongside the French Alps. Industrially produced, St. Marcellin is made with pasteurized milk and available all year round; hers is made of raw unpasteurized milk, *lait cru*, milk that only keeps twenty-four hours in the refrigerator, and has a natural fermentation and ripening. The first true St. Marcellins arrive mid-February and the season ends late November.

King Louis XI of France served St. Marcellin as the royal favorite at his table in the Palace of Versailles. It was the one cheese Fernand Point served at La Pyramide, as Paul does today at Collonges and in his three brasseries—"*Saint Marcellin Mère Richard*," the label says—"*half 19 Frs whole 28 Frs.*"

You will find it at Patrick Henriroux's La Pyramide, at the Mère Brazier's, at Jean-Paul Lacombe's Leon de Lyon, at Pierre Orsi, and of course, if you visit the Mère Richard and her daughter in the Lyon market hall. But, sadly, beyond Lyon, even in Paris, you may find only the St. Marcellin made from pasteurised cow's milk.

Madame Renée recommends a bottle of Beaujolais, Côtes du Rhône, or a fruity white Condrieu to go with her cheese.

Cheese Soufflé

Soufflé de Fromage

**Paul Bocuse,
Brasserie L'Est,
Lyon**

MANY RECIPES BY THE CHEFS *conclude with "serve without delay," "must be served very hot, on hot plates," or "serve immediately to the guests who have been waiting for it." Fernand Point, never one to mince words, said it best, "The* grande cuisine *does not wait for the customer."*

Piping hot soufflés are the speciality of the newest of Paul's brasseries, and the menu advises "Our soufflés require fifteen minutes to cook so to avoid waiting, please order yours at the start of the meal."

SERVES 4

Béchamel sauce

1¹/₂ tablespoons plus 1 teaspoon
　　unsalted butter
2 tablespoons all-purpose flour
1 cup warm whole milk
1 cup water

Soufflé

3 egg whites
4 egg yolks
1¹/₄ ounces freshly grated
　　Gruyère cheese
Salt and freshly ground pepper
　　to taste
Pinch freshly grated nutmeg

Preheat the oven to 360°F. Butter a soufflé mold or baking dish.

To make the béchamel sauce, heat the butter in a large saucepan over low heat. Add the flour, stirring constantly with a wooden spoon. When the mixture starts to stiffen into a froth, without letting it color, stir in some warm milk with the water added. Cook for 5 or 6 minutes, continuing to stir. Remove from the heat and add a pinch of salt.

To make the soufflé, in a mixing bowl using an electric beater, beat the egg whites until firm. Put the egg yolks into a separate bowl and add the grated cheese, salt, pepper, and nutmeg and whisk lightly. Using a spatula, carefully fold the mixture into the egg whites.

Fill the baking dish three-quarters full with the mixture. Place in the part of the oven at lowest heat so that it does not encrust too rapidly.

Cook for 20 minutes, or until the top takes on a golden brown color. Serve immediately.

CANTAL CHEESE, *LE FROMAGE CANTAL*
MARGARIDOU, AUVERGNE

Cantal is a country cheese from the Auvergne region, where the hillsides of the Massif Central are also the grazing grounds for Salers cows that are, along with neighboring Charolais, the best beef in France.

"We Parisians like these cheeses a little aged," a distinguished cheese purveyor in Paris once told me, "when they are six months or even a year old and a little *piquant*. The locals in Auvergne eat them at 3 months old when the crust is still thin and has that soft, milky taste."

Margaridou defends the Cantal in her journal. "It is the richest and one of the most healthy of cheeses. Doctors prescribe it in diets. There are as many different Cantals as there are grazing pastures around here. A good Cantal should be neither fermented nor piquant. It has a light taste of hazelnuts and gentiane, echoes of the mountains. Yes, it is a big peasant, *un gros paysan*."

Cantal can replace Gruyère or Emmenthal in many dishes: Gratinée Soup, Potato or Macaroni Gratin, Cheese Tart, and Croque-Monsieur or Croque-Madame.

A Côte du Rhône, Côte Rotie, or a Loire Valley rosé wine go well with this cheese.

Bread

For every recipe so far in this book on French chefs cooking, I must add Bread. For all the soups, eggs, fish, meat, poultry, game, vegetables, pastas, cheeses, you need bread on the table . The only exception is desserts.

In France, people buy bread fresh every day. In America, it is easy to take bread for granted. Mass-produced bread is on the scale of mass-produced cars, while bread from the little baker on the corner who works through the night to produce the morning loaves has gone the way of other small corner stores. Since the last century, American and Canadian big granaries producing strong flour, gaining the English market, too, largely replaced the soft flour that produced finer, tastier bread but did not have "long shelf-life." All-purpose flour is bleached, scientifically homogenized, sucked of natural qualities, replaced with preservatives, and tasteless.

"White is not the normal color of wheat flour; it is obtained by artificial bleaching," wrote Elizabeth David, the highly respected English post-World War II food writer in her classic, *English Bread and Yeast Cookery* in 1977.

Bread has been the "staff of life" of every nation for centuries. Once it was made at home by every family. Or as it still happens in a little village in France in Provence, once a month a batch of bread is baked for the community.

The flour was stone-ground by artisan millers. Paul Bocuse's ancestors were millers. They became restaurateurs and cooks while waiting for their customers' grain to be ground into flour.

The good news today is that there is a return of the artisan—manual workers, Paul calls himself and his chef colleagues. People are looking for authentic bread that was once the work of some artisans called bakers.

The chefs in this book are flagbearers for natural quality. They go to the market every day, early, to get the freshest and the best. They await the seasons and celebrate each year's arrival of the new crop by rewriting their menu. They choose the best artisan baker in town. Or more and more of them make their own daily bread. The best cooking schools in America, like the French Culinary Institute and the Culinary Institute of America, include bread-making as a major part of a student-chef's curriculum today.

I have chosen one bread recipe. It calls for one flour—stone-ground whole wheat flour. This is bread from natural flour; no white or all-purpose flour need be added. This is the flour recommended to us by Lionel Poilane, the most distinguished name in bakers in the world. The flour used to make whole wheat bread by the leading artisan bakers across America today.

"Stone ground whole wheat flour, nothing else, was what we used in our village," says the baker Michel Peden of Le Croissant Shop, who makes bread for many of the leading restaurants of New York—Celebrités, Bernardin, Lespinasse, Absinthe, Acacia, Caravelle, Lenox Room and others. He comes from Brittany where, he recalls, "We had a stone bread oven in our home, I remember, as a child." Steve Sullivan of Acme Bread in Berkeley, one time chef at Alice Waters' Chez Panisse, where some of the great chefs of France sent their sons to apprentice, told me he was inspired to be a baker on reading Elizabeth David's *Bread* and knows her whole wheat recipe by heart. Just as Amy Scherber of Amy's Bread in New York was inspired by Lionel Poilane. For a list of artisan whole wheat producers, see page 300.

Join the return of the bread that is natural, full-bodied, full of flavor, and certainly, a little rustic French on the side.

A Simple Wheat Bread

Un Simple Pain de Blé

Adapted from Lionel Poilane
Boulangerie Poilane,
Paris

MASTER BAKER OF PARIS, LIONEL POILANE *has his centuries-old ovens in the basement of his bakery on the rue Cherche-Midi. In the days of Pan Am, Paul Bocuse used to arrive with a large carton under his arm of Lionel's pain de campagne for me. Cutting it in half, I would put half away in the freezer.*

When I first lived in Paris in the fifties, in the hotel of the rue Dragon, on Christmas morning we took our turkey up the street to the friendly Poilane bakery in the rue Cherche-Midi to roast after they had finished baking. I remember the smell of roast turkey escaping from the covered casserole we carried back from the boulangerie run by Lionel's father and mother.

I called up Lionel and asked him if we could have the recipe for the pain de campagne. "Michel, yes, but it is a question of quantity. Would you cook a choucroute for two people?"

Lionel decided at the age 15 to learn the profession under his father's head baker. He worked years night after night, stripped to the waist, kneading dough, loading the red hot ovens, pulling out the finished loaves.

The great French actor Raimu in Marcel Pagnol's film, The Baker's Wife (La Femme du Boulanger, 1932) said it all when in the final scene his runaway wife returned and together they relit the oven. "Excuse me, cherie, I don't know why, but lighting the oven always brings tears to my eyes."

Based on all I have gleaned from Lionel over the years, respecting this great artist of breadmaking, here is one of his first steps in breadmaking I have adapted for our kitchen in the countryside, with bread enough for us and our neighbors.

1 teaspoon dry yeast

3 cups of Evian or Volvic natural spring water, about half a 1.5 liter bottle

3 pounds stone-ground whole wheat flour

3 large pinches sea salt

One day ahead, store all the ingredients at 75° to 80°F.

Dissolve the yeast in 1 cup barely warmed spring water. In a warmed bowl, hand knead half the flour with up to half the Evian water. Make a well in the flour and knead, adding enough water to make a smooth dough. (Bakers call this dough the "poolish," *poolisch* in French, as it was first developed in Poland in the 1840s.)

Set the dough in the mixing bowl, covered with clean cheesecloth or kitchen towel, to rest for 3 hours in a 78° to 80°F room, away from drafts of cold air. The dough should rise to double or triple in size, but watch it. As soon as the rising stops and the dough starts to dip down, changes into a concave shape, you know it is ready.

Immediately add the remaining flour and the sea salt. Knead again with your hands until you have a homogeneous dough. If it seems a little dry, add more water; if too soft, add some flour. Let it rest, covered with the clean cheesecloth, for 2 to $2^{1}/_{2}$ hours in the same 78° to 80°F room. After 1 hour, or about halfway through the second rising, take the dough and lightly knead and turn it. Michel Peden recommends this to give a little fresh air inside the dough. Replace it in the bowl to finish resting, covered.

At the end of this time, divide the dough into roughly round, square, or long shapes, and let rest for 20 minutes. Then comes the final hand shaping into the loaves. Sprinkle one or more baking tins with flour and place the loaves in the pans and let rest for 2 to $2^{1}/2$ hours more. Depending on the room temperature and the humidity, they will rise one-third to one-quarter more.

Preheat oven from 420° to 430°F, the same temperature for roasting a chicken. The oven must reach and heat at the temperature for at least 20 minutes, Michel stresses. This is the moment to "slash" the loaves several times with a sharp knife or razor, to permit the steam to escape during baking. Put the loaves in the oven. Baking time depends on the oven, the dough, and so much more, but when the loaves sound hollow when tapped on the bottom you know the bread is done. Set the loaves aside to cool on a rack.

❄ Just before placing the loaves in the oven, spray the oven with a little water. In Michel's village, they didn't have sprays. They placed a small, empty cast iron pot in the oven when they heated the oven. Just before they put the loaves in, cold water was ladled into the iron pot and water sprayed over the inside of the oven, producing the necessary humidity.

❄ Stone-ground whole wheat flour is the natural flour that contains all the nutrients in wheat that our ancestors made bread, until the big graneries of America and Canada brought in mass-produced, "enriched" white flour that took over the market. The distinguished health editor of The New York Times, Jane Brody, in her Good Food Book, described by Pierre Franey as "A great American cookbook," wrote, "The history of wheat is marked by the bad pushing out the good...Unfortunately, 80 percent of the wheat Americans now consume (a total of 150 pounds per capita per year) is refined—stripped of bran and germ and most of its valuable nutrients."

❄ For some small, good-quality producers of stone-ground whole wheat flour in America, see page 300. Unless your store has just received a new supply of flour, you will have a fresher batch of flour when it is shipped to you as you need it, directly from the mill.

❄ If you wish to make a lighter whole wheat bread, Michel recommends using 60 to 55 percent of the stone ground whole wheat flour and 40 to 45 percent nonbleached, nonenrichened, 100 percent white whole wheat.

❄ The famous Poilane miche de campagne loaf, baked in Paris, is now being flown into New York once a week, on Thursdays and can be shipped overnight. (See page 301.) It is about $35 a loaf, but it can be cut in half and frozen in your refrigerator. Don't miss the taste of bread.

Some words from Lionel Poilane:

☀ *Never hesitate to make your own bread—it can hardly be worse than some of the bread being sold as bread today.*

☀ *For centuries mothers made the family bread in the French countryside.*

☀ *Making your own bread strikes mysterious chords within us, bringing with it a sense of deep-bedded prehistoric physical satisfaction.*

☀ *The more bread you make at a time, the better your bread will be.*

☀ *Making bread is a serious affair: Make a supply for 10 to 15 days, for your family and for your neighbors. (For anything beyond a couple of days, store in the freezer.)*

☀ *In Jeannie's cottage in Pennsylvania, for our bread, we have spring water coming from back beyond the woods. Water from a spring, Lionel in Paris and Margaridou in Auvergne tell us, is the purest of all.*

Chapter Ten

Desserts

THE GRAND DESSERT TROISGROS

JEAN AND PIERRE TROISGROS, ROANNE

APPLE TART

PAUL BOCUSE, COLLONGES-AU-MONT-D'OR, LYON

WINE TART

JEAN-PAUL LACOMBE, LYON

PEARS IN BEAUJOLAIS

PAUL BOCUSE, COLLONGES-AU-MONT-D'OR, LYON

ICED MERINGUES

ALAIN CHAPEL, MIONNAY

MERINGUE HEARTS OF PASSION FRUIT

PIERRE TROISGROS, ROANNE

CHOCOLATE TRUFFLES

MAURICE AND JEAN-JACQUES BERNACHON, LYON

BITTER CHOCOLATE MOUSSE

ROGER VERGÉ, CÔTE D'AZUR

CHOCOLATE GÂTEAU ST. ELYSÉE

GEORGES PERRIER, PHILADELPHIA

CARAMEL BRULÉE, SIRIO

SIRIO MACCIONI, NEW YORK

CANDIED PINK GRAPEFRUIT

ALAIN CHAPEL, MIONNAY

CUSTARD CREAM

PAUL BOCUSE, COLLONGES-AU-MONT-D'OR, LYON

The Grand Dessert Troisgros

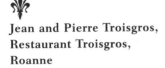

Jean and Pierre Troisgros,
Restaurant Troisgros,
Roanne

AMONG THE RECIPES THAT JEAN TROISGROS SENT ME *for chef Jean Laffont to look over before he and Pierre arrived for the last of my Great Chefs' dinners at Oz Restaurant in Dallas in the seventies was their grand finale,* Le Grand Dessert Troisgros.

"Cher ami, *this is not one single dish," Jean wrote me, "but an array of sweets, cakes, poached fruit, petit fours."*

Here are his directions:

"You compose an ensemble in various colors of poached fruit: half a pear, half a peach, strawberries, wild strawberries, raspberries, slices of orange, pineapple, cooked apricots, and figs, and other fruits available in winter, on one large plate.

"In the center, place a vanilla ice cream and a sorbet, covered with raspberry juice, and if you like, some heavy cream.

"On another plate, place a choice of small cakes like tarts, chocolate gâteaux, perhaps offer some peaches in wine, floating islands, chilled melon, and to accompany it all, make some petits fours."

This was how they presented their dessert in Roanne. At Paul's in Collonges, after the cheese course, the waiter wheels across to your table a cart of silver tubs filled with diverse fresh fruits, joined by a cart of cakes, tarts, and puddings, followed by a third cart of sauces, creams, and the *crème à l'anglaise.* Les twenty-one desserts de Paul Bocuse requires no translation.

The eleven desserts that follow are sufficient in themselves, served individually, one dessert a meal. You do not have a half-dozen young chefs working alongside you in your kitchen to produce all eleven at once.

However, one day, you might venture into assembling some of them into an array of desserts, une dégustation, a tasting on a large dinner plate for each guest. An assortment of colors, as Jean saw them.

As they say in Lyon, "Bon appétit! Bon soif!"

Which Wines to Serve with Desserts?

Cookbooks used to recommend sweet wines with what they called sweets or desserts, in particular the sweetest of all, the Sauternes from Bordeaux. Sweet on top of sweet is overloading. "Sauternes go perfectly with foie gras," says Jean-Pierre Haeberlin. Twenty years ago, Comte Alexandre de Lur-Saluces, owner and winemaker of the greatest sweet white wine in the world, Château d'Yquem of Sauternes, left the dining room when, at a dinner given in his honor by a wine and food society, they served his wine with a chocolate dessert. No wine goes well with chocolate.

The *Grand Dessert Troisgros* calls for one more wine, but served at the end of the meal. Champagne. "In the old days, in France, we used to open a bottle, after the coffee," said Prince Alain de Polignac, the winemaker at his family's house, Pommery.

I am just back from a week in St. Petersburg, where champagne was the drink of the czars for more than 100 years. I watched the Kirov dancing Prokofiev's *Romeo and Juliet* in the gold and blue Marinsky Theatre, and knew this was the place for champagne. In 1909 the Marinsky ballerina Kschessinska invited the other great dancers—Pavlova, Karsavina, Trefilova, and Preobrajenska—to join her in a *grand pas de deux* before the Czar. After the performance, Kschessinska took all the *premieres danseuses* for supper in St. Petersburg's finest restaurant. "When coffee had been served," she wrote in her memoir, *Dancing in Petersburg*, "the men were allowed to sit at our table and I offered them champagne." Surely a great champagne, like Clicquot's Grande Dame or Pommery's Louise, named after two of the legendary great ladies of Champagne.

Apple Tart

Tarte aux Pommes

**Paul Bocuse,
Restaurant Paul Bocuse,
Collonges-au-Mont-d'Or, Lyon**

IT GOES WITHOUT SAYING THIS APPLE TART RECIPE *comes from the same Bocuse family orchard and kitchen, as their compote of apples (see page xv).*

SERVES 6

4 tablespoons butter

5 cups all-purpose flour

Pinch salt

1/2 cup water

2 pounds Granny Smith apples

1/2 cup sugar

Blackcurrant, gooseberry, strawberry, or apricot jam or preserves

Preheat oven to low heat.

Remove the butter from the refrigerator an hour before use.

Put the flour into a large mixing bowl and add the salt. Work in the butter with your hands, and add the 1/2 cup water. Gently knead the dough with your hands so that all the ingredients mix in perfectly. If the dough sticks to your fingers, add a little more flour. Working the flour, butter, and water together ensures the pastry will be crumbly and taste of butter rather than flour.

Once the dough has a certain consistency, but not too firm, place it on the pastry table or board to rest for about an hour, covered with a clean kitchen cloth. Just before preparing the apples, warm the dough in the oven. Test the dough to determine its warmth.

Peel and core the apples and cut into slices the size of a silver dollar.

Remove the dough from the oven. Increase the temperature to 375°F. Grease and flour a 12-inch flan dish.

Gather the dough into a ball. Roll it out 1/4 inch thick about 12 inches round and carefully lay the dough into the flan dish. Fold excess dough over the edge and trim it with a knife. Prick the bottom of the dough several times with a fork. Place the apple slices in a flower formation on the dough, partially over-lapping, and sprinkle with sugar.

Bake for 35 to 40 minutes, checking from time to time. Remove the apple tart from the oven and glaze according to taste with jam or with preserved fruit, while still warm.

❈ *Fresh heavy cream,* crème fraîche, *or English custard in a bowl goes well with apple tart, served on the side.*

❈ *For a dinner party, you might try a dégustation of apple tarts made from different apples. A slice from each tart, and that cream!*

Wine Tart

Tarte au Vin

Jean-Paul Lacombe,
Restaurant Leon de Lyon,
Lyon

WHEN THE G7 HEADS OF STATE *held their 1996 meeting in Lyon, Paul Bocuse gave a cooking lesson to their wives in the morning, and they dined that evening chez Jean-Paul Lacombe with this* tarte au vin *on the menu.*

SERVES 4

Dough

1 pound sifted all-purpose flour
2/3 cup granulated sugar
14 tablespoons (1 1/2 sticks plus
    2 tablespoons) butter
1/2 cup cold water

Tart

4 tablespoons (1/2 stick) butter
4 tablespoons granulated sugar
4 apples, unpeeled,
    cut in small pieces
8 tablespoons *crème de cassis*
    (see note)
1 bottle Beaujolais wine
4 teaspoons all-purpose flour

To prepare the dough, place the flour and sugar in a bowl. Rub in the butter with the fingertips, taking care not to work the dough too much. Make a well in the center of the mixture, pour in 1/2 cup of cold water, and blend it into the mixture with the fingers until it is moistened. Knead it twice and set aside in a cool place for at least 30 minutes.

Preheat the oven to 325°F.

To prepare the tart, heat the butter in a saucepan over low heat, add the sugar and the apple. When the pieces of apple are caramelized and golden, add the *crème de cassis* and continue to cook over low heat for 5 minutes more so that they turn into a compote.

Pour the wine into the compote and stir in. Bring the compote to a boil over a high heat and reduce by three-quarters. Remove from the heat and stir into the flour. Cook for 2 minutes more. Put through a fine-mesh sieve and set aside.

Line 4 flan rings with the dough, forming a crest around the edge and pricking the bottom of each ring. Cut 4 circles of parchment paper slightly larger in diameter than the rings, and place one on each ring. Cover the paper with dried beans or pie weights to add weight.

Bake the rings in the oven for 20 minutes. The surface of the tart should be golden.

Remove flan rings from the oven and remove the beans and parchment paper. Spoon the Beaujolais compote onto the rings and return to the preheated oven for another 2 minutes before serving.

✳ *Jean-Paul recommends cooking the tarts at the last moment so that the pastry is crunchy and the dish retains all its aroma.*

✳ Crème de cassis: *There are two, one from Alsace by Massenet, the other by Faively in Burgundy. (See page 301.)*

✳ *If you wish to serve champagne after this dessert, if you have seven world leaders coming to dinner, there are some lovely light* rosé *champagnes by Clicquot, Pommery, Bollinger, Henriot, Krug, Möet & Chandon, Pol Roger, Perrier-Jouet, Taittinger, Laurent-Perrier, Roederer, Mumm, and others. They should all be drunk young.*

Pears in Beaujolais

Poires à la Beaujolaise

Paul Bocuse,
Restaurant Paul Bocuse,
Collonges-au-Mont-d'Or, Lyon

SERVES 4

4 medium pears, peeled,
  with stems left on

1 bottle Beaujolais wine

1/2 cup sugar

Juice 1/2 orange
  and 1/2 lemon

2 black peppercorns

1 whole clove

4 tablespoons *crème de cassis*
  (see page 301)

One day ahead, place the pears, standing upright, in a large, deep saucepan. Pour in the wine. Add the sugar, orange and lemon juice, peppercorns, clove, and *crème de cassis*. Bring to a boil, cover, and cook for 15 minutes.

Remove the pears with a slotted spoon to a serving dish. Pour the syrup in the saucepan over the pears and set aside. From time to time, baste the pears with the syrup. When cool, place in the refrigerator. Baste before serving next day. Serve cold.

❋ *This dish may be prepared the same day, some hours before serving. But it tastes best, prepared 24 hours in advance.*

Iced Meringues

Meringues Glacees

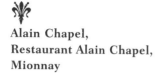

Alain Chapel,
Restaurant Alain Chapel,
Mionnay

HIS RESTAURANT STANDS ON A BEND OF A LONELY ROAD *thirty miles north of Lyon. In January, in this countryside of small lakes, it looms out of the mist like an oasis in the desert. Alain was delighted to fly to Dallas for my series of Great Chefs' dinners and promised to bring Burgundy's grand old man of the wines of Chassagne-Montrachet, Pierre Ramonet.*

We waited weeks for Monsieur Ramonet to receive his passport. Finally, I called his house and Madame Ramonet answered the phone. "Monsieur Ramonet is in the cellar. Non, monsieur, he cannot come up to talk to you. And monsieur, he'll not be going to America." She was adamant. So his son André was allowed to fly to Dallas, his first time in a plane, but it was Pierre Ramonet who chose the Chassagne-Montrachets for Alain's dinner.

The Chapel cuisine was a new experience for Dallas. After the dinner, Alain said to me, "Whenever you have a ticket for America, call me, I'll fly over." But he died of a heart attack in 1989.

Today his wife, Suzanne, is in charge at Mionnay. Philippe Jousse, Alain's second-in-command, is in the kitchen. Suzanne sent me two recipes (see also page 277), writing, "I know Alain would like you to have these."

SERVES 4

1 cup egg whites
2/3 cup confectioners' sugar

Vanilla ice cream

2 cups whole milk
3 vanilla beans
1/2 cup granulated sugar
5 egg yolks
1/2 cup light cream

Preheat the oven to 300°F.

Beat the egg whites in a mixing bowl (copper, if possible), and slowly add the confectioners' sugar. Spoon the whipped egg whites into a pastry bag.

Form the meringues by squeezing the egg-white mixture onto a baking sheet, each about 1 to 1 1/2 inches long. Sprinkle them with confectioners' sugar and wait 10 minutes, then sprinkle them again and wait. Remove any excess sugar. Put them in the oven and bake for about 45 minutes. Cool them and put them in an airtight storage container.

To prepare the vanilla ice cream, heat the milk. Split the vanilla beans and infuse them in the saucepan of hot milk and cook over medium heat for 15 minutes. Mix the sugar and the egg yolks in a bowl and beat with a wooden spoon until the mixture becomes thick and creamy and almost white, like a custard, *sauce anglaise*. Pour the sugar-egg mixture into a saucepan. Slowly add the milk over a gentle heat. Better still, use a double boiler, stirring constantly so the eggs do not not stick on the pan sides. It must not boil.

As the egg yolks warm and thicken, and coat the back of a spoon, remove from the heat and pass it through a fine-mesh sieve and pour it over the cream. Freeze in an ice cream freezer following manufacturer's instructions, or let it chill in the freezer and then whip it in a blender.

Put the ice cream in a pastry bag, and pipe some on the bottom of one meringue or carefully spoon it on. Cover it with another meringue to make a small sandwich with the ice cream in the center. Repeat for four iced meringues. Serve immediately.

✲ *The chefs use a copper bowl for mixing as it gives a little acidity to the egg white, preventing it from separating. If you do not have a copper bowl, Hervé advises, add a dash of lemon juice or a pinch of salt before starting to mix the eggs. Do not use a copper bowl to mix egg yolks.*

✲ *Confectioners' sugar, also known as icing sugar in restaurant kitchens, is the finely milled sugar used for dusting, decorating, or icing cakes.*

✲ *Chefs use pastry bags. "There are disposable pastry bags," recommends Hervé, "but a spoon can do the job well, carefully so as not to break the meringue. I must warn though, never, never, touch ice cream with the hands. There is always the risk of germs."*

Meringue Hearts of Passion Fruit

Il Passiflor

**Pierre Troisgros,
Restaurant Troisgros,
Roanne**

SOME MONTHS AFTER JEAN TROISGROS'S DEATH, *I was able to fly Pierre and his family down to Rio for a weekend of Pan Am gala dinners in his son Claude's restaurant. Pierre, Michel, and Claude cooked in the small kitchen and their wives, Olympe, Marie-Laure, and Marlene, were out front of the house greeting guests. On the Sunday, Claude's friend the bishop of Baja flew down to baptize Claude's first child and celebrate Michel's engagement to Marie-Laure. Today Pierre sends me this souvenir of Brazil and its passion fruit, O passiflor!*

SERVES 8

15 passion fruit
Sugar (see note)

Meringue

4 egg whites
2/3 cup confectioners' sugar
2/3 cup superfine sugar
    or caster sugar

**Pastry cream
(*crème patisserie*)**

6 tablespoons fine sugar
    or caster sugar
3 egg yolks
1/4 cup all-purpose flour

Preheat the oven to 212°F.

Open up the passion fruit and empty their pulp into a pan. Add sugar to balance the acidity of the fruit and set them over medium heat until they start to bubble. The pulp will thicken slightly. Remove and set aside.

To make the meringues, beat together the egg whites and sugars and continue to whisk them over low heat until the temperature reaches 140°F, measuring with a cooking thermometer. Set aside and continue beating the mixture until it is completely cold and very firm.

Butter lightly a sheet of aluminum foil and cut out 8 round shapes, 4 inches in diameter. Around the circles spread small petals of meringue using a pastry bag, finishing with a stem and some leaves. Heat in the oven for 1 hour.

To make the pastry cream, *crème patisserie,* beat the sugar and egg yolks in a small saucepan until they become white. Add the flour and blend with a whisk. In another saucepan, bring the milk to a boil with the vanilla bean and pour slowly into the other saucepan, bringing the mixture to a boil for several minutes, stirring constantly so it does not catch on the bottom. Pour into a bowl to cool into a thick paste.

To prepare the light cream, beat up the light cream with a whisk into a whipped chantilly cream (see page 10) and add it to the cold pastry cream. When ready to serve, place a meringue on each of the 8 plates. Garnish the heart of each meringue with the pastry cream and spoon over it the pulp of the passion fruit.

2 cups milk

1 vanilla bean, cut in half

8 tablespoons light cream

❉ *Sugar: You add a little sugar at a time and taste to see when you have balanced the acidity. Taste again, the only way to know "how much" sugar.*

Chocolate Truffles

Les Truffes au Chocolat

**Maurice and Jean-Jacques Bernachon,
Maison Bernachon,
Lyon**

"I MADE MY FIRST CHOCOLATE TRUFFLES ON DECEMBER 25, 1934," *Maurice Bernachon recalled.
"Apprenticed at fourteen years old, son of a railway signalman, chocolate was a luxury for me."*

*Today he is the finest chocolate maker in Lyon, one of the few in the world who insists on buying
his own beans, making his own blends and roasting the beans himself. "I import my beans from South
America, the best come from the middle of the jungle in Ecuador," he said, dropping his hand lovingly
into one of the sacks at the back of his store to bring out a handful. His almonds are from Spain,
vanilla beans from the island of Reunion, pistachios from Sicily, hazelnuts from the Piedmont,
while his cream and butter are from Echiré in Charentes and Isigny in Normandy.*

This traditionalist has no time for the nouvelle cuisine, *such as chocolate with thyme or rosewater
or spinach, of some colleagues. "Ridiculous," he storms. "When you have beans of such fine quality,
what more do you need? Would you dare to change the taste of Petrus or Yquem?"*

*Paul Bocuse (whose daughter, Jeanne, is married to Maurice's son Jean-Jacques), walks through
the Bernachon kitchen, dipping his fingers in each vat of chocolate and tasting as if he was at home
in the kitchen at Collonges.*

*Last year, at seventy-nine years old, having spent sixty-three years as chocolate maker without a
Sunday or holiday off, Maurice decided to hand over the house of Bernachon to Jean-Jacques.*

"Once chocolate was a luxury," Maurice concluded. "Today all the world eats chocolate."

FOR 70 TRUFFLES

1 pound extra heavy cream
    or *crème fraîche*

1 pound, 3¹/₂ ounces or 1 pound,
    3¹/₂ squares cooking
    chocolate or bittersweet
    chocolate (squares or bar)

³/₄ cup confectioners' sugar

7 squares bitter chocolate

8 ounces or 8 squares
    unsweetened or
    powdered bitter cocoa

One day ahead, put the heavy cream in a heavy
saucepan and cook over medium heat for 1 minute,
stirring constantly with a wire wisk. Remove the saucepan
from the heat.

Break the cooking chocolate into small pieces and add
to the saucepan of boiled cream while it is off the heat,
stirring continuously until the mixture is smooth. Cover
and refrigerate for at least 12 hours.

On the day, remove the saucepan from the refrigerator and slowly warm it over boiling water at 122°F, measured with a cooking thermometer, until the paste softens. Using a spoon or pastry bag, shape into small chocolate balls and roll them in the confectioners' sugar, at the same time rolling them into a ball in the palm of the hand.

Break the bitter chocolate into small pieces and melt them slowly over boiling water at 122°F. Drop the chocolate balls into this melted bitter chocolate and remove each one with a fork. Put them onto a plate. Roll them in the cocoa powder. Remove any excess cocoa by shaking the balls in a wire sieve.

※ *It is important your hands should not be warm while handling the truffles. Whenever the hands feel warm, run them under cold water and dry.*

※ *A cooking thermometer is indispensable when working with chocolate. (See page 297.)*

※ *Selection of chocolate: If you visit Lyon, definitely bring back some chocolate from the Bernachon store. Otherwise, Jean-Jacques Bernachon advises, "Buy the best quality you can find."*

※ *Warning: The European Common Market (EEC) recently passed a law permitting 5 percent vegetable fat to replace the cocoa butter used traditionally in chocolate. Some countries permit flour. "They will replace everything," say the Bernachons, "and you'll get industrial chocolate." Or as chef Raymond Oliver once said about nouvelle cuisine, "Put in muck and out comes muck."*

Bitter Chocolate Mousse

Mousse au Chocolat Amer

Roger Vergé,
Restaurant Le Moulin de Mougins,
Côte d'Azur

MAISON PRUNIER IN ST. JAMES STREET IN LONDON *was my first big dining experience. My grandmother knew Madame Prunier, daughter of the celebrated Paris restaurateur, who came and sat with us at the end of the meal. I remember her saying, "You can judge a restaurant by its salad dressing and its chocolate mousse."*

In Madame Prunier's Fish Cookbook, her pre-World War II recipe for mousse au chocolat *serves 10 people. I've adapted it to serve 5: Melt ¹/₂ pound chocolate and ¹/₂ cup heavy cream in a little milk over a low heat and leave to cool. Heat 1¹/₂ pint of light corn syrup on a very low heat, stir in 8 egg yolks, then place saucepan in a double boiler, taking care not to boil, and whip in 1 cup of heavy cream. As it starts to thicken, remove from heat and allow to finish thickening. When cold, place in the refrigerator.*

My grandmother Winifred Buller made chocolate mousse on her Aga cooker, the most well-tempered, desirable of ovens. She was the first English female professional pilot in 1911, learning to fly in France under under Breguet, as well as a spy for the Foreign Office and friend of Czechoslovakia's President Masaryk. She lived between the wars in Nice and learned her chocolate mousse from the Emperor Joseph of Austria's chef, who had retired there. In the eighties I lived in Nice, working with Roger Vergé creating Pan Am's First Class menu. Here is his chocolate mousse.

SERVES 5

4¹/₂ ounces (4¹/₂ squares) bitter chocolate, broken in pieces

3 generous tablespoons very strong hot black coffee

1 generous tablespoon unsweetened cocoa powder

¹/₂ lemon

Put the chocolate pieces, the hot black coffee, and cocoa powder in a large bowl.

Place the bowl in a double boiler or large saucepan and slowly heat to melt the chocolate. When melted, stir the mixture well so it is smoothly blended. Remove the bowl from the saucepan and set aside.

Using a very clean bowl, rub the insides with the ¹/₂ lemon, rinsing it under cold water and drying. Add the egg whites with a pinch of salt and whisk until they resemble soft peaks of light snow. Add the sugar and continue to whisk until the egg whites are quite dry and very firm.

Using the whisk, incorporate a quarter of the egg white mixture into the warm chocolate mixture. Using a spatula and not a whisk, fold in the remaining egg whites carefully to prevent deflating. Transfer the mousse to a china bowl and refrigerate for an hour to chill.

8 egg whites, at room temperature
Pinch salt
4 tablespoons superfine sugar

✻ *Bernard Duclos of Valrhona Chocolat recommended the Caraque 56 percent Cacao. (See page 301.)*

✻ *This light, slightly sweetened mousse should be eaten the same day.*

✻ *I can see Paul serving this chocolate mousse chez Roger and asking for some* crème fraîche. *Roger, who knows Paul, smiles and brings out the cream. A little more is a wonderful thing.*

Chocolate Gâteau St. Elysée

Gâteau St. Elysée

**Georges Perrier,
Le Bec Fin,
Philadelphia**

I HAD ONE QUESTION I NEEDED TO ASK ONE OF MY CHEFS. *Georges Perrier is from Lyon and often, when Paul Bocuse comes to America and assembles a gathering of chefs, Georges is there, so I ask him who is the man behind the name Paul Bocuse?*

"For me, Paul Bocuse is the great ambassador of cuisine in the world," replied Georges. *"Without him, the cuisine would not be where it is today. He's a grand prince of the cuisine. Above all, he's honest, has a lot of class, and knows how to receive those who come to him. He's very generous, very open, he's a monsieur, a grand monsieur. At the same time, there's a certain humility and simplicity about him. But his great talent, his genius, has been in recognising talent in other chefs, young chefs especially, and help them to move on."*

SERVES 6 TO 8

4 squares semisweet chocolate, Valrhona Chocolat Equatoriale 55 percent Cacao (see page 301)

2 cups butter

2 cups granulated sugar

4 eggs yolks

1 tablespoon flour

4 egg whites

1/2 cup cocoa or confectioner's sugar for dusting

Preheat the oven to 350°F. Butter and flour an 8-inch-round cake pan.

Heat the chocolate and butter together in a double boiler or heavy pot. Beat the sugar and egg yolks together. Combine these two mixtures in a bowl, and add the flour. Beat the egg whites until soft peaks form; do not beat until stiff; fold into above mixture.

Pour the mixture into the buttered and floured cake pan. Bake for 10 minutes in the oven at 350°F and then at 300°F for 20 minutes. Remove the cake from the oven. Let the cake cool slightly in the pan before removing.

Sprinkle the top with cocoa or powdered sugar before serving.

Caramel Brulée Sirio

Crème Brulée à la Cassonade, Sirio

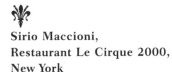

Sirio Maccioni,
Restaurant Le Cirque 2000,
New York

FOR AS LONG AS SIRIO MACCIONI HAS HAD A RESTAURANT IN NEW YORK, *first Le Cirque and now Le Cirque 2000, Paul has been dropping in for lunch when he is in town. Sirio visits Collonges, Paul visits Sirio's home in Italy. When Sirio celebrated Le Cirque's 15th anniversary in 1995, Paul flew in specially with Roger Vergé, Gerard Boyer, Alain Ducasse, Gaston Lenotre, and Roger Jaloux to cook the gala dinner organised by Marvin Shankin's* Wine Spectator *team in aid of the James Beard Foundation.*

Sirio's popular dessert, the caramel custard crème brulée à la cassonade Sirio, *is always on the menu. Sirio discovered this caramel custard in a restaurant in Spain. Paul asked Sirio for the recipe and put it on the menu at Collonges. Chefs across France heard about it and adopted it, though cassonade—raw crystallized sugar from the juice of the sugar cane—has long been part of Europe's culinary history, in civets of hare and tarts.*

SERVES 6

2 cups heavy cream or
    crème fraîche
Half a vanilla bean, scraped
1/3 cup granulated sugar
4 egg yolks
1/3 cup brown sugar

Preheat to 300°F.

Warm the heavy cream in a double boiler over hot water with the vanilla bean. Mix the granulated sugar and egg yolks together. Remove the vanilla bean and pour the cream into the sugar and yolk mixture and stir carefully with a wooden spoon.

Fill six 1 1/2-ounce molds and set them in a baking pan with water half way up the sides of the molds.

Bake for 30 minutes, or until they are set in the center of the mold. Remove and cool for 30 minutes.

Shake the brown sugar through a sieve to eliminate lumps. Sprinkle a thin even layer over the tops of the custards. Glaze for a few seconds under the broiler or a grill, until the sugar melts and forms a glassy crust.

❈ *The custard should be smooth, and free of bubbles and lumps.*

❈ *Caramelize the top of the* crème brulée *under the broiler just before serving or it will turn soggy.*

Candied Pink Grapefruit

Pamplemousses Roses Confits

**Alain Chapel,
Restaurant Alain Chapel,
Mionnay**

SERVES 4

2 pink grapefruit

3 pounds granulated sugar

1 cup water

8 tablespoons sugar crystals,
crushed

Two days ahead, cut off the top and bottom of each grapefuit, then cut each grapefruit into 12 quarters.

Blanch the grapefruit pieces in a saucepan of cold water, brought slowly to a boil over medium heat and cool 4 or 5 times, each time starting with cold water. This will remove the bitterness in the peel. Remove grapefruit quarters and set aside.

Make a syrup, mixing the sugar and water in a saucepan and over high heat, cook for 5 to 10 minutes. Set aside to cool, then add the blanched grapefruit quarters. Bring slowly to a boil over medium heat and set aside to cool. Repeat this operation 6 or 7 times twice a day for 2 days.

The grapefruit is now candied, *confit*—the liquid will be like a syrup and the grapefuit will be translucent. Leave the fruit to drain on a grill over greaseproof paper, for a whole day, then roll them in crushed crystallized sugar.

A plate of candied grapefruit pieces is a delicacy most appreciated at the end of the meal.

❋ *Jean Troisgros named his grapefruit dish "Pamélas" in his Grand Dessert Troisgros. He took small strips of candied grapefruit, including the peel and about one-third of the fruit. Two grapefruit cut in quarters and again in quarters would give a total of thirty-two strips. He cooked the grapefruit very slowly, from fifty and sixty minutes in a saucepan with the sugar, but no water. After draining off any excess syrup, he rolled the* pamélas *in sugar and served them, as did Alain, a little chilled along with the coffee.*

❋ *André Soltner at Lutèce would use just the rind and store the candied grapefruit in the syrup covered with plastic wrap, in the refrigerator. All it required when he needed some was to drain off the excess syrup, roll them one by one in granulated sugar and, when it was time for coffee, the waiter took them to the table "avec les compliments du chef." Pamélas and* Crème à l'Anglaise *are a perfect way to end an evening, and to end a cookbook.*

Custard Cream

Crème à l'Anglaise

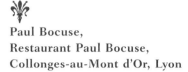

Paul Bocuse,
Restaurant Paul Bocuse,
Collonges-au-Mont d'Or, Lyon

DINING CHEZ PAUL AT COLLONGES *at least once or twice, sometimes more, every year between 1975 and 1996, I confess unashamedly, I always choose Bresse chicken roasted on the spit and, among desserts, a plate of* crème à l'anglaise.

YIELDS 1 QUART

2³/4 cups milk
1 vanilla bean, split
8 egg yolks
1¹/2 cups sugar

Boil the milk, add the split vanilla bean, cover and set aside.

Put the egg yolks and sugar in a bowl and beat with a wooden spoon until it becomes thick and creamy, and almost white in color. Remove the vanilla bean and slowly add the milk over a gentle heat. Or better yet, use a double boiler, stirring constantly so the eggs do not stick to the sides. It must not boil.

As egg yolks warm and thicken, finally coating the back of the spoon, remove from the heat and strain into a bowl, stirring while it cools.

❊ *The richness of* crème à l'anglaise *at Collonges comes from Roger Jaloux and the team in the kitchen, increasing the number of egg yolks to up to 20 yolks for 1 quart of milk. "The way that Monsieur Paul likes it," says Roger Jaloux. When the custard is cooled, in the tradition of Point and Brazier and Bocuse, they add 1 cup of heavy cream.*

AT THE TABLE

Driving back to Collonges on a visit with Paul to the market in Lyon, I asked him if he ever thought of the time ahead when he will be making fewer trans-Atlantic crossings and retire from this restaurant.

"One day, I hope to buy a house in the country," he said. "I will build a kitchen according to my tastes. I will install a stove and a very beautiful wooden table, and if I still have the health and spirit, I will always have four or five seats at the table, and I will serve Bocuse cooking. Not a big table—seating six—the ideal number, six, as if you cook two roast chickens, there always remains two quarters you can serve again. A table of wood of course, *bien sûr*, as wood is a living material and it's agreeable to eat on wood."

When a meal is over, Paul said, he likes to stay at the table. I remember the chefs' table in Troisgros kitchen in Roanne where I began working with the chefs.

"The table is a meeting place," Paul continued. "Often a lot of things happen during a meal. There is a moment in the composition of the dishes, of the menu and the wines, a link that is very strong."

In the living room of Jeannie's century-old little cottage in the country, stands a long, dark wooden table. I had always wanted a long wooden table and Jeannie found this one for me. I wrote much of this book seated here, in this house that must be about the same age as Fernand Point, the Mère Brazier, and Paul's grandmother, Grandmère Bocuse.

This is our home, where we come to find peace away from the city. Deer, and occasionally a black bear, walk the path I cut through the acre of woods behind the house. The bear stops to look at us and goes on his way. Jeannie's garden of flowers, salads, and herbs, is all in pots that we will soon bring in for the winter, filling the back porch with glorious colors.

Crossing the Atlantic, for both of us, has been an adventure that gave us the best years of our lives, with its treasure-house of good memories, *bons souvenirs*.

"And you, Helen," wrote my favorite World War I poet, Edward Thomas, to his wife, "What would I give you? If I could choose freely in that great treasure-house anything from any shelf..."

For you, Jeannie, I would choose a recipe from the cookbook Jean Troisgros gave me that has been by our bedside these years. Along with the three recipes Paul sent me last summer, it could have come right out of our garden this autumn evening.

"When they burn the weeds from the garden," wrote Margaridou in her journal, "I shall never forget the day we roasted the potato in the embers. It is the gourmandise from my childhood and I know of nothing better, smelling of the burning and the smoke and the grass and the wilderness. Afterwards you have to go and drink from the well in the palm of your hand the clear water of our fountains, and people can talk all they like about the end of the world, but this is all about the beginning of time."

The wooden table is laid. The candlelight beckons. The roasted chicken in the oven smells good, telling us it is ready to be served.

Stocks, Sauces, Marinades, and More

Some Basic Stocks

"THESE ARE THE STOCKS I LEARNED IN MY APPRENTICESHIP AS CHEF IN FRANCE," says Hervé Riou. "In those days, you were delegated to spend the week making stocks. Stocks and nothing else. It took hours. Today, in my kitchen at home, I decide on a day once a month or every two months to make my stocks. I make my demi-glace in an ice cube tray. When it is frozen, I put it into a clear plastic bag, so that when I need them I have only to take out a cube. I make all my stocks that way, so I always have some at hand."

WHITE CHICKEN STOCK

FOND DE VOLAILLE BLANC

3 medium-sized onions

1 medium-sized carrot

1 stalk celery

2 medium-sized leeks

2 pounds chicken carcass and giblets

3 quarts water

2 whole cloves

4 garlic cloves

1 bouquet garni: sprig of thyme,
    tarragon, parsley, and bay leaf,
    tied together

Peel and slice the vegetables, and place in a soup kettle or stock pot.

Remove the fat and skin from the chicken, rinse under cold water, and put it in the soup kettle. Cover with the water and bring to a boil for 1 minute. Skim, and reduce the heat to medium. Add the vegetables, cloves, garlic, and bouquet garni and continue to simmer for about 3 hours, skimming frequently.

Remove from the heat and when the stock is cool, strain through a cheesecloth or fine sieve into a bowl that has been prechilled so as to hasten the cooling of the consommé.

White chicken stock is excellent as the liquid for thick soups and poached fowls.

※ *Some of these stocks are now being sold in good gourmets stores, like Citerella and Zabar's on New York's West Side.*

WHITE VEAL STOCK

JUS AU FOND BLANC

2 medium-sized onions

1 medium-sized carrot

1 stalk celery

2 medium-sized leeks

3 pounds veal bones—
    rump, neck, or shoulder

3 quarts water

2 whole cloves (optional)

4 garlic cloves

1 bouquet garni: sprig thyme,
    tarragon, parsley, and bay leaf,
    tied together

Peel and slice the vegetables and place in a soup kettle or stock pot. Prick the onions with the cloves (optional).

Blanch the veal bones in a saucepan of salted boiling water for 1 minute and rinse in cold running water for 15 minutes. Place them in the stock pot, cover with water, and bring to a boil for 1 minute. Skim, and reduce the heat to medium. Add the vegetables and bouquet garni and continue to cook for about 3 hours, skimming frequently.

Remove from the heat and when the stock is cool, strain through a cheesecloth or fine-mesh sieve into a bowl.

White veal stock can also be used in soups and for poaching.

※ *To clarify stock, refrigerate for 12 hours, then skin off the fat that has risen to the top. See also page 81.*

BROWN STOCK WITH BEEF
FOND BRUN

2 pounds lean beef, brisket or shin, cubed

2 bones beef bones

2 onions, unpeeled and sliced

2 carrots, sliced

2 stalks celery, sliced

2 leeks, white part only,
    washed thoroughly and sliced

4 quarts cold water

2 tomatoes, sliced

1 garlic clove

10 peppercorns

1 bouquet garni: sprig thyme, tarragon,
    bay leaf, and parsley, tied together

2 tablespoons tomato paste

Preheat oven to 400°F. Place beef meat and bones in roasting pan and brown. Do not let them scorch or the stock will be bitter. Turn the bones from time to time. When the meat starts to brown, add the onions, carrots, celery, and leek. When the meat and vegetables are just brown, after a total of about 15 minutes, remove the solids from the pan and place them in stock pot. Cover with the water and slowly bring to a boil.

Deglaze the roasting pan on top of the stove with a little water and add the liquid to the stockpot.

Add the tomatoes, garlic, peppercorns, and bouquet garni and stir in the tomato paste. Simmer for 8 to 12 hours, skimming the grease from the surface frequently with a slotted spoon or skimmer.

Strain through a fine-mesh sieve into a bowl sitting on a large pan of ice cubes, so that the stock will cool before placing in the refrigerator, where it will keep up to 3 or 4 days. To make cooking easier, stock can always be made 1 or 2 days before use.

Brown stock with beef can be used for making glazes after the reduction, for moistening meat before braising, and for sauces.

BROWN VEAL STOCK
FOND DE VEAU BRUN

Proceed as above, but replace the beef with 2^1/2 pounds veal meat, cut in cubes, and ^{1}/2 pound veal bones, and after cooking for about 5 hours, this consommé should be a fine amber color.

Brown veal consommé can also be used for poultry and for poaching game.

DEMI-GLACE

Reduce the above stock by half and you have a demi-glace. The chefs know when it is sufficiently reduced—when it evenly coats a spoon. When it is cool, cover and refrigerate, where it will keep for one week as compared to the stock or *fond* that only keeps days.

When you need some stock, or *fond*, add a little water to the demi-glace, either allowing it to melt naturally or gently over a low heat.

FISH FUMET
FUMET DE POISSON OR FOND DE POISSON

5 pounds bones and heads of white flesh fish
    (sole, turbot, flounder, cod, bass, whiting)
3 tablespoons butter
1 pound onions, peeled, sliced
1/2 pound mushrooms, peeled and sliced
1 bouquet garni: 1 sprig each of
    tarragon, parsley, thyme, and a bay leaf,
    tied together
Juice of 1 lemon
15 peppercorns (optional)
Pinch salt
5 quarts water

Remove the gills from the fish and rinse the fish in cold water to remove any traces of blood.

Heat the butter in a skillet over medium heat and cook the onions and mushrooms under a closed lid.

Put all the ingredients in a deep stockpot, add water to cover, and bring to a boil. Reduce the heat to low and simmer for 30 minutes. Skim from time to time. Remove from heat and strain through a cheesecloth into an earthenware bowl. Store clear fish stock in a cool place.

Fish fumet is used in poaching fish.

❋ *For other stocks, see pages 45, 55, 64, 106, 135, and 168.*

Sauces

ONE SUMMER WHEN SHE WAS A YOUNG GIRL, Eugenie Brazier went to look after a family's children in their villa in Cannes. She also cooked for them. One day, Mademoiselle Brazier learned they expected a hollandaise sauce for dinner. She asked the concierge to help her. "Finally, it was quite easy," The Mère Brazier recalled in her memoirs. "In a copper casserole, I gently heated eight egg yolks in a little water, without letting them boil and added, little by little, a kilo of butter. No, it's more difficult than that. You must take care it doesn't turn into scrambled eggs."

SAUCE BEARNAISE

"To make a perfect bearnaise," said Fernand Point, "you need a yolk of egg, some shallots, some tarragon, and years of patience. But look away for a moment and all is lost."

10 tablespoons (1 1/4 stick) butter
2 shallots, chopped
1 bunch tarragon, chopped
1 teaspoon freshly ground pepper
1/2 cup white wine vinegar
3 egg yolks
1 tablespoon cold water
1 bunch parsley, chopped
Salt and freshly ground pepper to taste

Heat the butter in a skillet over high heat and melt without stirring. Add the chopped shallots, tarragon, and pepper, then pour in the white wine vinegar and reduce by three-quarters. Remove from the heat and cool slightly.

Add the egg yolks and setting the bowl on the edge of the oven and using a small whisk, whip them, adding 1 tablespoon cold water. When the sauce starts to thicken, add little by little the melted butter mixture, constantly whisking the mixture until it takes on the consistency of mustard.

Put sauce through a fine-mesh sieve or cheesecloth, add chopped parsley, salt, and pepper.

❊ *This sauce accompanies grilled meat and fish, soft-boiled eggs, and pig's trotters.*

BÉCHAMEL SAUCE
SAUCE BÉCHAMEL

1¹/2 tablespoons butter
2 tablespoons all-purpose flour
1 cup whole milk, warmed
1 cup water
Pinch salt

Heat the butter in a casserole over a low heat, add the flour, stirring constantly with a wooden spoon.

When the mixture starts to stiffen into a froth, without letting it color, stir in some warm milk and water. Cook for 5 or 6 minutes, while continuing to stir. Remove from the heat and add the salt.

❊ *See béchamel sauces in Paul Bocuse recipes on pages 235 and 249.*

❊ *Béchamel sauce goes with soft-boiled eggs, oeufs mollets, poached fish, string beans with a béchamel sauce, and gratins.*

❊ *Escoffier wrote for the chefs, "Any sauce whatsoever should be smooth, light, glossy to the eye, and decided in taste." If sauces interest you, Michel Roux, the distinguished chef and owner of The Waterside Inn on the banks of the Thames and, with his brother Albert, of Gavroche in London, has written a beautiful book on sauces. (See the bibliography, page 302).*

SUPREME SAUCE
SAUCE SUPRÊME

When making Christian Bouvarel's Bresse Chicken in a Soup Tureen (page 170), use some of thecooking liquid in which the chicken is poached in place of the stock below.

7¹/2 tablespoons butter
1 tablespoon all-purpose flour
1 cup chicken stock (see page 282)
¹/4 cup heavy cream or *crème fraîche*
1 egg yolk
¹/2 teaspoon lemon juice
Salt and freshly ground pepper to taste

Heat the butter in a small saucepan, mixing in the flour. Before the mixture browns, remove from the heat.

Strain 1 cup chicken stock and add it to the saucepan, whisking with a wooden spoon or spatula. Bring the saucepan to a boil and cook slowly for 10 minutes, whisking constantly.

Mix the cream and egg yolk in a small bowl and add this mixture to the saucepan on a low heat, still whisking. Bring to almost a boil, remove from heat, strain through a fine sieve or cheese cloth, add the lemon juice and season with salt and pepper. The sauce should be white and creamy. If too thick, dilute it with more chicken stock.

※ *For other sauces by the chefs, see pages 26, 28, 30, 96, 112, 136, 207, and 241.*

GRIBICHE SAUCE
SAUCE GRIBICHE

3 fresh eggs, hard-boiled, cold, and separated, whites and yolks
1 teaspoon Dijon mustard
Salt and pepper, to taste
2 tablespoons red wine vinegar
1 cup olive oil
Juice of 1/2 lemon
1 teaspoon capers
1 tablespoon chives, chopped

In a bowl, mash the yolks with a fork adding the mustard, salt, and pepper. Mix in the vinegar well. With a wooden spoon, beat the yolks, adding the oil, little by little, as in making a mayonnaise. Add in the mixture of lemon juice, capers, chives, and finely diced egg whites. Set aside.

※ *A sauce used with fish and with beef tripe (see page 121). Paul Bocuse calls it a mayonnaise using cooked eggs.*

FLAKY PASTRY
PÂTÉ BRISÉE

Carème said, "When the dough has been given its last turn, it should be used at once." Paul

Bocuse calls it a simple recipe, but requiring lot of experience. Here is a simplified version for the recipes on pages 5, 46, and 196.

1/2 pound unsalted butter, cut in small pieces, chilled
21/2 cups all-purpose four, sifted
1/2 teaspoon salt
2 eggs
2 tablespoons ice-cold water

Knead the dough for a minute, coating with 1/2 cup flour, and set aside.

Spread the remaining flour onto a board, make a well in the middle for the butter and salt. Knead with your hands until it is becomes fine and crumblike. Add the eggs and cold water. Continue kneading, moistening your fingers if necessary, and work into a smooth ball. As soon as you have a ball, stop working the dough[md]never overwork it. Wrap in plastic and refrigerate for at least 3 hours before using.

Remove from the cold and roll out on a lightly floured surface to form a rectangle about 24 by 14 inches and 1/2-inch thick. Fold into three—first left to right, right to left, left to right. Rest dough for 10 minutes. Repeat five more times, resting each time. Shape and bake without waiting.

MAYONNAISE
SAUCE MAYONNAISE

1 egg yolk
2 teaspoons Dijon-style mustard
Salt and white pepper to taste
1 teaspoon tarragon vinegar or lemon juice
1 cup olive oil

Put the egg in a bowl, add the mustard, salt, pepper, and the vinegar or lemon juice, and start to whisk constantly. Add the oil drop by drop at the beginning, then as the mayonnaise thickens and the volume increases, pour the oil in gradually a little faster in a fine stream, while still stirring.

※ *For the best results, Hervé recommends, the egg, vinegar, oil, and mustard should be at room temperature. If curdling occurs, the oil may have been added too rapidly or the oil is too cold. Put 1 tablespoon of warm water in a bowl and add slowly to the curdled mayonnaise, whisking vigorously at the same time. The finished mayonnaise should be light, smooth, and creamy.*

※ *Paul Bocuse uses a wooden spoon for the whisking.*

SALAD DRESSING
VINAIGRETTE

Roger Vergé, who cooks in Provence where the olive trees grow, makes his dressing with a good fruity extra-virgin olive oil, wine vinegar, finely chopped Italian parsley, a handful of little black Niçoise olives (pitted or not pitted), a finely minced garlic clove, salt, and freshly ground pepper. Here is another version.

3/4 cup olive oil or 1/2 cup peanut oil
    and 1/4 cup walnut oil
1/4 cup lemon juice
1/2 teaspoon Dijon-style mustard
Salt and freshly ground pepper
1/2 teaspoon chopped chervil
1/2 teaspoon chopped chives
1/2 teaspoon chopped parsley
1/2 teaspoon chopped tarragon

Put the ingredients in a bowl, mixing well, and pour over the salad.

※ *The oil and lemon juice above can be replaced by 1 tablespoon red wine vinegar and 3 tablespoons oil, or by the juice of one lemon (replacing the vinegar) and 3 tablespoons cream (replacing the oil).*

※ *For other vinaigrette recipes, see pages 212, 213, 216, 217, and 218.*

ANCHOVY SPREAD
ANCHOIADE

Roger Vergé, Restaurant Le Moulin de Mougins, Côte d'Azur

Roger Vergé serves this at his Le Moulin de Mougins as the Grande Anchoiade, a meal in itself. Alongside slices of toasted bread, he serves a basket of raw vegetables, crudités of all kinds of tomatoes, mushrooms, celery, radishes, fennel, cucumbers, red, green and yellow peppers, lettuce hearts, tiny artichokes, spring onions, fresh broad beans, lemon quarters, hard-boiled eggs and black Niçoise olives.

The bowl of anchoiade *should be large enough for guests to dip their vegetables in. The wine should be served cool—a young fresh red, white or rosé of Provence—and in abundance. Ideally, place the table in the garden in the shade of a large tree. Laid out just out just before the guests arrive at the table, the colors and sunshine lead to thoughts of a siesta.*

Chefs Michel Bourdeaux and Hervé Riou made this anchoiade *for a dinner I organized in New York in honor of Roger and his latest cookbook a few years ago. Everyone agreed, we could have stayed with* anchoiade *on little toasts and the glass of Provence rosé till the sun went down.*

SERVES 4

4 ounces tinned anchovy fillets in olive oil
1 cup finest first-pressing virgin olive oil
2 cloves garlic, peeled and chopped
1/4 teaspoon each chopped thyme and basil
1 teaspoon Dijon-style mustard
1 tablespoons red wine vinegar
1/2 teaspoon freshly ground pepper

Using the a food processor, put all the ingredients in the container and process until smooth. Alternatively, place the ingredients in a mortar and pound to a paste with the consistency of a mayonnaise.

Serve from a bowl.

❋ *Alongside, serve hot toasted country-style bread,* pain de campagne, *or other French bread. Or serve a salad of mesclun, black olives, quartered tomatoes, and hard-boiled eggs.*

❋ *Save any extra sauce in a wide-mouthed airtight preserving jar in the refrigerator.*

❋ *In England at tea-time, we served an anchovy paste, called Gentleman's Relish.*

GARLIC BUTTER
BEURRE D'AIL

For recipe, see Le Coze (page 74).

MINT SAUCE
SAUCE MENTHE

8 large sprigs fresh mint leaves
2 tablespoons sugar
5 tablespoons red wine vinegar
Pinch salt

Remove the mint leaves from the stems and chop. Combine all the ingredients in a mixing bowl. Let stand at least 30 minutes before serving, allowing flavors to blend.

Serve on the side in a sauceboat, with hot or cold roast lamb. Note use wild, common, or garden mint. The fancy flavors are for curries.

The Marinade

A NUMBER OF THE RECIPES call for a marinade—from the Mére Brazier's herrings marinated in white wine to the venison of Jean Banchet in Chicago.

"In the old days, they marinated everything," explained Paul Bocuse, "because we didn't have coolers and refrigerators. In my countryside, when we went out hunting and my grandfather shot a hare, if by chance it was my grandmother's birthday fifteen days later, he said we must keep the hare. We hung it up in its skin for as long as possible in a cool part of the cellar. After a time, we had to remove the skin and cut up the meat and put the pieces in wine and alcohol to marinate and preserve."

"Try this test: Cook a boeuf bourguignon with beef that has been marinated first and cook another that has not been marinated and compare them. I personally prefer the one unmarinated. Whereas fresh herrings in a marinade of white wine I find excellent. But all tastes are permitted. That is what cooking is about."

CREAM

For an English schoolboy on vacation, adventure was rising at dawn to join my grandmother's farmer bringing in the herd of Guernseys and Jerseys for milking time. I was a welcome hand tying them up, feeding them, and cleaning them out. Sitting on a stool with a pail between my legs, I was taught to milk. The pail of warm milk fresh from a cow smells as beautiful as the aroma of a young wine. We took the milk that was not picked up by a truck up to the dairy of the "big house" where I was allowed to work the milk separator that turned out the cream and the hand-turned churn that made the butter.

A birthday treat was to cycle up the valley to a farmhouse where they served "cream teas" of clotted cream and jam on hot scones. Inside the farmhouse on the kitchen stove sat large wide pans of milk simmering for the cream to rise like a skin and be skimmed off and cooled in the larder.

Where has the cream of yesterday gone? In France, the land of *la laiterie* and *la crèmerie*, little stores overflowed with creams and butter. Civilized people, the French, they cut the butter you needed from one of a half-dozen mounds of different butters—sweet butter, salted butter, *demi-sel* (2 grams of salt to 100 grams of butter), table butter, kitchen butter, nonpasteurised farm butter from "raw" cream. Bowls and tubs of cream with single cream, double cream, sour cream, *crème fraîche, crème fleurette,* or chantilly cream, pastry cream and small cardboard pots of a light, foamy dream of whipped fresh cow's milk, wrapped in a cheesecloth and called a *Fontainebleu.*

"France is a country of cream, wine, butter, and many cheeses," Paul Bocuse told his first audience of young student chefs at Brooklyn Community College in 1976. "None of these are dietic foods. France is the only country in the world to use all these products within such a small area. Since calories are not my problem—I am a chef not a doctor—I shall continue to use butter and cream and wine, and in this way we can continue to do good things in the kitchen."

Our chefs share their joy of cream throughout these pages, and you will miss the true essence of the dish if you skimp on the cream in dishes such as Jean and Pierre Troisgros' Salmon Escalopes with Sorrel Sauce, Fernand Point's Potato Gratin, Roger Vergé's Scrambled Egg in the Shell with Caviar, Maurice Bernachon's Chocolate Truffles, Paul Haeberlin's Salmon Soufflé Auberge de l'Ill, André Soltner's Onion Tart, Pierre Troisgros' Meringue Hearts of Passion Fruit, Paul Bocuse's Gratin of Macaroni, Chicken in Creme Cooked in a Wok, and *Crème à l'Anglaise.*

For more on cream, Paul Bocuse assembled over fifty recipes *à la crème* in his cookbook, *Paul Bocuse's French Cooking.*

Cooking Times and Weights and Measures

Cooking Times

"WATCH YOUR COOKING TIMES," says Paul Bocuse. "A vegetable has a time for cooking just as a fish or meat. Too often we don't pay attention. We put the beans to cook and after a time we say, 'They should be cooked.' No. Green beans, when they are young and fresh should be watched carefully and should be a little hard in the mouth, crunchy, *craquant*, when ready."

First, warm the oven to the required heat. Never start to cook from a cold oven.

OVEN TEMPERATURES: CONVERSIONS

Degrees Fahrenheit (°F)		Degrees Celsius (°C)
32	Freezing	0
40		4
140		60
150		65
160		70
170		75
212	Low Heat	100
275		150
325	Medium Heat	165
350		175
375		190
400	Hot	205
450	High Heat	230
475		245
500		260

Source: The New Professional Chef (Culinary Institute of America)

Weights and Measures

"EXPERIENCED CHEFS KNOW PRECISELY when what they are cooking is ready, they know instinctively the proportion of ingredients they need to use and never go to a pair of scales," wrote Ali-Bab in his classic, *Gastronomie Pratique*, in 1907.

The Mère Brazier gave measures for some of her ingredients, Fernand Point never did. It would surely depend on what they found at the market and how they felt in the kitchen that day. Instinct played a large role. We do know that Madame Brazier liked her soles to weigh 14 ounces, her lobsters 1 3/4 pounds, and her chickens 3 1/2 pounds. Otherwise, it was "A lobster well and truly alive," "a large gigot," "a beautiful woodcock."

The French buy and cook butter by the gram or kilo, and like the English, have a pair of scales in the kitchen to weigh the ingredients. Americans weigh and cook by the cup, tablespoon, or teaspoon. Though cooking in America was for a long time influenced by the English settlers, scales in the kitchen never caught on this side of the Atlantic.

"I have never been very successful in measuring cooked ingredients such as chopped meat or diced potatoes in cups," recalled the English food writer Elizabeth David in her cookbook about spices. "Do you cram the stuff down? Do you give it a good rattle so that it settles—or alternately flies all over the place? Just press lightly, my American colleagues tell me. How light is lightly? And how much does it matter?"

The following measures are offered to help:

3 teaspoons = 1 tablespoon
= 1/2 ounce = 15 grams

8 tablespoons = 1/2 cup = 4 ounces
= 1 stick of butter = 55 grams

The French also measure by the soup ladle (about 2 ounces). It would take a load of fun out of our chefs' cooking if we got into how much, precisely, was their few drops lemon juice; their knob, nut, or *noix* of butter; their thin, thick, or nice slice; their dash, pinch, or a little bit of; their piece, handful, large, small, some, several, as much as desired.

"Quantities in my first cookbook were approximate," Bocuse explained. "If I wrote '12 onions' this does not mean that the dish will not come out right if you use 9 or 14 onions. Do not, therefore, take what is written absolutely literally. I give you the outline of a certain kind of cooking, and you, with your taste, your imagination, will do your own cooking."

SOME MORE PRECISE MEASURES AND EQUIVALENTS

Pinch	less than 1/8 teaspoon
3 teaspoons	1 tablespoon
1 tablespoon	1 fluid ounce
2 tablespoons	1/8 cup
4 tablespoons	1/4 cup
8 tablespoons	1/2 cup
1/2 cup	4 fluid ounces
10 2/3 tablespoons	2/3 cup
12 tablespoons	3/4 cup
16 tablespoons	1 cup
1 cup	8 fluid ounces
4 cups	1 quart
8 cups	2 quarts
1 quart	32 fluid ounces
4 quarts	1 gallon

WEIGHT: MEASURES AND CONVERSIONS

U.S.	Metric (rounded)
1/4 ounce	8 grams
1/2 ounces	15 grams
1 ounce	30 grams
4 ounces	115 grams
8 ounces (1/2 pound)	225 grams
16 ounces (1 pound)	450 grams
32 ounces (2 pounds)	900 grams
40 ounces (2 1/4 pounds)	1 kilogram

To convert ounces and pounds to grams multiply ounces by 28.35 and multiply pounds by 453.59

Source: The New Professional Chef (Culinary Institute of America)

VOLUME: MEASURES AND CONVERSIONS

U.S.	Metric (rounded)
1/4 ounce	8 grams
1/2 ounces	15 grams
1 ounce	30 grams
4 ounces	115 grams
8 ounces (1/2 pound)	225 grams
16 ounces (1 pound)	450 grams
32 ounces (2 pounds)	900 grams
40 ounces (2 1/4 pounds)	1 kilogram

Source: The New Professional Chef (Culinary Institute of America)

Measures in Wine

THE FRENCH, WHEN GOING TO COOK *with wine,* buy wine by the bottle, that is 24.5 fluid ounces = 24 ounces per bottle. Beaujolais, Bordeaux, Alsace, even champagne are in this bottle called a fifth, and usually it has a cork. However, good, lighter, and less expensive wines, often with screw caps, are in 1 or 2 litre (1 or 2 quart) bottles. Depending on which size of bottle you buy, half a bottle is therefore 12 ounces or 25 ounces—we round off figures as every French chef does.

When they say a glass of wine (in their Bordeaux glass) it measures 4 ounces = 8 tablespoons = 1/2 cup.

Some Basic Kitchen Equipment and Culinary Glossary

Equipment

TAKE FOUR CHEFS—Paul Bocuse, Jean and Pierre Troisgros, André Soltner—and their list of kitchen equipment, assembled below, includes few gadgets. A blender and electric mixer can be useful, but often they prefer to handle a good, old wooden spoon or wire whisk.

Here is a basic list of what will help you prepare the recipes in this book.

aluminium foil

baking dishes

blender

bowls—large and small

can opener

cast-iron casseroles, *cocottes*

cheesecloth

colander

corkscrew

cutting board

double boiler, *bain marie*

electric mixer

egg dishes (ramekins)

food scale (see Weights and Measures page 291)

forks, large

grater, four-sided

knives (stainless steel), 1 large knife, 1 bread knife, 1 serrated knife, 2 medium all-purpose knives

ladle

measuring cup

measuring spoons

parchment paper

pepper mill

plastic bags (for stocks)

plastic wrap

roasting pan

rolling pin

saucepans—stainless steel, heavy bottoms or copper pans lined with stainless steel—ideally, 4 with diameters 8 inches (20 cm) to 5 inches (12 cm)

sieve, fine-mesh

skillet, frying or sauté pan

skimmer

slotted spoon

soufflé mold

spatula

spoons, large

stock pot, *marmite*

strainer

vegetable peeler

wire whisks, large and small

wooden spoon

SPECIAL EQUIPMENT FOR CERTAIN RECIPES IN THIS BOOK

candy thermometer

couscous pan

gratin dish

tajine dish

tartlet molds

Glossary: Some Basic French and English Culinary Terms

"I HAVE ALWAYS REGRETTED I never learned another language," said Paul Bocuse. Here are some English and French cooking words and terms that appear in these recipes.

À L'ANGLAISE To cook plainly in water.

BAIN-MARIE A double boiler, the lower of the two pots containing hot water, to keep hot or reheat food in the top pot.

BARD To wrap fresh pork fat around meat or poultry before cooking.

BASTE To pour its own juice or fat over meat, poultry, or fish, at regular intervals in cooking.

BEURRE MANIÉ Softened butter, that has been kneaded with an equal amount of flour.

BLANCH To briefly plunge into boiling salted water.

BLEND To mix ingredients smoothly.

BOUILLON The clear stock or broth from a pot-au-feu.

BOUQUET GARNI Sprigs of herbs tied together with string or in cheesecloth (see page 12).

BRAISE To cook with a little liquid in a closed container inside or on top of the oven.

BROACH To place on a spit.

BROWN To cook lightly under a broiler or in a skillet.

BRUNOISE Shredded or diced vegetables.

BUTTER To coat thoroughly with melted butter, spread with brush.

CARAMELIZE To boil sugar until it turns brown, for coating molds and coloring.

CARCASSE The body and bones of poultry, game, lobster.

CHAUD Hot.

CLARIFIED BUTTER Butter melted on low heat, foam skimmed off, strained, leaving milky residue.

CLARIFY To make clear i.e stock, by filtering or decanting coat cover with a thin layer of egg, butter, oil.

COLOR see Brown.

CONFIT Preserved, cooked in its own fat.

COURT BOUILLON A light broth used to poach and cook fish.

CROUTONS Small cubes or even slices of toasted or fried bread, for soups.

DEBONE To remove the bone in a piece of meat.

DEGLAZE To add liquid to a pan and heat so as to remove particles of food stuck to the pan during cooking.

DEGREASE To skim off the grease.

DICE To cut meat and vegetables into small cubes.

DREDGE To sprinkle lightly with flour, sugar.

ESCALOPE To cut in slices.

FILLET A piece of fish from a boned fish; to fillet; fillet of beef, the tenderloin.

FINES HERBES A mixture of finely chopped parsley, tarragon, chives, chervil.

FLAMBER To set aflame with cognac.

FOIE GRAS The liver of a goose or duck, specially fattened (see page 198).

FONDS Basic stocks used in soups and sauces.

FROID Cold.

GARNITURE Vegetables, rice, pasta accompanying a main dish.

GRATINÉE Sprinkled with breadcrumbs and butter and browned in the oven; grilled, by cooking under the direct red heat of a grill.

JULIENNE To cut in large thin, match-like strips, about 2 inches (5 cm) long.

LIAISON The binding or thickening of a sauce by adding a thickening ingredient.

MACERATE To soak in wine or liqueur to add desired flavor.

MARINATE To soak meat, game or fish in wine or spices to enrich flavor before cooking, producing a marinade (see pages 288–299).

POACH To cook in a liquid below boiling point.

POT-AU-FEU A traditional French stew of meat and vegetables.

PURÉE Cooked food passed through strainer or sieve and reduced to a fine pulp, preferably using a food mill, potato masher or wire whisk.

QUENELLE Forcemeat ball used for garnishing soups (see page 55).

REDUCE To boil a liquid so that part of the liquid evaporates, thickens, and intensifies the flavor.

ROTI To roast, to cook in an oven or on a spit.

ROUX The thickening element for soups and sauces brown: roux brun, for brown sauces; pale, roux blond, for cream sauces; white, roux blanc, for white sauces and Bechamel sauce.

SAUCE Juices from cooked foods, brown or white sauces to accompany cooked food.

SAUTÉ To brown food in a sauté pan or shallow dish of hot fat.

SEAR To cook over high heat for a short time.

SEASON To salt and pepper to taste.

SIMMER To cook, gently bubbling, over low heat.

SOUFFLÉ A purée thickened with egg yolks and beaten egg whites, baked in oven.

SPIKE To insert truffles, garlic cloves, strips of meat into fish, meat, poultry.

STRAIN To pass through a sieve.

SUER To sweat, cook meat or fish in a tightly closed container until the first drops of moisture appear.

TRUSS To tie up poultry with string to preserve shape while cooking.

À LA VAPEUR Steam-cooked.

WHISK To beat, whip up with a wire whisk (preferable to an electric beater).

ZEST The outside rind of a lemon and orange.

Suppliers for Produce and Kitchen Equipment

IMAGINE THIS SECTION OF THE BOOK a walking through a wonderful marketplace. You can go from stall to stall, producers and suppliers, and discover old friends and new. What they have may depend on the seasons, on what is new and just arriving. Just as you go regularly to your stores and markets, return here regularly. As Jean Troisgros recommended so strongly, it can give you ideas.

Call or write for their catalogs for more details on produce and shipping.

Aux Delices des Bois

4 Leonard Street, New York, NY 10013

212.334.1230

Seasonal fresh wild mushrooms and produce imported from France.

Bridge Kitchenware

214 East 52 Street, New York, NY 10021

212.688.4220

Father-and-son family business. High quality European imports for the professional: copper cookware, French stainless steel, French porcelain, bakeware, knives, pastry supplies, glassware. Also 8-quart and 11-quart couscous pan, *couscoussière*.

Chef's Catalog

P.O. Box 620048, Dallas, TX 75262-0048

800.338.3232; fax 800.967.3291

Large range of professional kitchen equipment for home chef including copper and stainless steel double boilers; stainless steel mixing bowls, stockpots; pots and pans; soup pots; deep casseroles; sauté pans; warming tray; knives; baking and kitchen scales; cooking twine; candy thermometer; copper; whipping bowl; storage bowls; steamers, braisers, roasters; indoor rotisserie.

Citerella

2135 Broadway, New York, NY 10024 and

1313 Third Avenue, New York, NY 10021

212.874.0383

Fresh farm-raised and seawater fish and shellfish; smoked fish; prime aged meat; fresh poultry and game; French cheeses, butter, organic milk, Vermont *crème fraîche*; fresh foie gras; truffles; olive oils and olives; fresh pastas; stocks, sauces; coffees.

D'Artagnan

280 Wilson Avenue, Newark, NJ 07105

800.DARTAGNAN or 973.465.1870

Imported French fresh duck and goose foie gras (as from Dec 23, 1998); goose and duck foie gras (mousse, terrine, and block of goose foie gras with truffles); chicken sausage; squab; muscovy, mallard, Long Island duck; duck confit, demi-glace, legs, wings, smoked magret and duck fat; hams; organic chicken and turkey; capon; goose; poussin; quail, guinea hen; imported Scottish grouse, partridge, pheasant, hare, wood pigeon; rabbit; buffalo, bison, wild boar, New Zealand red and fallow deer; free-range American and Australian lamb; baby lamb; ostrich; fresh cultivated and wild and dried mushrooms; black truffles and black truffle oil; Cavaillon melon; mâche; white asparagus.

The above can also be alternatives when a product is not available, or as a change of the major ingredient in a recipe with which you had a great success.

Kalustyan Orient Export Trading

123 Lexington Avenue, New York, NY 10021

212.685.3451

Specializing in rice, including high quality unpolished basmati rice, as used in Bernard Loiseau's recipe (see page 167). Also herissa, couscous, tajine and *couscoussière* pots, and much more.

Sur La Table

1765 Sixth Avenue South, Seattle, WA 98134-1608

800.243.0852

Kitchenware including roasting pans, spätzele maker, Opinel knife; candy thermometer, French ovens; *couscoussière*; *tamis*; *fait tout*; wok; kitchen scale; food mill; sea salt. And tableware.

Sur La Table stores are also located in Los Angeles, San Francisco, and Dallas.

Williams-Sonoma

P.O. Box 7456, San Francisco, CA 94120-7456

800.541.1262 (general); 800.699.0449 (food);

fax 702.363.2541

Prime beef, lamb, veal; organic turkey; rabbit, prosciutto; Scottish game, venison, poussin, and other D'Artagnan produce; fresh red snapper, lemon sole fillets, Maine lobsters; French walnut oil; grapeseed oil; Dijon mustard; sea salt; fresh truffles (in season). Kitchenware including roasting pans, soup pots, gratinee bowls, copper braiser, vegetable slicer (mandoline), colander, dutch ovens, bouillabaisse pot and bowls, chinois, warming tray, pie tins, stainless-steel bowls and cookware, knives, cheesecloth, whisks, rotisserie. And tableware.

Williams-Sonoma stores are located in all major cities across America.

Zabar's

2245 Broadway, New York, NY 10024

212.787.2000

French cheeses, butter, *crème fraîche*, heavy cream, organic milk; foie gras; coffees; French olive oils and olives; fresh and smoked ham, prosciutto di Parma and Daniele; French truffles; patés; fresh made stocks, sauces, and pastas; caviar; whole wheat flour and breads; chocolate; smoked seafood; sea salt; and more.

Also has a kitchenware department with kitchen scales, bain marie, 8-quart couscous pans, saucepans, skillets, knives, stainless-steel and copper cookware, dutch ovens; woks; tableware; and more.

Other High-Quality Gourmet Stores with Produce and Kitchen Equipment

Balducci's

426 Sixth Avenue, New York, NY 10011

212.673.2600; mail order 800.225.3822

Dean & Deluca

560 Broadway, New York, NY

212.226.6800

M. Slavin and Sons Fish

122 Thatford Avenue, Brooklyn, NY 11211

718.346.6734

Purveyors of high-quality fish to the top chefs of America.

Urbani Truffles USA

262 Mott Street, Suite 206, New York, NY 10012

212.696.2433

Fresh black truffles, canned black truffles, truffle juice, truffle oil.

Valrhona Chocolat

1901 Avenue of the Stars, Suite 1774,
Los Angeles, CA 90067
301.277.0401; fax 301.277.7304

French producer of fine chocolate—
supplying the great chefs of France and
America. Call or fax for local distributor.

Vermont Butter & Cheese Company

Pitman Road, P.O. Box 95, Websterville, VT 05678
800.884.6287, 802.479.9371; fax 802.479.3674

Hervé and I highly recommend their
crème fraîche and Vermont butter.

Villeroy & Boch Tableware

Showroom at 41 Madison Avenue,
New York, NY 10021
212.988.7011 (and also in San Francisco)

Fine quality tableware for the great
restaurants and hotels worldwide, including
the Alain Vavro designed tableware.

Whole Foods

2421 Broadway, New York, NY 10024
212.874-4000

117 Prince Street, New York, NY 10012
212.982.1000

Organic produce: milk, butter, eggs,
tomatoes, carrots, green salads, potatoes,
onions, celery, leeks, mushrooms, herbs, garlic,
great northern beans, lemons, oranges, grapefruit, apples, pears; chicken; olives, olive oils,
vinegars; stone ground whole wheat flour;
pastas, couscous, basmati rice; seaweed
(wakame, kombu, nori); sea salt (French
Atlantic, Pacific); Evian, Volvic.

Some organic produce is now on sale in
good gourmet stores. Try organic milk, butter,
or young carrot juice and taste the difference.

Farmers Markets

Starting with the farmers market in Union
Square in New York City, where produce has
to be grown locally and is largely seasonal.

Some Other Mills with Stone-Ground 100 Percent Whole Wheat Flour

Amy's Bread

75 Ninth Avenue, New York, NY 10001
212.462.4350

Arrrowhead Mills

Box 2059, Hereford, TX 79045
713.364.0730

Baker's Catalog

King Arthur Flour, Norwich, Vermont 05055-0876
800.827.6836

Stone-ground whole wheat flour,
unbleached, 100 percent of wheat flour &
germ; organic stone-ground whole wheat flour,
100 percent white whole wheat flour, rye flour,
unbleached all-purpose flour; loaf pans,
dough baskets; yeasts; baker's scales; digital
thermometer; liquid measures; mini tart pans;
bread pans; Guerande sea salt (fleur de sel,
fine, extra fine)

Bread Alone

Rte 28, Boiceville, NY 12412
914.657.3228

Campagna Home

29 East 21 Street, New York, NY 10010

212.420.1600

Campagna ships the Poilane *miche de campagne* packaged in its box overnight outside New York. Also stocks olive oil, cheeses, kitchenware, and pottery from France.

The Great Valley Mills

1774 County Line Road, Barto, PA 19594

800.688.6455

Paula's Products (for Guisto's Flour)

156 Utah Avenue, South San Francisco, CA 94080

415.852.4541

Poilane Boulangerie

8 rue du Cherche-Midi, 75006 Paris, France

011.33.1.4.798.81.84

The Poilane's 4-pound *miche de campagne,* country loaf—brown flour, hand-molded, baked in a wood fire oven—flown in from Paris.

Wines and Liqueurs

Sherry-Lehmann Inc.

679 Madison Avenue at 61 Street, New York, NY 10021

212.838.7500 or 800.811.WINE; fax 212.838.9285

If your interest in fine wines extends to perusing the latest catalog, you cannot do better than ask to be placed on their mailing list. Or visit the store. America has fine wine stores like no other country.

Bibliography

Cookbooks

THE TROISGROS BROTHERS WERE IN THEIR KITCHEN, *cooking, testing, making the finishing touches to the recipes in their first cookbook.*

"A cookbook is not just something you copy," said Jean. "If a cook at home who is not a professional takes a cookbook and it gives her ideas, that means the book is good. If she copies the recipes just as they are, then she has not understood. When you go to the market, if a fish looks fresh, you buy it. If it's not fresh, you buy another fish. A recipe calls for a certain blue cheese, but you can always use another blue cheese. Or a salad that calls for carrots, turnips, leeks. When there are no more leeks you use artichokes. The head is made to think."

"You cook according to the seasons," added Pierre.

Many of the books listed below, alphabetically by author, are out of print, but hunting for them in secondhand bookstores on both sides of the Atlantic can bring as much pleasure as going to the market for food.

Assire, Jerome. *The Book of Bread.* Paris: Flammarion, 1996.

Bittman, Mark. *How to Cook Everything.* New York: Macmillan, 1998.

Blanc, Georges. *The Natural Cuisine of Georges Blanc.* New York: Stewart, Tabori, Chang, 1987.

Bocuse, Paul. *Paul Bocuse's French Cooking.* New York: Pantheon, 1977.

Bocuse, Paul. *Paul Bocuse in Your Kitchen.* New York: Random House, 1982.

Bocuse, Paul. *Paul Bocuse's Regional French Cooking.* New York: Flammarion, 1996.

Boulud, Daniel. *Cooking with Daniel Boulud.* New York: Random House, 1993.

Brody, Jane. *Good Food Cookbook.* New York: Norton, 1985.

The Culinary Institute of America. *The New Professional Chef,* sixth edition. New York: Van Nostrand Reinhold, 1996.

David, Elizabeth. *Classics of Mediterranean Food, French Summer Cooking.* New York: Knopf, 1980.

David, Elizabeth. *Country Cooking.* New York: Alfred A. Knopf, 1980.

David, Elizabeth. *English Bread.* London: Penguin, 1977.

David, Elizabeth. *French Country Cooking.* London: Penguin, 1966.

David, Elizabeth. *French Provincial Cooking.* New York: Harper & Row, 1960.

Ducasse, Alain. *Alain Ducasse Flavors of France.* New York: Artisan, 1998.

Escoffier, Auguste. *The Escoffier Cook Book.* New York: Crown, 1941.

Escoffier, Auguste. *Ma Cuisine.* New York: Bonanza, 1984.

Fisher, M. F. K. *The Art of Eating.* New York: Macmillan, 1990.

Franey, Pierre. *Pierre Franey's Healthy Cooking with Friends.* New York: Artisan, 1996.

Franey, Pierre and Miller, Bryan. *Seafood Cookbook.* New York: Times Books, 1986.

French Culinary Institute. *French Culinary Institute's Salute to Healthy Cooking.* Emmaus, Pa.: Rodale Press, 1998.

Guerot, Alfred. *French Cooking for Everyone.* New York: Flammarion, 1963.

Kovi, Paul. *Transylvanian Cuisine.* New York: Crown, 1985.

Le Coze, Maguy and Rippert, Eric. *Le Bernardin Cookbook.* Maguy Le Coze and Eric Rippert. New York: Doubleday, 1998.

Merimée, Prosper. *Larousse Gastronomique.* Edited by Jenifer Harvey Lang. New York: Crown, 1988.

Oliver, Raymond. *La Cuisine.* Edited by Nika Hazelton. New York: Amiel, 1969.

Olney, Richard. *Reflections.* New York: Brick Tower Press, 1999.

Olney, Richard. *Simple French Food.* New York: Macmillan, 1986.

Palladin, Jean-Louis. *Jean-Louis Cooking with the Seasons.* New York: Lickle, 1996.

Pellaprat, Henri-Paul. *Great Book of French Cuisine.* New York: Vendome, 1994.

Pepin, Jacques. *Cooking with Claudine.*
San Francisco: KQED Books, 1996.

Pepin, Jacques. *La Technique.* New York:
Knopf, 1997.

Perrier, Georges. *Georges Perrier Le Bec-Fin
Recipes.* Philadelphia: Running Press,
1997.

Prunier, Madame. *Madame Prunier's
Fish Cookbook.* London: Penguin, 1938.

Rosengarten, David. *Taste.* New York:
Random House, 1998.

Roux, Michel. *Sauces.* New York: Rizzoli, 1996.

Soltner, André. *Lutèce Cookbook.* New York:
Knopf, 1995.

Troisgros, Jean and Pierre. *Cooks in Roanne.*
New York: Morrow, 1987.

Vergé, Roger. *Cuisine of Sunshine.* New York:
Morrow, 1988.

Vergé, Roger. *Entertaining in the French Style.*
New York: Stewart, Tabori, and Chang,
1984.

Vergé, Roger. *Roger Vergé's Vegetables in the
French Style.* New York: Artisan, 1995.

Vergnes, Jean. *At Le Cirque Restaurant.*
New York: Fine, 1980.

Wells, Patricia. *Bistro Cooking.* New York:
Workman, 1989.

Wells, Patricia. *Food Lover's Guide to France.*
New York: Workman, 1987.

Wolfert, Paula. *Cooking of South-West France.*
New York: Harper & Row, 1988.

Winebooks

Bespaloff, Alexis. *Complete Guide to Wine.*
New York: Signet, Penguin, 1994.

Buller, Michael. *The Winemakers' Year Four
Seasons in Bordeaux.* New York and
London: Thames & Hudson, 1991.

Buller, Michael. *The Winemakers Year in
Beaujolais.* New York & London: Thames
& Hudson, 1993.

Johnson, Hugh. *Wine.* New York:
Simon & Schuster, 1984.

Johnson, Hugh. *World Atlas of Wines & Spirits.*
New York: Simon & Schuster, 1990.

Lichine, Alexis. *Alexis Lichine's Guide to
Wines and Vineyard's of France.* New York:
Knopf, 1982.

Lichine, Alexis. *New Encyclopedia of Wines &
Spirits.* New York: Knopf, 1984.

Peynaud, Emile. *The Taste of Wine.* London:
Macdonald Orbis, 1987.

French Cookbooks

HUNTING THROUGH BOOKSTORES in France and
even over here you may also discover, as I did,
some of these French cookbooks.

Ali-Bab. *Gastronomie Pratique.* Paris:
Flammarion, 1928, 1993.

Ali-Bab, Escoffier, Gilbert, Montagne,
Pelleprat, Urbain-Dubois, *L'Art Culinaire
Francais.* Paris: Flammarion, 1950.

Bernachon, Maurice. *Bernachon La Passion du Chocolat*. Paris: Flammarion, 1985.

Blanc, Georges. *Ma Cuisine des Saisons*. Paris: Laffont, 1984.

Bocuse, Paul. *Bocuse à la carte menus pour la table familiale*. Paris: Flammarion, 1986.

Bocuse, Paul. *Bocuse dans votre cuisine 222 recettes*. Paris: Flammarion, 1982.

Bocuse, Paul. *Bon appetit*. Paris: Flammarion, 1989.

Bocuse, Paul. *Cuisine de France*. Paris: Flammarion, 1990.

Bocuse, Paul. *Bocuse La Cuisine du Marché*. Paris: Flammarion, 1980, 1987.

Bocuse, Paul et Perrier, Louis. *La Cuisine du Gibier*. Paris: Flammarion, 1984.

Bocuse, Paul and Vallaeys, Anne. *La Bonne Chére*. Paris: Flammarion, 1995.

Brazier, Mère. *Les Secrets de la Mère Brazier*. Paris: Solar, 1977, 1992.

Chapel. Alain. *La Cuisine c'est beaucoup plus que les recettes*. Paris: Laffont, 1980.

Ducloux, Jean. *Cuisinier à Tournus*. Paris: Solar, 1984.

Ducloux, Jean. *La Cuisine Traditionelle*. Paris: Solar, 1977, 1994.

Guide Gault-Millau. (bi-monthly). Henri Gault & Christian Millau. Paris.

Haeberlin, Paul & Jean-Pierre. *Les Recettes de l'Auberge de l'Ill*. Paris: Laffont, 1982.

Meilherat, Alain, Vavro, Alain, and Heimerman, Etienne. *Dedicaces Gourmandes 15 chefs du Rhone*. Lyon: MP Plus, 1996.

Michelin. *Guide Michelin*. France (annual). Paris: Michelin, 1999.

Peynaud, Emile. *Le Gout du Vin*. Paris: Dunod, 1983.

Peynaud, Emile. *Le Vin et les Jours*. Paris: Dunod, 1988.

Poilane, Lionel. *Guide de l'Amateur de Pain*. Paris: Laffont, 1981.

Poilane, Lionel, Mathois, Ginette, and Michel, Albin. *Pain, Cuisine et Gourmandes*. Paris: Albin Michel, 1985.

Point, Fernand. *Ma Gastronomie*. Paris: Flammarion, 1969.

Margaridou. *Journal et Recettes d'une cuisiniere au pays d'Auvergne*. Edited by Suzanne Robaglia, notes by Jean and Pierre Troisgros. Nonette, Auvergne: Créer, 1977.

Troisgros, Jean and Pierre. *Cuisiniers à Roanne*. Paris: Laffont, 1977.

Troisgros, Pierre and Michel. *Cuisine de Famille chez les Troisgros*. Paris: Flammarion, 1998.

Vergé, Roger. *La Cuisine de Soleil*. Paris: Flammarion, 1986.

Vergé, Roger. *Fêtes de Mon Moulin*. Paris: Flammarion, 1986.

Vergé, Roger. *Les Legumes de Mon Moulin*. Paris: Flammarion, 1992.

The Chefs and Their Restaurants

Telephone and fax numbers are given with France's country code (33), regional number (i.e., for Lyon, dial 04 when in France, 4 from the United States) and restaurant number.

Champagne

Gerard and Evelyne Boyer

Restaurant Hotel Les Crayères, 64 boulevard Henry Vasnier, 51100 Reims.
(33) 3.26.82.80.80; fax (33) 03.26.82.65.52.

Alsace

Jean-Pierre, Paul and Marc Haeberlin

Auberge de l'Ill, 68970 Illhaeusern.
(33) 03.89.71.89.00; fax (33) 03. 89.71.82.83

Luxembourg

Lea Linster

Restaurant Lea Linster, 17 route de Luxembourg, 5752 Frisange.
352.66.84.11; fax 352.67.64.47

Paris

Alain Ducasse

Restaurant Alain Ducasse, 58 avenue Raymond-Poincaré 75116 Paris
(33) 1.47.27.12.27; fax (33) 1.47.27.31.22
(also Monaco)

Lionel Poilane

Boulangerie Lionel Poilane, 24 rue du Cherche-Midi, 75006 Paris
(33) 1.45.79.11.49

Burgundy - Beaujolais

Bernard Loiseau

Restaurant La Côte d'Or, 21210 Saulieu
(33) 3.80.90.53.53; fax (33) 3.80.64.08.92

Georges Blanc

Restaurant Georges Blanc, 01540 Vonnas
(33) 04.74.50. 90.90; fax (33) 04.74.50.08.80

Jean Ducloux

Restaurant Greuze, 1 rue Albert-Thibaudet, 71700 Tournus
(33) 03.85.51.13.52; fax (33) 03.85.51.75.42

Lyon

Paul Bocuse

Restaurant Paul Bocuse, 40 rue de la Plage, 69660 Collonges-au-Mont-d'Or
(33) 04.72.90.90; fax (33) 04.72.27.85.87

and

l'Abbaye de Collonges quai de la Jonchere, 69660 Collonges-au-Mont d'Or

Paul Bocuse also has three brasserie-style restaurants in Lyon, directed by his chefs, Roger Jaloux, Jean Fleury, and Christian Bouvarel:

Brasserie Le Sud, 11 Place Antonin-Poncet, Lyon
(33) 04.72.77.80.00

Brasserie Le Nord, 18 rue Neuve, Lyon
(33) 04.78.28.24.54

Brasserie L'Est, Gare des Brotteaux, Lyon
(33) 04.37.24.25.26

Jacotte Brazier

Restaurant Mere Brazier, 12 rue Royale,
69001 Lyon
(33) 04.78.28.15.49

Jean-Paul Lacombe

Restaurant Leon de Lyon, 1 rue Pleyney,
69001 Lyon
(33) 04.78.28.11.33; fax (33) 4.78.39.89.05

Pierre Orsi

Restaurant Pierre Orsi, 3 place Kleber, 69006 Lyon
(33) 04.78.89.57.68; fax (33) 04.72.44.93.34.

Renée Richard

Fromages Mère Richard, 102 Halles de Lyon,
cours Lafayette, 69003 Lyon
(33) 04.78.62.30.78; fax (33) 04.78.71.75.09

Maurice Bernachon

Chocolats Maison Bernachon, 42, cours de
Franklin-Roosevelt, 09006 Lyon
(33) 04.78.52.23.65; fax (33) 04.78.52.67.77

In the Region Around Lyon–Rhone–Roanne

Michel Chabran

Restaurant Michel Chabran, RN 7, Ave 49 Parallee,
26600 Pont de l'Isere
(33) 04.75.84.60.09; fax (33) 04.75.84.59.65

Madame Alain Chapel

Restaurant Alain Chapel, route nationale 83,
01390 Mionnay
(33) 04.78.91.82.02; fax (33) 04.78.91.82.37.

Patrick Henriroux

Restaurant La Pyramide, 14 boulevard Fernand
Point, 38200 Vienne
(33) 04.74.53.01.95; fax (33) 04.74.85.69.73

Regis Marcon

Auberge des Cimes, 43290 St. Bonnet-le-Froid
(33) 04.71.59.93.72; fax (33) 04.72.44.93.34

Pierre and Michel Troisgros

Restaurant Troisgros, Place Jean Troisgros,
42300 Roanne
(33) 04.77.71.66.97; fax (33) 04.77.70.39.77

Côte d'Azur

Alain Ducasse

Restaurant Louis XV Alain Ducasse, Hotel de Paris,
Monte Carlo, Monaco
377.92.16.68.15; fax 377.92.26.69.21

Roger Vergé

Restaurant Moulin de Mougins, quartier
Notre-Dame-de-Vie, 06250 Mougins
(33) 04.93.75.78.74. fax (33) 04.93.90.18.55

Roger Vergé

Restaurant L'Amandier de Mougins,
06250 Mougins
(33) 04.93.90.00.91

Brazil

Claude Troisgros

Restaurante Claude Troisgros, rue Custodio
Serrao 82, Jardin Botanico, Rio de Janeiro
55.21.537.8582 fax 55.21.537.8574

United States of America

Jean Banchet

Restaurant Le Français, 283 South Milwaukee
Avenue, Wheeling, IL 60090
847.541.7470; fax 847.541.2043

Daniel Boulud

Restaurant Daniel, 60 East 65 Street,
New York, NY 10019
212.288.0033; fax 212.737.0612

Café Daniel, 20 East 76 Street, New York 10021
212.772.2600; fax 212.772.7755

Maguy Le Coze

Restaurant Le Bernardin, 155 West 59 Street,
New York 10019
212.489.1515; fax 212.265.1615

Ariane Daguin

D'Artagnan Inc, 280 Wilson Avenue,
Newark, NJ 07105.
800.DARTAGNAN or 973.344.0566;
fax 973.465.1870

Sirio Maccioni

Restaurant Le Cirque 2000, Villard House,
455 Madison Avenue, New York 10022
212.794.9292; fax 212.303.7712

Jean-Lois Palladin

Napa Restaurant, Rio Suite Hotel,
3700 West Flamingo, Las Vegas, NV 89103
800.777.1711

and

Restaurant Palladin, 224 West 49 Street,
New York, NY 10019
212.320.2929; fax 212.320.2989

Georges Perrier

Restaurant le Bec Fin, 1523 Walnut Street,
Philadelphia, PA 19102
215.567.1000 fax 215.568.1151

and

Brasserie Perrier, 1619 Walnut,
Philadelphia 19103
215.568.3000; fax 215.568.7855

Tip: please call or fax confirming your reservation a week before the date
or on your arrival in France. Bon voyage! Bon appetit!

Further Acknowledgments

ON COMPLETING THIS BOOK, it became clear that thanks are due also to a whole world of good people whose hospitality, generosity, encouragement, and love warmed my heart and guided me along the road.

The ladies are always there to welcome at the restaurants, including Simone Soltner; Raymonde and Martine Bocuse; Olympe, Martine, Marlene, Marie-Laure, and Anne-Marie Troisgros; Denise Vergé; Elyanne Boyer; Jacotte Brazier; Fabienne Lacombe; Maguy Le Coze; Suzanne Chapel; and Mado Point.

Thanks also due to Ferdinand Metz, The Culinary Institute of America; Dorothy Cann Hamilton, Jacques Pepin, Alain Sailhac, French Culinary Institute; Paul Kovi and Tom Margittai, Four Seasons, New York; Sirio Maccioni, Le Cirque 2000, New York; Raymond Oliver, Lionel Poilane, Christian Millau and Henri Gault, Paris; Marc Sarrazin; Jules Epstein, Wine & Food Society; Peter M. F. Sichel; Michael Aaron, Sherry Lehmann; Douglas Fairbanks, Jr.; Ed Acker, Peter Sheahan, Jean Khalifé, Pan Am; Richard Olney; Michel Bourdeaux, Vatel Club; Michel Peden, Le Croissant Shop; Cathleen Riou; Dominique Vavro, Collonges-au-Mont-d'Or; Lalou Bize-Leroy; Comte Henri and Irline de Rambuteau, Georges Duboeuf, Gerard Canard, Beaujolais; Alain and Danielle Querre, Jacques Hebrard, Pierre Lurton, St. Emilion; Corinne Mentzelopoulos, Emile Peynaud, Peter Alan Sichel, Henri Martin, Jean-Eugene Borie, Jean-Michel Cazes, Alexis Lichine, Comte Alexandre de Lur-Saluces, Jean Cruse, Bordeaux; Hubert Trimbach, Jean Hugel, Alsace; Robert and Michael Mondavi; Doris Tobias; Elizabeth Granirer; Jennie Bagwell; Ronald Harwood; Monica and Ronald Searle, Valerios Caloutsis, Dan Sturge-Moore, Jacques Esterel, Jean Rouvet, Paris; Winifred and Donald Buller, London.

Thanks also to those at IDG Books who worked on the book in its final stages, especially Alexandra Greely, Lisa Nicholas, Margaret Durante, Arun Das, and finally, Amy Trombat for her beautiful book design.

Index